# GREY CUP
# CENTURY

Feb19
16c
6/12/18
u=4

# GREY CUP
# CENTURY

Michael Januska

## DUNDURN
TORONTO

Front cover images: Top (left to right): The Fog Bowl of 1962; Michael "Pinball" Clemens; 1968 Grey Cup action; Roughrider kicker Dave Ridgway. Bottom right: Russ Jackson (#12) and Ken Lehmann (#41) receive the Grey Cup, November 30, 1969. *All images courtesy of the Canadian Football Hall of Fame.* Cover image © Andrew Rich / iStockphoto.com

Project Editor: Michael Carroll
Copy Editor: Allison Hirst
Design: Jesse Hooper
Printer: Webcom

**Library and Archives Canada Cataloguing in Publication**

Januska, Michael
        Grey Cup century / Michael Januska.

Issued also in electronic formats.
ISBN 978-1-4597-0448-0

        1. Grey Cup (Football)--History. 2. Canadian Football League--History. 3. Canadian football --History. I. Title.

GV948.J36 2012        796.335'648        C2012-900130-9

1    2    3    4    5        16    15    14    13    12

We acknowledge the support of the **Canada Council for the Arts** and the **Ontario Arts Council** for our publishing program. We also acknowledge the financial support of the **Government of Canada** through the **Canada Book Fund** and **Livres Canada Books**, and the **Government of Ontario** through the **Ontario Book Publishing Tax Credit** and the **Ontario Media Development Corporation**.

Care has been taken to trace the ownership of copyright material used in this book. The author and the publisher welcome any information enabling them to rectify any references or credits in subsequent editions.

*J. Kirk Howard, President*

Printed and bound in Canada.

VISIT US AT
*Dundurn.com | Definingcanada.ca | @dundurnpress | Facebook.com/dundurnpress*

| Dundurn | Gazelle Book Services Limited | Dundurn |
| --- | --- | --- |
| 3 Church Street, Suite 500 | White Cross Mills | 2250 Military Road |
| Toronto, Ontario, Canada | High Town, Lancaster, England | Tonawanda, NY |
| M5E 1M2 | LA1 4XS | U.S.A. 14150 |

*This book is for all the fans of Canadian football who for generations have cheered on their heroes in pursuit of the glorious Grey Cup.*

# FOURTH QUARTER: 1983–2011     175

**10 1983–1992:**     177
A Decade of Uncertainty

**11 1993–1999:**     202
The American Experiment

**12 2000–2011:**     219
A New Golden Age

**Epilogue**     241

**Appendix 1:**     245
Grey Cup Winners,
1909–Present

**Appendix 2:**     249
Grey Cup Most Valuable Player Award Winners,
1959–Present

**Index**     253

# FIRST QUARTER:

1909–1927

# 1
## 1909: "UNDISPUTED RUGBY CHAMPIONS OF THE DOMINION"

The greatest of traditions often stem from the humblest of beginnings, and the Grey Cup is no exception. Born in the mid-19th century, Canadian football struggled to define itself against its parent, rugby, and underwent decades of changes in rules and scoring as coaches and players worked to refine the game and establish standards that would enable the best team in the Dominion to rise to the top.

The first organized competitions were established in 1883 when the Ontario Rugby Football Union (ORFU) and the Quebec Rugby Football Union (QRFU) were formed. The following year these two unions came together to form the Canadian Rugby Football Union (CRFU), and at the end of that season the Montreal club defeated the Toronto Argonauts 30–0 to win the first ever CRFU championship. Despite the interest and fervor, the CRFU collapsed before the end of the decade. It was reorganized in 1891 as the Canadian Rugby Union, but the ground beneath it continued to shift.

The proverbial game-changer came in 1903 when the ORFU became the first major competition to adopt the rules that University of Toronto coach Thrift Burnside had derived from those already in place in the United States. The adoption of the Burnside Rules was considered a radical move, but by 1906 they were in force throughout Ontario and Quebec and it was from these very rules that the modern Canadian football code evolved. From this point the game evolved more rapidly.

In September 1907, the Hamilton Tigers and the Toronto Argonauts of the ORFU joined with the Montreal Foot Ball Club and Ottawa Rough Riders of the QRFU to form an elite competition: the Interprovincial Rugby Football Union (IRFU), also known as the Big Four. On December 1 of that year the Montreal Foot Ball Club defeated the Peterborough Quakers and won the first-ever Dominion Championship. In 1908, the Hamilton Tigers won the championship, defeating the University of Toronto's Varsity Blues. These matches were the genesis of today's Grey Cup.

Albert Henry George Grey, the grandson of a former British prime minister and the son of Sir Charles Grey, who served for a time as a member of the Special Council of Lower Canada, was born in 1851 in London. In his early career he served as a member of British Parliament, and at the age of 43 he inherited the Earldom Grey. He was also one of the first four trustees responsible for the administration of the funds that established the Rhodes Scholarship. In 1904, King Edward VII appointed Grey the ninth governor general of Canada, succeeding his brother-in-law, Lord Minto.

As governor general, Grey was a vigorous promoter of Canadian unity and strived to help the young nation forge its identity. He travelled the country extensively, and while he was unsuccessful in negotiating Newfoundland's entry into Confederation, it was with his granting of Royal Assent to the appropriate Acts of Parliament that Alberta and Saskatchewan joined Canadian Confederation in 1905. He helped plan Quebec's tercentenary in 1908 and led the negotiations between the Canadian and British governments that resulted in the creation of the Royal Canadian Navy.

While he was a well-known patron of the arts, having established, for example, the Grey Competition for Music and Drama, Grey was also interested in sport. He had wanted to sponsor a trophy to honour Canada's top amateur hockey team but was beat to it by Sir Hugh Montague Allan, who made his formal announcement early in 1909. It was very soon after that that Grey was persuaded to donate a trophy tied to the Dominion Football Championship of Canada — an amateur competition played between members of the Canadian Rugby Union.

With the regular season drawing to a close, excitement began to build around the playoffs. The Interprovincial final between the Ottawa Rough Riders and the Hamilton Tigers was scheduled to take place on November 20 in neutral territory — Toronto's Rosedale Field. Approximately 7,000 fans witnessed the match, 2,000 of whom had arrived from out of town. According to the *Globe*, it took "two special trains to carry the Hamilton contingent, while a train load came from the capital. And they came to make merry, with bands and banners."

It was a well-played game, and in the end it was the Rough Riders' persistence that paid off. They won 14–8, capturing the IRFU championship title. The ecstatic crowd swarmed the field and carried off the victors.

Meanwhile, on Varsity Field at the University of Toronto, the Ontario final was being fought between the Parkdale Canoe Club and the Toronto Amateur Athletic Club (TAAC). In Parkdale's brief three-year history they had already won two senior championships and had lost only one game — ironically, to this very club three weeks earlier. With a score of 3–0 at the half, the TAAC were looking the winners again, much to the dismay of Parkdale. But in the second half the Paddlers fought back and with only minutes to go made good on a TAAC fumble and carried the ball over their opponent's line for a touchdown. With a final score of 9–3, the Parkdale Canoe Club won the ORFU championship title.

That night the executive committee of the Canadian Rugby Union met at the King Edward Hotel in downtown Toronto and, on the back of a cocktail napkin, cobbled together the remainder of the playoff schedule. It was decided that the senior finalists, Ottawa and Varsity, would meet the following weekend and the winner of that game would advance to battle Parkdale on December 4 for the Dominion Championship.

The University of Toronto Varsity Blues had a rugby football tradition that extended back before Confederation. The Ottawa Rough Riders, on the other hand, had just soundly defeated the Hamilton Tigers — another team with a rich football history. Many believed that this upcoming match would come to represent the pinnacle of amateur football in Canada.

> THE FIRST DOCUMENTED GRIDIRON FOOTBALL MATCH PLAYED IN CANADA OCCURRED ON NOVEMBER 9, 1861, AT THE UNIVERSITY OF TORONTO. HOWEVER, MODERN CANADIAN FOOTBALL IS WIDELY REGARDED AS HAVING ORIGINATED FROM A GAME OF RUGBY PLAYED IN MONTREAL IN 1865.

The game took place once again on Rosedale Field. It should be noted that while the venue had a 3,400-seat capacity, reports set the attendance somewhere upward of 12,000. Walking around the present-day grounds — now ringed by tree-lined streets tightly packed with grand homes — a crowd like this is almost impossible to imagine.

But this small section of Rosedale had been annexed only recently and was still surrounded for the most part by open field. Images survive of fans watching the game perched in trees and atop half-constructed homes. Indeed, if Varsity's Hugh Gall had punted the ball hard enough, he probably could have kicked the leather clear out of the city limits.

The Rough Riders were favoured to win but the game ended in an upset, with Varsity soundly defeating the Ottawans by a score of 31–7. And so it was decided: the competition for Lord Grey's trophy would be played between the Parkdale Canoe Club and the University of Toronto's Varsity Blues.

In the week that followed, a sub-plot developed. Robert Patchin, an Ottawa-based foreign correspondent for the *New York Herald*, had a keen interest in Canadian football and managed to convince the paper to support — editorially as well as financially — his efforts to secure two of the leading Canadian teams for an exhibition match to be played in New York City on December 11. Varsity and the Rough Riders were chosen since they had each won their respective titles.

But Patchin arrived in Toronto the Friday before the big game only to learn that the Varsity club decided to turn down his invitation. The organization had a number of reasons, one being that several of the players had exams on the proposed date, another being that the academic calendar had no more room left for football. And, with all due respect to the *Herald*, the university said they would have rather the invitation came from one of the American colleges.

This left Patchin scrambling. He immediately approached the Hamilton Tigers club about taking the place of the Varsity team. A meeting was held Saturday morning at 11:00 between the executive of the Tiger club, Patchin, and Harry Griffith, the Varsity coach. Much to Patchin's relief, the Hamilton club embraced the offer. Ottawa was immediately notified by long-distance telephone and, while the Dominion Championship was being contested in Toronto, these two clubs hammered out the details of their trip to New York.

There were 3,807 in attendance at Rosedale Field — quite modest compared to the attendance the previous couple of weekends. Clearly this Dominion Championship game, not yet referred to as the Grey Cup, was being considered something of an anticlimax to the season. And, to be fair, it was entirely possible that the fans were suffering from a bit of football burnout after the playoffs.

The event was covered not only by the Toronto dailies but by other papers, as well, both nationally and abroad, including the *Ottawa Citizen* and *Hamilton Spectator*, and the *New York Herald* and *New York Times*.

The game was set to commence at 2:30 p.m. Conditions were ideal: cloudy skies, a dry field, and temperatures above freezing. Varsity won the coin toss and chose to start at the west end of the field to allow whatever light winds were available to help carry the ball. Bill Ritchie kicked the oval to Percy Killaly of Parkdale, who took a few steps before losing the ball to Varsity's Jack Newton, who was then tackled at the Parkdale 30-yard line. The game was afoot.

Varsity scored the first point — a *rouge* in rugby football parlance. On the first down Parkdale gained some yards, but then fumbled the ball to Varsity. The oval came to Hugh Gall, who manoeuvred around the end for a touchdown — or a *try*. Ritchie attempted to convert but the angle was too difficult to manage and he missed the mark. The score remained 6–0 for Varsity until the end of the first quarter. The "tricky" Parkdalers answered in the second quarter, however, with a touchdown scored by Tom Meigham after a Varsity fumble. There was no conversion. Several more scrimmages followed, but neither team was able to make further gains before the end of 30 minutes.

With the score at halftime a close 6–5 in favour of the students, the Paddlers received a standing ovation. This wasn't going to be the drubbing that everyone was expecting. According to the *Toronto Star*'s report, "there was some anxiety in the Varsity camp as to the final outcome." No doubt Coach Harry Griffith had a few words for his players.

The cloud cover had broken and the second half opened with Varsity staring down autumn's late-afternoon sun. Despite the distraction, the Blue and White came out charging, searching for opportunities to widen the gap. The first one came when Parkdale's halfback, Moore, fumbled a pass at his own 40-yard line. Varsity's Murray Thomson seized the ball and was allowed to trample over his opponents and fall on the ball for a touchdown. With Ritchie's kick, Varsity climbed to a 12–5 lead. It continued to be a lively quarter with Varsity scoring three more rouges, the last of which came off a 45-yard kick from Gall. Parkdale managed to score a point, but the Paddlers' frustration was showing, with two of their players taking the only penalties of the game. The third quarter ended with the score 16–6.

After a few kicks into the final quarter it was more than apparent that Varsity was in control of the game. The students kept the ball at the Paddlers' end, and after a rouge, a touch-in-goal, and yet another rouge they were suddenly up 20–6. The Canoe Club was playing a losing game but fought to keep the damage to a minimum by punting the ball as far as possible downfield. Varsity, however, made good returns on each kick, allowing their backfielders to move closer to the Parkdale line.

Parkdale needed to finish with a few more points on the board. They struggled to get something happening. On the final play the ball was kicked out of scrim to Varsity quarterback William Foulds. Parkdale managed to break through and cornered Hugh Gall. This was Parkdale's chance. But Foulds had called Smirle Lawson's number. Lawson, the player they called the Big Train, secured the oval, crashed through the entire Canoe Club team and, with the clock running out, launched into one of his spectacular 50-yard runs for a touchdown.

According to the *Toronto Star*, the timers were "on the field trying to notify the referees." Finally, just as the ball was touched down over the line, the officials blew the whistle, bringing to an end what was the first Grey Cup. No attempt was made to convert the goal and the final score was 26–6, ending a perfect season for the Blue and White. Police Sergeant Armstrong gave the nod to his 50 men to allow the crowd onto the field to surround their champions.

The two rather conspicuous absences from the game were the trophy itself and its sponsor. Apparently Lord Grey had forgotten to place his order for the sterling silver cup with Birks Jewelers. In the meantime, the Varsity players were each awarded a miniature silver cup, cufflinks, and a football-shaped watch fob.

> THE RECEIPTS FROM THE FIRST GREY CUP GAME WERE $2,616.40, OR ABOUT $52,590 IN 2011 DOLLARS. THAT PUTS THE AVERAGE TICKET PRICE AT LESS THAN 70 CENTS AND, CONVERTED TO TODAY'S COINAGE, THAT PROBABLY WOULDN'T EVEN COVER YOUR PARKING.

Monday brought the verdict in the papers. In the *Star*'s assessment of the game, Varsity's Charlie Gage, an outside wing, was singled out as the "most sensational player on the field," an athlete who "played like a fiend to the very end."

Credit was also given to Murray Thomson, who couldn't let go of the ball if he tried. Hugh Gall was praised for his remarkable punting ability. Jimmy Bell, who despite his cracked ribs "was always in the midst of the doings, tackling fearlessly," was also given a nod, and Bill Ritchie was cited for his skill at keeping the team on its toes.

While Ritchie had praised Parkdale, saying they had a "better line than Ottawa," the *Star's* reaction was a bit more tepid, saying that Percy Killaly "punted very well," halfback Alex Cromar played a very "useful game," and that quarterback Jimmy Dissette played a "good game, his passing being accurate." The *Star* was saving its hyperbole for Varsity, going on to remark how their defence was solid and they were on the Paddlers "like wolves."

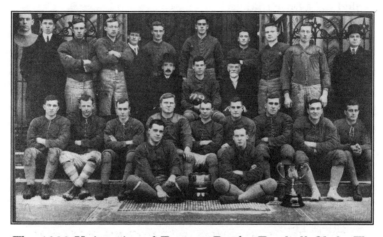

*The 1909 University of Toronto Rugby Football Club. The image of the Grey Cup has been super-imposed.*

In contrast, there was no shortage of criticism for the Varsity team from the *Ottawa Citizen* or the *Hamilton Spectator*. The *Citizen* opened their report with "conquerors of Ottawa team took things carelessly at beginning of match ... Lawson and Gall were both off color, fumbling repeatedly," generally describing it as a "distinctly off day" for the victors, and concluding with the statement that the "interest in the struggle was probably the least ever shown in a Canadian senior rugby final. Even the college choruses lead by the Highlanders band lacked spirit."

The *Spectator* opened with a headline saying that the "Varsity Team Was Way to the Bad." The correspondent went on to report that, "while the Parkdale crew created a surprise by their good showing, the work of the college team was very ragged and far from the brilliant standard they established in the game against Ottawa." It's interesting to find out how old a creature that cynical sports enthusiast is: "The crowd, as usual, was eager to see the favorites lose, and at half-time pulled hard for Parkdale."

While it seemed that none of the newspapers thought Parkdale deserved to lose, none of the papers seemed to think that Varsity deserved to win.

There are many footnotes to this inaugural Grey Cup. Here are just a few:

- The Hamilton Tigers and the Ottawa Rough Riders got to play their exhibition game in Van Cortlandt Park in New York City the following weekend in front of an audience of 15,000. The Tigers beat the Rough Riders 11–6.

- On March 10, 1910, the University of Toronto's Varsity Blues were finally awarded the actual "Grey Cup." The invoice from Birks came to $48.

- A number of Canadian football stars emerged out of the match, and several of them — all from the Varsity club — were inducted into the Canadian Football League Hall of Fame: Smirle Lawson, Jack Newton, quarterback William Foulds, coach Harry Griffith, and Hugh Gall, who still holds the record for number of single-point kicks in a Grey Cup game (eight).

- In the early part of the century, Lord Albert Grey, in the capacity of governor general, worked tirelessly at strengthening the bonds within the young Dominion. But it is through his sponsorship of a trophy awarded to amateur football champions that he is most remembered, because that simple gesture has evolved into a sporting event that on an annual basis unites millions of Canadians.

And so the tradition began.

# 2
## 1910–1920: THE FIRST GREAT RIVALRY: TORONTO VS. HAMILTON

The rich history of football in the city of Hamilton reaches almost as far back as Confederation. Shortly after the first club was established, the team played a match against the Toronto Argonauts, switched their colours from black and orange to black and yellow, and after that was known as Hamilton's "Tigers."

The Tigers were a founding member of the Ontario Rugby Football Union in 1883, winning their first championship in 1890 over Queen's University. They struggled through the turn of the century, but came roaring back in 1903, dominating competition in ORFU for a time and winning four consecutive provincial championships. Sitting out the nationals until 1905 because of a rules dispute with the Quebec Union, they relented in 1906, rejoined the game, and went on to defeat McGill University and claim their first Dominion Championship. The Tigers were also founding members of the Interprovincial Union in 1907, earning the Dominion Championship title again the following year.

• • •

Rain poured down in the days leading up to the second Grey Cup, and the clay field at Hamilton's Amateur Athletic Association Grounds — the Tigers' jungle — was puddling much of the moisture. The game took place the last Saturday in November and there was a chill in the air. That didn't discourage the several thousand Varsity Blues fans from travelling to the Mountain City by car, boat, or special train to witness what was being dubbed the "Battle of Hamilton."

*The 1910 Grey Cup: University of Toronto's Hugh Gall executing one of his sensational kicks.*

Tickets quickly became scarce and sold at a premium in the hours leading up to the game, with forgeries going for a tidy sum. And then there were the scalpers. It was reported that a Varsity fan paid $100 for four tickets, more than $2,000 in today's currency.

Hamilton's Rooters' Club, led by mounted police, left Gore Park for the AAA Grounds around 1:30. Official estimates put attendance at just over 10,000, but that was before the gates were crashed and fences toppled. Police reserves were called in to control the surplus crowd that swelled the audience. Meanwhile, back in Toronto, Varsity fans packed the streets, eagerly awaiting updates from the newspaper offices, cheering wildly with every advance and score made by the Blue and White.

The students took an early 11–0 lead before the end of the half following Jack Maynard's reception of a lateral pass from Hugh Gall that he ran past the posts. Maynard also made good on the convert. But in the second half, the Tigers began to gnaw away at their deficit, scoring four consecutive rouges. In the fourth quarter, "Kid" Smith's touchdown cut Varsity's lead to four points. By this time the gate-crashers were crowding the gridiron, blocking the view for spectators in the lower grandstand. Toward the end, these same interlopers spilled onto the field and play had to be stopped for several minutes as a feeble attempt was made to drive them back.

University of Toronto put the Tigers on the defensive for the remainder as Gall kicked five unanswered rouges to secure a victory for the Varsity squad. In the end, the Blue and White tamed the Tigers by a score of 16–7.

The Toronto contingent swarmed their heroes and carried them off the muddy field. Football fans of all stripes soon fell into their well-known snakedance formation and paraded behind the 48th Highlanders' Band through the streets of downtown Hamilton for an evening of celebrations.

• • •

On November 18, 1911, the Toronto Argonauts defeated the Hamilton Alerts 9–2 in the Eastern semi-final. The Calgary Tigers of the newly formed Western Canada Rugby Football Union offered a challenge for the Grey Cup, but the CRU rejected it because the WCRFU was not a full member of the CRU. That year it would instead come down to a meeting between the Argonauts and the Varsity Blues at the Dominion Championship.

The bookmakers were favouring the University of Toronto's Varsity Blues over the Argonauts, offering bettors 10–7 odds. Forty newspaper representatives from across

Canada and the United States applied for reservations to the press box while others subscribed to bulletins. Interest was diverse and widespread.

Six tons of straw had been spread across the Varsity Stadium field in an effort to keep the moisture in check in the days leading up to the final. Before the teams held their respective practices on Friday afternoon, the straw was removed and any conspicuous water was lifted from the field with giant sponges.

Club and season ticket holders received their passes early in the week. Tuesday afternoon the queue started forming for the general public, though the box office wasn't set to open until Thursday morning. Scalpers bought up blocks of seats and standing-room tickets. Friday night, anxious fans were paying them as much as $10 for the privilege of seeing the game. In an effort to meet demand, carpenters worked overnight to complete the last section of the new bleachers, providing an additional 500 seats that would go on sale first thing Saturday morning, just as the sawdust was being swept away.

According to an account in the *Globe*:

> There was pandaemonium outside the Stadium for hours before the game. Sellers of pennants, programs and colours vied with ticket speculators in making themselves heard. The street railway supplied a special service, and cars unloaded thousands at the gates, while there was an almost endless line of automobiles, carriages and pedestrians from all directions.

As the teams made their way to their respective benches, a steamroller was finishing smoothing the surface of the field. It was dry, at least until the start of intermittent snow flurry activity. There was not an empty seat in the stadium. Thousands more stood along the gridiron, stamping their feet and passing around hot Thermoses.

The Argos were the first to make their mark on the scoreboard after Ross Binkley booted one over to Varsity's Jack Maynard who was downed for a rouge. The quarter ended with Varsity's Allan Ramsey and Maynard exchanging punts, but no more points were gathered. Ramsey scored the first touchdown of the game in the second quarter and it was breezily converted by Maynard. The score at the half was Varsity 6, Argos 1.

In the second half, a pair of singles from Binkley nudged the Argos closer to Varsity on the board. However, the wind was quickly let out of the Argos' sails after Maynard kicked the ball over Binkley's head for a single and Frank Knight scored a touchdown on a Binkley fumble. Maynard's conversion wrapped up the scoring in the third: Varsity 13, Argos 3. Binkley tried to make amends, opening the last quarter with a field goal. An air-tight Argos defence and costly Varsity fumbles stalled the students' offence, however, and the game ended with the teams splitting a pair of rouges. The final score was University of Toronto 14, Argonauts 7. It was the students' third consecutive Dominion Championship.

Unofficial figures set the attendance at almost 14,000, with ticket sales exceeding $12,000. After nominal expenses, the teams split the balance. The students turned their share over to the university's athletic fund. Football helped pay for a number of Varsity athletic organizations that were not self-sustaining. The Argos, meanwhile, had enough money to buy themselves a flotilla of new boats with enough left over for a trip to the Olympic Games' regatta in Sweden the following summer.

• • •

The Varsity Blues' reign ended abruptly in 1912 when McGill University brought them down at the Intercollegiate final. In an interesting turn of events, McGill then refused to challenge for the Grey Cup, saying, "In view of the fact that our examinations are fast approaching, we do not deem it advisable to prolong further an already lengthened football season, which has cost us considerable sacrifice in respect to our graduate work."

This meant that, ready or not, the Toronto Argonauts were leapfrogging into the Dominion Championship where they would confront the Hamilton Alerts. But there was yet another twist. The Ontario final had been a bitter battle fought between the Alerts and the Toronto Rowing and Athletic Association. The final straw for Toronto was in the last quarter when a whistle disallowed a touchdown. It was Toronto's contention that there was no reason for the whistle and the play was legal. Hamilton, however, obeyed the whistle and let the Toronto player run the ball without confrontation. The Alerts won the game 9–7.

Following several days of grievances both on and off the field, the Hamilton squad finally met the Argonauts on the AAA Grounds on Saturday November 30. This was only the Alerts' second season in the Ontario Union and already their second trip to the Dominion Championship final.

> THE FOURTH GREY CUP WAS DELAYED AN HOUR AS THE GROUNDSKEEPER FORGOT TO PROVIDE THE BALL FOR THE COMBATANTS. THERE WAS PANIC UNTIL EVENTUALLY SOMEONE KICKED IN THE DOOR OF A LOCKED DRESSING ROOM, HOME TO THE ONLY AVAILABLE FOOTBALL ON THE PREMISES.

Ignoring the fact they were marked as underdogs, the Alerts took the lead in the opening quarter after scoring a pair of rouges. They very nearly stretched that lead after Murray Mulligan ran the ball in for a touchdown, but the play was called back on an offside penalty. The Argonauts tried to narrow the gap before the half was up, swarming the ball after Tout Leckie mishandled a punt behind the Alerts' goal line. The opportunity evaporated when, at the last second, Leeming Carr kicked the ball behind the dead line for a safety. Hamilton added another pair of rouges to secure a 4–2 lead before the break.

In the second half, penalties against the Alerts offered the Argonauts chances on which they failed to capitalize. Hamilton achieved their touchdown in the third quarter when Ross Craig broke through the line and passed the posts. His try was good for a two-point conversion, stretching the Tigers' lead to 11–2.

The Double Blue went on to score two more rouges in the fourth, but it was all in vain; they were simply no match for the hungry Tigers. Fans at AAA Grounds were treated to the first upset in Grey Cup history. The final score was 11–4.

Hamilton was asserting itself on many fronts, rightly earning its nickname of the Ambitious City. In the field of sport alone, that Saturday they had representatives playing in all three Dominion Championship series, not just the fourth Grey Cup.

A boisterous crowd followed the Alerts in a procession to the Waldorf Hotel where they were met by the Rough Riders — the intermediate squad that had just defeated Royal Military College — for dinner and celebrations. To cap things off, the junior Alerts defeated their opponents at the Ontario Agricultural College in Guelph. Hamilton had won a triple crown, firmly establishing its pre-eminent status in the football realm.

• • •

Following the collision the previous season, early in September 1913 the Hamilton Alerts made a formal request to rejoin ORFU but were denied. Players immediately began defecting to the Hamilton Tigers.

In November, the Tigers went on to win the Interprovincial title and awaited the outcome of the ORFU final to learn whom they would be playing in the Dominion Championship. The ORFU contest was between Toronto's Parkdale Canoe Club and the Rowing and Athletic Association. Tigers' manager Dave Tope was in Toronto to catch the game and size up his opponents. It was a close contest, but the Parkdale Paddlers outplayed the Oarsmen and won 8–3. When after the game a *Montreal Daily Mail* correspondent approached Tope and asked him for his thoughts, Tope predicted that the Tigers would "win handily over Parkdale."

Naturally, both teams were expressing confidence, but complicating matters further for bookmakers was the fact that the analysts were declaring the teams evenly matched. The outcome, however, told a different story.

The Tigers kicked things off in the first quarter with a Ross Craig touchdown converted by Sam Manson. After a trio of rouges, two for the Tigers and one for the Canoeists, the quarter ended Hamilton 8, Parkdale 1. The next quarter saw the second Tiger touchdown, which was also converted, followed by a Parkdale rouge. The Tigers' third touchdown came after Parkdale fumbled a pass: Art Wilson's powerful charge was converted by Manson. Rounding out the half, the Tigers took possession after a blocked kick and from 25 yards out Manson booted it for a single. It was Hamilton 21, Parkdale 2.

After the break, Parkdale worked the kinks out of their defence and managed to hold the Tigers at bay through a scoreless third. But it didn't hold for long. The final quarter was where the Tigers really ran up their tally, pretty much scoring at will. They started off with three rouges, then Bob Isbister plunged for a touchdown. On the heels of that play, Harry Glassford intercepted a Parkdale pass at midfield and sprinted down the line for another touchdown. The Canoeists perked up and moved the ball into Tiger territory only to have Manson run it back. A fumble by Parkdale's Herb Zimmerman resulted in yet another Tiger touchdown, and just before the final whistle, Craig bucked over for Hamilton's final major.

The fifth Grey Cup holds the record for providing the second-largest margin of victory: the Hamilton Tigers defeated Parkdale Canoe Club by a score of 44–2.

Perhaps the gap may not have been quite so wide if the Parkdale captain and star punter was not playing disabled. Hugh Gall was still undergoing treatment for a hip injury he sustained in a motorcycle accident before the start of the season. He injured it again during the game. Not only that, but during the previous week he had crushed the index finger of his right hand in the engine of his car. He had played the game with the digit wrapped in splints and bandages. Needless to say, Gall had difficulty handling the ball and was unable to tackle. It was understood that in future, prior to any major tournament, Gall should avoid contact with any and all mechanical devices.

And when it comes to analyses and predictions, a fan can't believe everything they read in the papers. Football die-hards in Hamilton knew the score, so to speak, and to them it was a foregone conclusion. There had been rows of vacant seats in the grandstands and bleachers at AAA Grounds and only about 400 fans arrived by train from Toronto, nudging the attendance up to a very modest 2,100.

If the game accomplished anything it was that it gave a sportswriter a chance to dust off his thesaurus. The now pedestrian "outclassed" was being replaced with labels such as "joke," "farce," and phrases like "utter, ignominious rout," "absolutely decisive beating," and "utterly miserable showing."

It was the Tigers' first Grey Cup win and the Parkdale Canoe Club's final appearance at what was quickly becoming the Fall Classic.

• • •

The Toronto Argonauts went into the 1914 Dominion Championship already beat, so to speak. They were coming out of a pair of matches against solid Hamilton contenders. The first match took place Saturday November 28 against the Tigers, whom the Boatmen defeated 11–4, and the second took place the following Wednesday against the Hamilton Rowing Club, from which the Argos surfaced after a tense 16–14 contest.

On the other hand, the Blue and White, U of T's Varsity team, were coming off a two-week break feeling focused and invigorated and were heavily favoured to win. The Argos were put through a light workout on Rosedale Field on Thursday and Friday. There was no ball involved, just exercises meant to keep limber their stiff and sore muscles. The rest of the time was devoted to chalk talk.

Slightly more than 10,000 filled the stands at Varsity Stadium to witness the sixth Grey Cup. Fans arrived from all corners of the province; even the Hamilton Tigers turned out. The rooting was performed by U of T students, and the rest of the entertainment was provided by the 48th Highlanders' Band. The weather was fair and dry for the time of year; ideal conditions for football.

In the *Globe* account, the game was described as "loose, rough, and at times even dirty." Both of the Argos' touchdowns were the result of Varsity mishandles. The first came after less than a minute of play: Red McKenzie's fumble on a punt return was picked up by the Argos' Glad Murphy, who snatched it up and hauled it 15 yards to the end zone. Jack O'Connor made the convert and it was 6–0 Argos. Freddie Mills turned another fumble into the Argos' second touchdown of the day. O'Connor failed to convert but later made good with a lucky field goal. The score at the half was 14–0, enough to muffle the student rooters.

The Blue and White held the Argos scoreless in the second half, and they themselves got on the board with a pair of rouges. It wasn't the prettiest game ever played, but it was played well enough to win the Argos their first Grey Cup in three tries. This meant that the University of Toronto would have to hand over the Cup, which they were refusing to relinquish until they were challenged for it and lost. They had won it back in 1911, when they last played the Argonauts in the final.

• • •

In these early years there was no question that it was the college teams that drew the crowds. The second-smallest audience in the history of the Dominion Championship turned out on November 20, 1915, to witness the Hamilton Tigers defeat the Toronto Rowing and Athletic Association by a score of 13–7. The game was played at Varsity Stadium, but without a college team on the ticket only about 1,000 spectators populated the stands and 1,800 more warmed the bleachers. The damp weather didn't help either.

Certain members of the Hamilton contingent, who numbered in the several hundreds, had brought with them carrier pigeons enlisted to bring word back to the Ambitious City on the progress of the team. The winged carriers hesitated at first, circling the stadium for a half-hour before heading west with their halftime report. They must have known that no one respects the bearer of bad news — the T.R. & A.A. were leading 4–1. However, Toronto was unable to maintain the pace.

After a bit of backing and forthing in the final two quarters, it was Norman Lutz's touchdown that ultimately sealed the victory for the Tigers. The final score was Hamilton 13, Toronto Rowing & Athletic Association 7.

Times were changing and the world was now marching into a war that stole the best and brightest of a generation. On the same page as the football scores were notices about all the young men, the likes of Hamilton halfback Sam Manson, who had just taken a commission in the army for service overseas.

• • •

By 1916, the Allied forces were entering the darkest days of the Great War and most senior-level football in Canada was coming to a standstill — including ORFU and the Interprovincial Rugby Football Union (the Big Four).

That didn't mean that there wasn't still a place for football. In Ottawa, the Overseas Football League was successfully organized as a replacement for the Big Four. The league consisted of teams made up from battalions in Ottawa, Hamilton, Toronto, and Montreal, and the games were played according to intercollegiate rules and open to any and all in uniform, both amateur and professional.

There was, however, no Dominion Championship played that year and the Grey Cup spent the rest of the war locked in a bank vault, more or less forgotten. Memories resurfaced briefly when, on August 29, 1917, the man that donated the Cup, Earl Grey, died. And two days before the Armistice in 1918, David Elliott of the victorious Hamilton Alerts was killed in action in France.

• • •

The autumn of 1919 saw the first regular football season played in four years. But while there may have been peace in Europe, lines were being drawn among the Canadian rugby football leagues.

On Saturday November 8, the Winged Wheelers of the Montreal Amateur Athletic Association (MAAA) defeated the Hamilton Tigers 13–6 to take the Interprovincial title. The following Saturday, two other decisive matches took place: McGill University's 21–1 victory over the Varsity Blues, which earned them the intercollegiate title; and the Toronto Rowing and Athletic Association's win over the Toronto Capitals, which saw the T.R. and A.A. take the Ontario honours in a 40–1 romp that had fans exiting the field before the end of the fourth quarter.

McGill had already announced that, should they win the Intercollegiate, they would not play for the Dominion Championship. Following the game, a meeting was held in the director's room at the MAAA clubhouse where McGill reaffirmed its decision. The consensus around the table was that a Dominion Championship series where McGill would not participate was a championship in name only and that a match between the Winged Wheelers and the T.R. and A.A. for the Dominion Championship title would be wholly unsatisfactory. On top of that, a Montreal championship played between the Winged Wheelers and McGill was viewed as "hardly fair" to the Canadian Football Union. This development, together with the onset of winter and everything it brings with it, led to the disbanding of the Wheelers for the season, and so Montreal was out.

According to the report in the *Globe*, the general mood was that a match should be scheduled that would "renew the games of yesteryears between the winners of the Interprovincial and Intercollegiate Unions."

The same page in the *Globe* carried an opinion piece that concluded by saying that the "Canadian Football Union should deal at once with the matter of national finals. It is proposed to inquire fully into variations in the rules and their interpretation in the respective unions. The West wants representation in the councils of the national body and the privilege of playing for the title.... The haphazard methods that apply to Canadian football should be put aside now."

## Clean It Up

THERE'S A GAME CALLED RUGBY FOOTBALL

THAT IS PLAYED NOW IN THE FALL

BUT THE RULES ARE SO CONFUSING,

THAT, BAH-JOVE, IT'S QUITE AMUSING,

AND OFFICIALS ARE AT LAST 'FUSING

TO CLEA-NI-TUP.


IN THE DOUBLE INTERLEAGUES AND THE O.F.U.

THERE IS STILL SO MUCH TO DO TO

CLEA-NI-TUP

THAT UNLESS A STAND IS TAKEN

WHEN THE RULES ARE IN RE-MAKING

THE BOYS THAT "GET THE BACON"

WILL CLEA-NI-TUP.


SO T.R. AND A.A. BEWARE!

WHEN YOU GET THE STONEY STARE

FROM ARGOS, M.A.A.A.

AND McGILL, THAT GIVES NO PAY,

THOUGH THEY CAN SCARCELY SAY,

CLEA-NI-TUP.

BUT A MOUNTAIN MAN DECLARES

FOUR M.A.A.A. PLAYERS

FOR "HAM" WILL PLAY NEXT FALL

TO HELP BENGALS CHASE THE BALL

TO MAKE THE WINGED WHEEL SQUALL,

SO CLEA-NI-TUP.

NOW THE REASON MAY NOT BE CLEAR

TO ALL WHO SEE AND HEAR

TO THOSE WHO ARE IN THE KNOW,

THERE ARE SOME TEAMS THAT MUST GO,

IF REAL SPORT IS TO GROW

SO AS A SCRIBE I WRITE

TO CLEA-NI-TUP,

TO WORK WITH ALL MY MIGHT

TO CLEA-NI-TUP,

FOR SURELY THERE'S A FATE

THAT WILL OVERTAKE THE LATE,

HENCE, MOVE ON, INCREASE YOUR GAIT,

AND "CLEA-NI-TUP."

There were signs that interest in the Dominion Championship was returning when, early in November, 1920, a new football attendance record of 15,000 was established in a match between the University of Toronto and McGill at Varsity Stadium. In the days leading up to the eighth Grey Cup, excitement continued to build. Tickets for the game, set for Saturday December 4, sold like hotcakes. On the Thursday prior, a block of 1,000 seats went on sale and sold out in an hour. One stealthy fan kept a keen eye on University of Toronto team manager Bill Blatz, and at the right moment made off with his overcoat — containing 50 tickets meant for team players, as well as a sum of money. By the end of the day, every seat in the grandstand was spoken for. In a panic on the Friday morning, the Canadian Rugby Union reserved two more sections of bleacher seats. It was expected to be the biggest crowd to ever witness a football game in Canada.

Die-hards and supporters were allowed into Varsity Stadium to watch the teams hold their practices. Analysts noted how the Argo management changed the lineup every few minutes, thereby speeding up the players on the field. It suggested that management would be putting every player to good use and the bookies took careful note.

Saturday morning, football fans poured into the city from all parts of Ontario and points beyond. By kickoff time, the Blue and White were 4–1 favourites. Continuing a tradition, rain fell steadily throughout the day.

The teams appeared evenly matched in the first quarter, the only point coming from the Argos when U of T's Joe Breen was downed just inside his goal line. But it was a sensational thrust and dash play by Varsity's Warren Snyder that brought about the game's first touchdown and put the students in the lead early in the second.

The Argos, however, kept pounding away until late in the third when a Dunc Munro fumble allowed Jo-Jo Stirrett to score a touchdown, raising the U of T tally to 11. It was a hopeless battle thereafter, and when the Argos' defence went to pieces for several minutes, the university team took full advantage, plunging through at will and ultimately scoring their final touchdown of the game. The Argos continued to fight admirably even though the game was irretrievably lost. Twice in succession Jack O'Connor broke through the centre, finally enabling the Boatmen to score their last point.

Weakened by injuries and the absence of some of the starters from the earlier part of the season, the Argos had fought against overwhelming odds only to be defeated by the University of Toronto 16–3.

Following the game there was a dinner held at Hart House at the University of Toronto. It turned out to be a celebration of good sportsmanship. The Argos freely admitted that the better team had won and they heaped praise upon the University of Toronto's "Laddie" Cassels, who was declared one of the best coaches in Canada. It was the last time these two Toronto teams would meet at a Grey Cup.

Rewinding, at the conclusion of the regular season, officials sat down to discuss the success or failure of changes that had been made to the code. Naturally there was a range of opinions, but debate seemed pointless as the majority of players and coaches had ignored the amendments. The most obvious violation was regarding the rule permitting interference four yards ahead of the scrimmage line. In the discussion it was agreed that the officials were responsible for making such calls. Little was settled upon and the debate continued inside and outside the boardroom.

A celebration dinner was held at Hart House and CRU president Hugh Gall confided that real effort was being made to secure uniform rules throughout the Dominion. Addressing criticism that this should have been done long ago, he remarked, "while there is life there is hope." And while there may have been nationwide confusion over contradictory regulations and a constant tinkering with the code, it should be noted that the game's popularity was growing with every passing year.

# 3

## 1921–1927:
## A CHALLENGE FROM THE WEST

On a Monday afternoon in mid-November 1921, a few hundred hearty spectators huddled together in stands overlooking a snow-covered gridiron in Winnipeg's north end to watch the Edmonton Eskimos battle the Winnipeg Victorias for the Western Canada Football Union title and a chance, for the first time, to show the East what the West was made of at the Dominion Championship.

Newspapers of the day remarked at the size of the players on the Edmonton team. *Husky* was a popular adjective. Their size must have worked to their advantage because the *Calgary Herald* reported that "the day was not one for much football strategy," and concluded that it was Edmonton's "aggressive tactics in the first period of play that really settled the argument in their favor." At any rate, the Eskimos never looked back from the 8–1 lead they established in the early minutes and ended up winning the game 16–6.

Jubilation was followed by what must have been a difficult decision: the Eskimos would not travel to Toronto to meet the Eastern finalists. The schedule had just come down and the Dominion Championship was to be played December 3, almost three weeks away. It was considered impossible to keep an idle team focused and in condition for such a length of time. And then there was the hard matter of the expense. The next day the Western champions packed up their gear and took the next train back to Edmonton.

But the Canadian Rugby Union had been working to make the Dominion final a national championship in more than name only. It was their mandate to grow the sport, apparently at any cost, and they very much wanted an East versus West contest for the Grey Cup. One possible solution was to compress the Eastern finals schedule. Intercollegiate champions the University of Toronto's Varsity Blues could play the Interprovincial title-holders, the Toronto Argonauts, on Saturday November 19. The victors would subsequently advance to play Parkdale Canoe Club, Ontario's standard-bearers, the following Wednesday. The winner of that match would then go on to play Edmonton in the Dominion Championship on Saturday November 26. The CRU immediately notified the Edmonton club of the plan.

Edmonton responded enthusiastically. Their decision to make the trip to Toronto was reached at the close of an intense six-hour fundraising campaign. Edmontonians came to the rescue of their Eskimos, the Rotary Club alone contributing $1,800 to the cause. Manager Moe Lieberman put forth some of his own money to make it happen, as did CRU president William Foulds. To seal the deal, the Eastern teams "guaranteed a huge amount to bring the team across the continent." The Eskimos would leave Saturday morning and arrive in Toronto the following Tuesday.

DARKNESS COMES QUICKLY IN THE NORTHERN LATITUDES IN LATE FALL. IN THE MONTH LEADING UP TO THE WESTERN FINAL IN 1921, THE EDMONTON ESKIMOS PRACTISED IN THE DARK OF THE LATE AFTERNOON BY MEANS OF A "GHOST BALL" — A BALL PAINTED WITH PHOSPHOROUS.

Sports journalists were suddenly standing on their feet and wanting to find out more about these men from the Mysterious

West. It was said the Eskimos would "demonstrate that Western football must be reckoned with." It was also pointed out that many of the players were graduates from American colleges. This would become a thorny issue in the years to come.

On the night of Thursday November 17, officials from the Canadian Football Union presided over a meeting of representatives from the University of Toronto, the Parkdale Canoe Club, and the Toronto Argonauts. It was a long, drawn-out affair. One of the clubs was apparently less than enthusiastic about bringing the Edmonton team across and the Parkdale club was opposed to playing a mid-week game. After much debate it was agreed that U of T's Varsity team and the Argonauts should indeed play their upcoming weekend match, but that Parkdale ought to play against Edmonton on Saturday November 26, with the winner going on to play the Varsity–Argonauts victor in the final on December 3. Not exactly the East versus West Dominion Championship envisioned by the CRU. Once again, they cabled Edmonton and awaited a response.

While they were waiting, there was yet one more meeting and another schedule change. The CRU and the Eastern clubs were now settled on having the winner of the upcoming game between Varsity and the Argonauts then meet Parkdale on Saturday November 26, with the winner of that match battling Edmonton for the Dominion Championship on December 3, as originally planned. They had come full circle. Already committed to travelling east, and not being available for the discussion, Edmonton had little choice but to agree to the terms.

"Now the championship of Canada will be officially decided and the fans of the East, who are prone to make little of the strength of the Western teams, will get a real line on both" [*Globe*, November 19]. This also represented an opportunity for a levelling of the proverbial playing field and adopting a nationally accepted set of rules. There was only hope.

The Western contingent consisted of 18 Edmonton Eskimos players, manager Moe Lieberman, coach Deacon White, and Western Canadian Rugby Football Union president I.S. Fraser. They headed east by rail and after passing through Winnipeg apparently saw nothing but snow. When they awakened in southern Ontario after a night's sleep to discover a climate comparatively milder than that under which they played the Western final, they breathed a sigh of relief.

The train pulled into Toronto's old Union Station the morning of Friday November 25. Greeted on the platform by the newspaper media, Coach White announced that his championship team was "here to do their best in an effort to win the Canadian football title." They were quartered a few blocks north at the Prince George Hotel and their first practice was scheduled for 10:00 the next morning at Varsity Stadium. However, they would have to practise without their official uniforms, which did not arrive with the rest of their luggage.

After practice, the Eskimos — along with about 9,000 other football fans — sat in the rain and watched the Argonauts drag Parkdale through the mud to win the semi-final, 16–8. Lionel Conacher was given much of the credit for leading the Boatmen to victory. Despite all that, a confident Coach White declared that his Eskimos had "little to fear" from the Argonauts.

Monday morning the Edmonton team held a signal drill on the Varsity gridiron and later a lineup practice at Broadview Field. Spectators weren't allowed at either and some of the newspapermen responded with a note of sarcasm. On Wednesday they reported that White had lifted the "veil of secrecy" and allowed fans "the privilege" of seeing his team go through their motions.

All said, the Westerners were becoming minor sports celebrities in Hogtown. Players were tossing superstition aside and agreeing to have their photos taken. After practices at Varsity Stadium, they would dress at Hart House and ride a tallyho — a large, horse-drawn touring carriage — back down to the Prince George Hotel. They wore the name "Edmonton" on their arms, and with their red and black mackinaw coats, they attracted a lot of attention. Tickets for the game were in hot demand and there was every indication it would be a sellout.

Conacher was scheduled to play two games in two different sports on Saturday and was anxious to be in top form for both. If the Argonauts took a day off, he didn't; he stayed sharp and went through his routine. At the same time he felt that if he didn't make hockey practice with the Toronto Aura Lees, he'd be of little help against the Granites and so he took to the ice in the evenings.

The ninth Grey Cup was played on Saturday December 3, 1921, at Varsity Stadium in front of a crowd of over 10,000 people. The Argonauts quickly got the scoring underway with a touchdown by quarterback "Shrimp" Cochrane: from three yards out he ran the ball around the end and across the Edmonton goal line. The Argos' second major came out of another misplayed Eskimo punt. Gordon Britnell made a lateral pass to Harry Batstone, who then passed to Conacher, who ran it in for the touchdown.

Spectators and sports journalist alike noted the heavy use of illegal interference by the Eskimos and how the pertinent rules were not being enforced by officials. It was as if two different games were being played on the field.

Edmonton's moment came after the break when Miles Palmer ran for a 25-yard touchdown. The Argos responded, and Conacher broke a number of tackles for his second touchdown in the third quarter to go along with his field goal and two rouges. His final tally was 15 points, tying "Husky" Craig's 1913 Grey Cup record. Conacher then left the game before the

*Sports legend Lionel Conacher was voted Canada's Athlete of the Half-century. He also served in the RCAF and became a member of provincial and later federal parliament.*

start of the final quarter to join the Toronto Aura Lee hockey team for a scheduled game.

With a final score of Toronto Argonauts 23, Edmonton Eskimos 0, it was the first shutout in Grey Cup history and an ignoble beginning for the West. What it came down to was a clash of football cultures: American tactics bowing to Canadian stratagems.

Regarding the Eskimos' style of play, two aspects that were widely noticed were the tackling and the excellent line-plunging. The tackling was wild and aggressive and Argo players were being grabbed below the knees and around the neck. The plunging, however, was admirable, with Vic Yancey, University of California star Curly Dorman, and Miles Palmer gaining ground virtually every time they were called upon.

It was widely recognized that White had been drilling his team in plays that were exhausted in the United States over the previous dozen years. With few exceptions, the Westerners showed little that was not already academic in the East. But conversely, the visitors gained invaluable experience they would take home and share with their prairie counterparts.

The Argonauts finished the season undefeated, propelled by the powerhouse trio of Conacher, Batstone, and Cochrane.

• • •

Renamed the Elks, the Edmonton club earned another trip to the Dominion Championship the following year.

On the morning of Saturday December 2, "Quilty, Murray Thompson and Rib Isbister, President of the Canadian Union, held a consultation, and decided on a uniform interpretation of the rules." Despite that, Elks coach Deacon White, who was described as a "thorough gentleman," admitted before the game that "his players were 'crude' in their tactics, and that he did not expect them to win."

The 10th Grey Cup was the only final played in Kingston, Ontario. The stands at Richardson Stadium were filled to capacity, just under 5,000, with the overflow standing around the field. But this must have represented every fan in the Limestone City because there was evidently very little interest in the match outside of the stadium. There was no doubt that the local boys — who had recently ended the season for Toronto's Varsity Blues and Argonauts squads — would have any trouble defeating the Elks.

Queen's was actually trailing 1–0 at the half but fought back. Not only that, the effects of the long trip were beginning to show on the Edmonton team and they started crumbling apart in the last quarter.

After a 29-year drought, Queen's overtook what was described as a "vastly over-rated Edmonton team" to take the title. The final score was 13–1.

It was later said that the locals "played the game because they felt that by so doing football would be helped all over Canada." Football was still struggling for respect and recognition. The lack of organization and the reliance on university and college students was not helping the cause. The Queen's students did not hide the fact that they would have preferred to pack up their uniforms after the game against the Argonauts and, following McGill's lead, go back to their studies. Then there were the lopsided matches. It was difficult to build an audience for a sporting event that was looked upon as a foregone conclusion, or at best a workout for the superior team.

There was no parade, no celebration after the game. A banquet was hosted by the university, but no one from the Edmonton team even attended: following the game, the Westerners left for Toronto and on Sunday morning entrained at Union Station for their long journey home, leaving promises to return the next year in their quest for the Grey Cup.

• • •

Edmonton did not qualify for the Dominion Championship in 1923. Instead, at the completion of the regular season, the West sent the Regina Rugby Club east into the lion's den.

On Saturday December 1, 1923, more than 8,600 fans packed Varsity Stadium to witness Queen's University demolish the Regina team 54–0 in what was described as a "farcical exhibition" and still stands as the largest margin of victory in Grey Cup history.

Queen's coach Billy Hughes summed it up well when he said, "There is nothing much to say about the game, but you've got to give Regina credit for being real sportsmen. Despite the big score against them, they went down fighting hard."

Regina's flying wing and future Saskatchewan Hall of Famer Howie Milne was credited with fighting a great single-handed battle. Prairie heavyweights Kerr, Rennebohm, and Crapper, along with other sizeable plungers, were helpless against the speed and skill of Queen's. Once again, Western brawn had failed against Eastern finesse and strategy.

The students finished their season undefeated. Their stars included former Argonaut Harry Batstone, best of the best in the backfield; captain Bill Campbell, their flying wing; "Pep" Leadley; Karl Quinn; and "Gib" McKelvey. Queen's said that it would be the last game they would play in an East versus West Dominion Championship final, and it was.

• • •

A year later, the farce that was played out on the field at the 11th Grey Cup was matched in spades by the one that was played out off the field at the next.

In mid-November, under blinding snow conditions, the Winnipeg Victorias defeated the Calgary 50th Battalion in their own backyard by a narrow margin, 11–9, to take the Western Canadian title. It wasn't exactly a shining victory. The Bisons — as they were nicknamed because of the logo on their jerseys — scored all but one of their points off fumbles that Calgary had made at their own end, and in the dying minutes of the game Calgary failed to capitalize on an opportunity for an easy touchdown. The win was a gift to Winnipeg. Many fans, as well as Winnipeg sportswriters, admitted that Calgary had the better team and should have won. Now the Victorias would be fighting to save not only the West's reputation in a Dominion final, but their own as well.

Two weeks later, the Queen's University squad fought a hard battle with the Balmy Beachers of Toronto, coming out the victors by a score of 11–2 to claim the Eastern title. Now it was settled: the Dominion Championship would be played between the Winnipeg Victorias and Queen's University on Saturday December 6, at Varsity Stadium.

While the Victorias worked on their strategies for defeating the brilliant Queen's squad, travel arrangements were made. There was an immediate disagreement over which of the two railways to use. A special meeting was held at the Western champions' club in Winnipeg, and as the disagreements could not be resolved, in a jaw-dropping move the Victoria club decided to cancel the trip. As it was described in the *Globe* on December 1, "the majority of the team wanted to go over one railway, while the officials were bent on going over the other. The players decided to go on their own accord, but the officials stepped in and prevented them from going as the Victoria Club."

A petty internal squabble then evolved into what can only be described as a communication breakdown of epic proportions. In that same edition of the *Globe* that reported the club's decision, Canadian Rugby Union Secretary Bob Hewitson announced that this fact "automatically" made Queen's University the senior champions. This, however, didn't seem to stop the Victorias from holding another meeting. The *Calgary Herald* reported that it was announced by "officials of the club, following a meeting at noon when all matters in dispute between officials and players were straightened out," that the Winnipeg Victorias would be travelling east to take on Queen's University in the Dominion Championship.

That night the Canadian Rugby Union was preparing to formally declare Queen's University the Dominion champions for the third consecutive year when a cable arrived from Winnipeg saying that the Victorias would be in Toronto as originally planned to take on Queen's. But the message arrived too late and the Westerners were notified that they need not come. The tickets for what would have been the 13th Grey Cup game were destroyed, and the vacancy at Varsity Stadium was given to the junior final. At Queen's University, training broke, the equipment was dismantled and packed away, and the team, anxious to get back to their studies, hung up their uniforms.

According to the *Globe* on December 3, several members of the Winnipeg team were "bitterly incensed at both the members of the team and club officials who were responsible for preventing the team from playing in the national final." The disappointment and outrage was not only felt among the organization and Bison fans, but among the citizens of Winnipeg. They, like the squad, had been looking forward to challenging the East and improving on that victory over Calgary. Another Winnipegger, C.E. Chown, president of the Canadian Union, was also keenly disappointed. To add insult to injury, there were murmurs that it wouldn't have been a good match anyway, that Queen's would have trounced the Victorias, and that the worthy battle had already been fought between the students and the Balmy Beachers.

This wouldn't be the first time that the winner of the Grey Cup was determined off the field.

• • •

*Varsity Stadium in 1925: The Toronto Argonauts versus the Hamilton Tigers in the regular season. (Left to right): Rayner (Tigers), Reeve (Argos), Weaver, Wale, and Breeh.*

Perhaps wanting to put the past behind them, the Winnipeg team renamed themselves the Tammany Tigers for the 1925 season. With the aid of such stars as their flying wing Dick Buckingham, they defeated Regina 11–1 to take the Western title.

At that time, the Ottawa Rough Riders were in decline and became uncompetitive during the 1910s. This was attributed to the Great War and professional hockey salaries luring Ottawa athletes away from football. During this period, another local team, the Ottawa St. Brigids, was on the ascent and developing top talent. In 1923, the St. Brigids and the Rough Riders merged and in the following year they changed their name to the Ottawa Senators. In 1925, the Senators defeated three-time defending champion Queen's in the Eastern semi-final.

The Dominion Championship, the 14th Grey Cup, was played for the first time in Ottawa, in Lansdowne Park, in the south end of the city, where Bank Street crosses the Rideau. About 6,900 spectators filled the stands on December 5.

BEFORE THE START OF THE 1925 GREY CUP GAME, WINNIPEG MANAGER "TOTE" MITCHELL PRESENTED TEAM CAPTAIN JOHNNY LAING WITH A HUGE FLORAL HORSESHOE, A GIFT FROM THE MAYOR OF WINNIPEG. AND FOR THE OTTAWA TEAM CAME A TELEGRAM FROM QUEEN'S THAT READ: "BEST OF LUCK FELLOWS. PLAY AS GOOD AS YOU PLAYED AGAINST US AND THERE WILL BE NOTHING TO IT."

The scoring opened with Ottawa's Charlie Lynch sending an onside kick flying toward the Winnipeg end zone. Senator Charlie Connell recovered and ran the ball in for a touchdown. Edgar Mulroney's 20-yard run around the right end secured Ottawa's second touchdown of the game before the break.

So confident in his team was Ottawa coach Dave McCann that he let his second-stringers play the second half of the game. The Senators went on to score their last two touchdowns in the fourth quarter. A Winnipeg mistake gave the Senators possession on the Tammany's five-yard line. Following a string of lateral passes, Connell scored his second major after running the ball around the end. Later, Don Young pounced on a loose ball in the Winnipeg end zone, netting Ottawa their last touchdown of the game. The final score was Ottawa 24, Winnipeg 1.

A disappointing day for football fans and a disappointing day for Tammany hopeful Dick Buckingham, who twisted his knee in the opening quarter and hardly set foot on the field after that.

In the evening, players from both teams, as well as officers from each club, sat down to a dinner in the Château Laurier. There were speeches, first from Dr. Jack Hand, president of the Ottawa Senators. He was followed by John DeGruchy, president of the Canadian Rugby Union, Tom Clancy, president of the Interprovincial Rugby Union, and Tote Mitchell, manager of the Winnipeg Tammany Tigers. Despite the lopsided victory, a good time was had by all.

• • •

Whenever the reputation of the Grey Cup seemed to be gaining ground and momentum was being created, league organizers and club executives fumbled the ball. As was the case with the 12th Grey Cup in 1924, the Grey Cup victors in both 1926 and 1927 were determined off the field.

In 1926 it was forfeiture. This from A.S. Matheson, president of the Western Canada Football Union:

> Recognizing that the [Regina] Roughriders have a good team, and further that they doubtless have been looking forward to the trip east since winning the Western title, I do not think they would be well advised to go east in quest of the Dominion honors this season ... in my judgment the Roughriders would have but a very slight chance of

winning out ... there is no question about
the rugby prestige of this section suffering
every time a poor showing is made against
the eastern champions.

And so, on Saturday December 4, the Ottawa Senators
came down to compete with the University of Toronto's
Varsity team for the Dominion Championship. To say that the
game was played under less than ideal conditions would be
an understatement. Apparently "hundreds of ticket-holders
stormed the box office at the Stadium before the game started
to get their money refunded." The scene became somewhat
chaotic and officials had to put a halt to it so that organizers
could get on with the game.

The *Globe* reported that the "players trod a frozen field
that had about as much smoothness and resilience as a cob-
blestone road. A thin layer of snow served only to make the
footing more treacherous. The ball was an oval cake of ice,
the moisture from the players' hands freezing to it.... The
cheerleaders were missing, and it was too cold for the U of T
band to pipe the popular tunes."

The first touchdown came in the opening quarter as a
result of a fumble by Varsity's Jack Sinclair. The rest of the
breaks in the quarter were Ottawa's, materializing in rouges
and amounting to a score of Varsity 5, Ottawa 3. The collegians
continued applying pressure, leaving the Ottawans feeling like
they had their backs against the wall. The Senators were kept
scoreless in the second quarter, while Varsity managed to put
away four singles. After only two periods and with a score of
Senators 7, Varsity 6, it was still anybody's game.

During halftime, spectators ran up and down and around
the field in an effort to keep warm while the game itself was
promising to heat up.

At the start of the third, Warren Snyder gave up an opportunity to make a kick on a third down, electing instead to run the end, only to be tackled, thereby handing the Senators another point. Varsity's France Trimble had to be carried off the field after a high tackle from Jess Ketchum. The third quarter very much belonged to Ottawa and ended with two more singles, rounding out the score at 10–6.

Varsity continued fighting though. It was on a third down in the final quarter that Warren Snyder executed a drop kick that was wide of the posts. Halfback Joe Miller elected to play it safe with a kick to the dead line for the students' only point in the half. Minutes later the game was over. The final score was Ottawa Senators 10, Varsity Blues 7.

• • •

The next season, the Western Canada Rugby Football Union, under new president Stan Milne, started taking steps toward getting its house in order. In a broad-ranging meeting it was decided for starters that the union should move up its schedule so that the Western final was to be played on either the first Saturday in November or Thanksgiving Day (starting in 1921, Armistice and Thanksgiving Day were both celebrated on the Monday of the week in which November 11 occurred). This was for the fans as much as the players.

While the executives were working through their agenda, the Western final was being fought on the gridiron at Athletic Park in Vancouver. At the end of 60 minutes, the Regina club reaffirmed its supreme status in the conference by defeating the University of British Columbia in a 19–0 rout.

Regina issued its formal challenge to the East a few days later. While the date of the Dominion Championship was set for December 3, Regina would have to wait for the outcome of Saturday's Eastern final to find out who their opponents would be — Toronto's Balmy Beachers or the Hamilton Tigers. Both teams had Grey Cup experience, the Tigers having already won it twice.

The Regina footballers were fired up. There was little doubt they were the strongest team the West had ever produced. Still, there was some hesitancy. The East was dubious, claiming that bad weather would hurt ticket sales needed to offset the cost of bringing the Regina team to Toronto. In the West, the *Regina Morning Leader* was running comments made by *Edmonton Journal* sportswriter George Macintosh, who opined that "the West would be foolish this year to take on a game in the East with the Dominion title at stake." Macintosh noted that the several Regina footballers who had migrated east had relayed back that "in the East are strong rugby squads and the training is much different and a much longer grind than that in the West, yet these boys aver that the West produces just as good rugby material as does the East."

The raw material was there. Macintosh went on to express his belief that it was a mistake leaving the Western teams isolated. He embraced the idea of East–West competition. How else will any team determine its worth, realize its true ability? "It may be determined at a loss, a heavy loss too," he said, "but there's only one way to really answer the question. Get out there and play them and find out how bad, or good we really are. Until this is done each year our contention is that the calibre of the Western teams will not be really known."

But money and weather weren't just excuses, they were very real factors. It was easier to come back from a disaster on the field than it was to come back after a disaster at the box office. Regina was looking for a commitment from the East. The East was looking for a fair and competitive football game.

While executives in the East and West reflected, argued, and crunched numbers, the way out came from the Eastern finalists. At the eleventh hour, Regina's manager received a telegram from the Toronto Balmy Beachers saying that Regina's request for a game had to be refused. As the *Regina Morning Leader* reported on Tuesday November 29, 1927, "owing to the their inability to field a strong team on account of injuries to players and the decision yesterday of 'Yip' Foster, back field star, and 'Scotty' Cawkwell, secondary defence player, to turn professional and play hockey this season, officials of the Balmy Beach club stated today that the players had been ordered to hang up their uniforms."

The Balmy Beachers were declared the winners of the 15th Grey Cup.

# SECOND QUARTER:

## 1928–1951

# 4

## 1928–1936: THE GREAT DEPRESSION AND ROUGHRIDER PRIDE

On a chilled-to-the-bone Saturday afternoon in late November 1928, on Hamilton's AAA Grounds, the Tigers defeated the University of Toronto's Varsity team, thereby capturing the Eastern title. The final score may have been an uneven 28–5, but tribute was paid to the young collegians, who made more than just a respectable showing on the gridiron.

And now the next Grey Cup era was set to begin, a gang of Regina Roughriders ushering it in with their first of an unprecedented five consecutive trips to the Dominion Championship.

There had been some skepticism about the East–West format, but its proponents won out. They recognized that efforts in the West to establish certain standards were setting their game on a solid foundation. It was also acknowledged that intersection competition was the only way — to borrow a familiar analogy — of levelling the playing field. Contrary arguments persisted, however. Some maintained that by the time the Eastern final would normally take place, a Dominion Championship in the West would likely be played under adverse weather conditions. The pro side countered, pointing out that the East had already hosted a number of finals on frozen fields and players were accustomed to it. It was also argued that a Dominion Championship in the West would not draw the bigger crowds. One reporter took the opportunity to remind fans that there was "more than gate money to amateur sport."

On the morning of the 16th Grey Cup, the Regina Roughriders arrived in Hamilton and checked into the Royal

Connaught Hotel. By 11:00 a.m. they were already on their way to the AAA Grounds for a workout. There was little time to find their legs and hone their strategy — kickoff was only a little more than three hours away. It was to be the first live, play-by-play radio broadcast of a Grey Cup game.

The Roughriders had not lost a game in three years and had not allowed a single touchdown to be scored against them in the same span. They had every reason to be confident.

In the first quarter a Roughrider fumble gave the Tigers possession on the Regina 35-yard line. Five plays later, Brian Timmis plunged through for the first touchdown of the game. After a scoreless second, the tally at the half was Hamilton 6, Regina 0.

Hamilton's Huck Welch opened the third with a rouge. Regina then fumbled a pass and Jack Baker dribbled the ball, which landed on the other side of the Roughriders' goal line. Jimmy Simpson pounced on it just in time for a touchdown. The Tigers continued their rampage, collecting 19 points in the third quarter alone, bringing the score to 25–0. Timmis scored his second and his team's last major in the fourth quarter. The final tally was Hamilton Tigers 30, Regina Roughriders 0.

It was unfair that some referred to the end result as a foregone conclusion. And, not surprisingly, some of the East–West naysayers felt the need to express their I-told-you-so attitude. But there were also converts who credited the Roughriders with playing a clean, hard game and demonstrating how football had indeed improved in the West. Spectators who had witnessed Western teams in action were universally of the opinion that these Roughriders were the best aggregate to ever roll out of the Prairies.

Afterward, a small but select gathering of football authorities held their perennial debate about rules and the football code, and suggested yet more changes intended for the betterment of the game. The latest view was that the defences were too strong and play could be opened up, making the event an even bigger draw. Apparently, marketing hadn't yet been discovered.

• • •

At Richardson Stadium at Queen's University in mid-November 1929, the reigning Grey Cup champions, the Hamilton Tigers, beat the students 14–3 to claim the Eastern title. And so it would be the Hamilton Tigers versus the Regina Roughriders in the first consecutive rematch in Grey Cup history.

The Roughriders' journey east began on Wednesday November 27. The Tigers, meanwhile, worked to perfect a defence against Regina's threatening onside pass. They were not going to make the mistake of underrating their challengers. They knew that Regina put up a better battle the previous year than the final score indicated. The Tigers' practice started at 4:00 p.m. that day and ran for more than two hours.

On Friday, the prairie boys received a royal reception from the Jungle Kings and there were plans for a sightseeing trip and theatre party. But before then, the Roughriders managed to squeeze in a short workout to loosen muscles stiffened by the days-long train journey.

When the players marched out onto the field on game day they were greeted by the icy blasts of a Great Lakes winter. The ground was as hard as pavement and the players' cleats hardly made an impression. Gazing up into the stands they would have seen less than 100 shivering fans huddled beneath rugs and blankets. That number would grow to barely reach 2,000 rather than the anticipated 5,000 to 6,000.

Hamilton's Ray Boadway had a couple of opportunities to leave a major mark on the scoreboard, but each time he lost his footing on the granite-like turf and was pulled down by any Roughrider with a free hand. On one of his later ventures, he slammed into a goal post and dropped the ball. And then referee John DeGruchy, while racing back with his eyes on a punt, collided with the same post, collapsed, and saw stars. It was said that in these conditions, "neither he nor Boadway could even dodge a stationary object let alone tacklers."

In the dying seconds of the game the Jungle Kings pounced once more when Huck Welch, after fumbling the ball, snapped from scrimmage, recovered it, and then passed to Jimmy Simpson, the diminutive outside wing. Simpson made the catch on the Regina 35-yard line, ran for 10 more, and passed to outside wing Alfred Henry "Cap" Fear, who then raced it across the line for a touchdown. Hamilton fans went berserk, but that wasn't the end of it: umpire Bob Priestly ruled that Simpson had made the catch within 25 yards of the Regina goal line, making the play illegal. While the Tiger fans could argue the call, what they could not argue was the potential value of this thing called the forward pass. The final score was Hamilton 14, Regina 3.

• • •

"Alvin Ritchie, the Regina coach, believes his Roughriders are just as good as any other team in Canada and hasn't hesitated saying so.... His players will be in good condition and imbued with that spirit which goes hand in hand with victories."

The Regina contingent arrived in Toronto on the Friday morning before game day and went through a noon workout at Varsity Stadium. Spectators, casual and vested, noted the Ruffies' speed and agility. There was a growing sense these Westerners were quick studies and had learned a few lessons from their Eastern adversaries. There was also the feeling among observers that Coach Ritchie would be sending onto the field a carefully considered combination of freshmen and veterans.

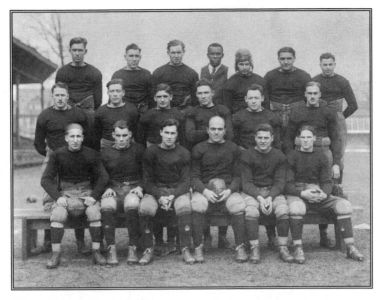

*The Regina Roughriders team photo, taken prior to practice at Varsity Stadium on the eve of their Grey Cup match against Toronto's Balmy Beachers, 1930.*

But there were still doubters. Eddie Baker, sports editor of the *Ottawa Citizen*, said that if the Roughriders should beat Toronto's Balmy Beachers, "there should be some kind of investigation, Federal or Provincial." This was fairly representative of the Eastern media's attitude toward the team, leaving the Roughrider nation "particularly riled." Consequently, Ritchie declined any social invitations while in Toronto.

When it came to concern over the gate receipts, weather was always a factor, but so now were the radio broadcasts. Officials from Toronto's Balmy Beachers, the host team, made it clear that in this lean season no one would be turned away. They hoped that attendance would at least cover expenses.

It was a mild Saturday early in December. The 18th Grey Cup was played in so much rain and mud that, five minutes into the game, the officials and fans could not tell the team players apart. The main stand was filled but only a few sat in the bleachers, and attendance was estimated at 3,900. As feared, many stayed home by their firesides and followed the match on the radio.

The Toronto Balmy Beachers' Albert "Ab" Box got things started, booting leather high to make the first three singles of the game. He was relieved when the count was 5–0 in the second quarter. By the intermission it was 10–0 for the Beachers.

Regina coach Alvin Ritchie presumably gave his team much to think about because his squad came out charging in the third quarter. Their efforts, however, gained them little ground. In the final quarter, with about six minutes left, and just when it appeared the 'Riders might actually pull their game from the fire, the Beachers' battle-weary star Teddy Reeve was sent to the rescue. He limped off the bench, put on his headgear, and ambled forth, crippled shoulder and all. He was given a remarkable reception and did not disappoint. The great middle wing plunged, tackled, and ultimately blocked a ball that was likely Regina's last opportunity to win the game.

The final score was Beachers 11, Roughriders 6. Despite their loss, it was widely felt that the 1930 Regina club had made the best showing of any Western team challenging for the Grey Cup. They cleverly and decisively outplayed Balmy Beach in the second half, demonstrating that the West's game was swiftly advancing and that they would soon receive the respect they so greatly deserved.

• • •

In 1931, the Regina Roughriders made their third consecutive trip east in their quest for what had become the Holy Grail of Canadian football. The 19th Grey Cup was the first and only one to be contested in Molson Stadium at McGill

University in Montreal. Over 5,000 filled the stands at the base of Mount Royal.

There was little doubt that the West had yet again turned out a most formidable football squad. It was also understood they would be facing what was being hailed as one of the "most powerful aggregations ever assembled in the Dominion" in the Montreal Winged Wheelers.

It turned out to be a game of Grey Cup firsts. The Canadian Rugby Union had only just started allowing the use of the forward pass across all leagues, and consequently the first touchdown pass — a 40-yarder — was thrown by Montreal's Warren Stevens to Kenny Grant in the third quarter.

The final score was Montreal 22, Regina 0 — which marked the first time the Grey Cup would leave the province of Ontario. It was a hard-fought battle and once again the score belied the supreme effort put forth by the Western challengers. The only blemish on the game was Montreal's Red Tellier getting banished for life for "attacking" a Regina player after the game. Tellier was later reinstated.

The Roughriders, perennial champions of Western Canada, had once again failed to capture the Cup. Their valiant effort against the fabled Winged Wheelers, however, did not go unnoticed.

• • •

On Tuesday night, November 29, 1932, the Regina Roughriders boarded the transcontinental once again and headed east to do battle in the Dominion Championship. It was another rematch with the Hamilton Tigers.

That same night, while the Ruffies were riding the rails, the Tabbies traded a field practice for a meeting in the clubhouse where they could draw and redraw their strategies in a chalk talk. Absent was Frank Turville, backfielder, still recovering from the previous weekend's victory against University of Toronto in the Eastern final.

The Depression was beginning to take its toll. The Canadian Rugby Union announced that there would be a new, reduced set of ticket prices. Premium seats would sell for $1.50 while general admission would go for 55 cents.

> IN THE FIRST CANADIAN PRESS WESTERN ALL-STAR FOOTBALL DREAM TEAM (1932) — FOLLOWING A POLL OF NINE WESTERN SPORTSWRITERS — THE REGINA ROUGHRIDERS HELD NINE OF THE 12 POSITIONS, AND ALVIN RITCHIE WAS UNANIMOUSLY CHOSEN AS COACH.

A stopover in Winnipeg on Thursday was meant to break up the long journey for the boys and provide them with an opportunity to stay limber. They spent the morning working out on St. John's Field and afterward attended a luncheon in their honour where they listened to speeches full of goodwill and support from Western football enthusiasts. They finally arrived in Hamilton early Friday morning and, sticking to their schedule, held a light workout at noon. Coach Ritchie, now being referred to as the Knute Rockne of the West, expressed his confidence and maintained that his key players — Dave Sprague, Brian Timmis, Ray Boadway, and Frank Turville — could break down anything Steeltown assembled.

But there were harsh words back east from the press: "It is only natural to expect that the same old fate will befall the Westerners when they meet Tigers today at Hamilton…. Fine phrases, indeed, and perhaps convincing to those who utter them, but not likely to impress Eastern football enthusiasts, who have been fed the same sort of chatter concerning the

Western champions on practically every Eastern jaunt that the Roughriders have made."

In the opening play of the game, the Roughriders' Curt Schave returned Frank Turville's kickoff to his 25-yard line and then promptly dropped the ball upon being tackled. Three plays later, Dinny Gardner took a pass on an extension play and crossed the goal line for a touchdown. The Tigers ran up two more points after Regina's Jersey Campbell snapped the ball over punter Charlie Harrison's head. Harrison bolted behind the goal line to retrieve it and ended up tackled for a safety. In the second quarter, Regina's Austin DeFrate had a short pass intercepted by Ike Sutton, which he ran 35 yards for a touchdown.

The Roughriders finally got on the board in the fourth quarter, registering a touchdown by Austin DeFrate. But in the end the Tigers did bring down the Roughriders handily, the final tally being 25–6, which to some suggested that the Grey Cup was in little danger of travelling anywhere west of the Great Lakes.

• • •

In 1933, the makeup of the Grey Cup changed yet again: the Dominion Championship was not to be an East–West show-down. The extended Eastern semi-finals, the weather, and yet more debates concerning the amount of American talent on Canadian teams led to the contest ultimately being played out between the Toronto Argonauts — who had already eliminated the Winnipeg squad — and the Sarnia Imperials. The Scullers left by train for Sarnia in the late afternoon, Friday December 8.

Vern DeGeer of the *Border Cities Star* interviewed Carl Cronin, coach and quarterback of the Winnipeg team, and Cronin made some interesting comments regarding the cross-border trade in athletes. He said he didn't care for the way newspapermen in the East were consistently referring to former American college players as imports. "Canada," he said "has been sending amateur hockey players across to the United States for years, and no effort has been made to treat these players as if they were violating some criminal code of the criminal law, but the inference here in the East seems to be that we Americans are nothing short of crooks." Point taken.

The Dominion Championship brought the small southwestern Ontario city to a near standstill, with spectators pouring in from Windsor and London and dozens of other neighbouring communities. The Argonauts were strongly favoured, but there was every reason to believe there might be an upset. Sure, the Double Blue had the proven ability, but it had been a tough season for them and it was possible they were at the end of their ropes.

Nineteen thirty-three may have been the year of the forward pass, but it made little impression on the outcome of the 21st Grey Cup. Perhaps more importantly, this Grey Cup marked the first time that no touchdowns were scored.

The Imperials dominated an unimpressive first half, leading 1–0 at the whistle. While the Oilmen added another point in the third quarter, the direction of the game seemed to be changing. Toronto's Tuffy Griffiths blocked Bummer Stirling's kick on the 40-yard line, giving the Argos the ball. Jack Taylor snatched a lateral pass from Andy Mullen and ran 20 yards around the end, after which Teddy Morris bought seven yards. With a beeline to the goal posts, Tommy Burns lifted the leather for a Toronto field goal. After three, the score was 3–2 for the Argonauts.

Sarnia later tied on a rouge, but after an Imperial fumble, Toronto replied with a single that once more put them in the lead. This turned out to be the winning point. The final score was 4–3 Argonauts. It was Argos' coach Lew Hayman's first

Grey Cup, but it was also the narrowest margin of victory to date in a Grey Cup match. The Sarnia Imperials were now viewed as a force to be reckoned with.

• • •

Shortly after midnight on Sunday November 18, 1934, a quarter of Sarnia's population, or about 5,000 people, jammed the city centre to greet their triumphant Imperials. Their Oilmen had beaten the Tigers 11–4 — in Hamilton no less — to claim the Eastern honours. The team paraded through the city on a fire truck. When they pulled up to City Hall, Mayor Blake congratulated them. Coach Art Massucci and Norm Perry, whose touchdown had won the day, spoke for the team. It was not until the early morning hours that the streets cleared and a semblance of normalcy returned to the "Tunnel City."

> VARSITY STADIUM HAS OCCUPIED THE CORNER OF BLOOR STREET AND DEVONSHIRE ROAD SINCE 1898. IT HAS PLAYED HOST TO MORE GREY CUP GAMES THAN ANY OTHER VENUE IN CANADA AND IS STILL HOME TO FOUR-TIME GREY CUP CHAMPIONS THE UNIVERSITY OF TORONTO VARSITY BLUES.

Two days later, the Regina Roughriders — the Western champs — began their journey east, with a stopover in Winnipeg the next day. They arrived in Toronto on the Friday and held a quick workout at Varsity Stadium. The Imperials arrived the same day and, after having held practices in the drizzling rain back in Sarnia, were relieved to find the weather in Toronto cold and clear. Massucci felt optimistic and promised that his team would be at full strength for the match.

Over 1,000 rooters from Sarnia and other communities in southwestern Ontario arrived Saturday by special train. In all, nearly 9,000 spectators packed Varsity Stadium to witness the 22nd Grey Cup. Conditions held and provided a fast field. According to analysts, the game could go either way, though the Canadian Rugby Union president had his money on the Roughriders. In the end, the Oilmen overpowered and outplayed the Roughriders. Sarnia's two touchdowns were converted by drop-kicks from quarterback Alex Hayes, and with the same foot he also realized a field goal. Five additional points were registered by the supreme punting ability of Hugh "Bummer" Stirling. Regarding the Western squad, the consensus once again was that this was the best team yet to make an appearance at the Dominion Championship — just not quite good enough. A standout among the Roughriders was backfielder Ralph Pierce, former University of North Dakota star, marvelled at for his speed and ability to run back kicks.

The final score was Sarnia Imperials 20, Regina Roughriders 12.

• • •

While en route east, 1935's Western title-winners, the Winnipeg 'Pegs, waited to learn the outcome of the Eastern final and the host city of the Dominion Championship. They were still waiting by the time they reached their stopover in Detroit. Soon the news came through that Sarnia experienced a reversal of fortune: the Imperials had been defeated 22–3 in an ambush of Tigers.

On Monday the Winnipeggers played an exhibition game against Assumption College across the river in Windsor. While the Westerners handily defeated the collegians 17–0, many — including their coach — felt that the 'Pegs, four weeks out of practice, were a little rusty and could do much better. Sitting in the stands was Hamilton coach Fred Veale, who must have also recognized this because upon his return home he warned his Tigers to expect a battle.

A decision finally came down from the Canadian Rugby Union regarding the venue. The game would be played in Hamilton and not a neutral territory. Sarnia protested, but the rules were quite clear: "the home club shall provide the grounds, subject to the approval of the union."

Winter came down heavy in 1935. The Winnipeg team held their penultimate practice on a snow-covered field at Wayne State in Detroit before retreating into the college gymnasium for their last. Meanwhile, the Tigers were practising on their own frozen field. The train carrying the Winnipeggers left for Hamilton on Friday afternoon and arrived in the early evening.

The temperature rose overnight and on a rain-swept field the 23rd Grey Cup was bitterly fought by the Winnipeggers for "dear old Minnesota, Manitoba and Canadian West."

Fritz Hanson proved to be the greatest Winnipegger of them all. Even brilliant Tiger tacklers like Jimmy Simpson, Jack Craig, and Seymour Wilson were baffled by little Fritz. Hanson caught magnificently and was good for yards anytime he had possession.

While Hamilton's Jack Craig failed to return the Winnipeg kickoff, on the next play Bomber quarterback Bob Fritz completed a 15-yard touchdown pass. There was no conversion. Hamilton responded with a field goal. In the second quarter, Winnipeg's Russ Rebholz completed a touchdown pass to Greg Kabat and this time the convert was good. Each team scored a single to make the halftime score 12–4.

In the third quarter, Wilf Patterson capped a four-play drive to haul it in for a touchdown. After the conversion and a Frank Turville single, Hamilton was within two points of a win. Winnipeg punt returner Fritz Hanson received a punt from his 30-yard line and returned it nearly 80 yards for a touchdown. Hamilton, however, forced Winnipeg to give up a safety, leaving them a converted touchdown behind. On the last play of the game, Hamilton again attempted an onside kick. This time Hanson recovered and ran the ball out of the end zone, denying Hamilton the rouge.

The final score was 18–12 for the Winnipegs, which meant that for the first time in its history, the Grey Cup trophy was going west. The verdict was that the better team had won. There were no alibis and no excuses.

Looking at the big picture, the outcome was widely viewed as beneficial. "No more will a Canadian final be regarded as a foregone conclusion that another Eastern team is about to win. Finalists henceforth will meet on an equal basis, and the Westerners ... will be commanding wholesome respect of their opposition."

And then there were the inevitable comments about the American players: "From a Western point of view the one regret was that the long sought-after victory was scored, not by a team of Western Canada athletes, but by a powerful football machine, principal cogs of which were imported duty-free from the United States market.... No Interprovincial Union team, despite all the trouble over imports, ever was as 'packed' with U.S. talent as the new Canadian champion." But there was a consensus that there was some real chemistry brewing here: "That of course, doesn't alter the fact that they are a great team. They overcame some very real handicaps to win, and in doing so produced some scintillating football that amazed the onlookers."

• • •

In 1936, the Sarnia Imperials returned in fighting form, anxious to reclaim the Grey Cup, but football bureaucracy was once again left to determine what shape the Dominion Championship would take.

On Wednesday December 2, the governors of the Western Canada Rugby Football Union voted 5–3 to withdraw the West's challenge for the Dominion Championship, the 24th Grey Cup, after refusing the Regina Roughriders permission to compete. This came about as a result of the Alberta governors' protest of the Regina Roughriders' entry into the final with a team handicapped by the ineligibility of five regular players. The discussion quickly degenerated into an open quarrel between factions within the Western football conference. On Friday it was agreed that the winner of the next day's match between the Sarnia Imperials and the Ottawa Rough Riders would take home the Grey Cup.

Sarnia was favoured. Though Ottawa had an impressive wing line, Sarnia had a strong backfield. The only flaw in the Riders' play seemed to be in its forward pass, considered the weakest among the nation's football unions. After some further consideration by armchair quarterbacks and the official oddsmakers, it was thought the game might actually be a close match. Damn the experts.

It turned out to be a game filled with more than its fair share of drama and excitement. Early in the first quarter, the Imperials took a 12–0 lead and looked as if they might just run away with it. But the Rough Riders were tireless and in the next set managed to close the gap. However, the Sarnians regained their lead, tilting it 24–12 going into the intermission. They cruised through the third quarter, adding a couple more points to the scoreboard, no doubt confident that they had the game in hand. But Ottawa refused to let go. In the fourth quarter, another eight points brought the Riders within striking distance. In the dying minutes, the gang from Capital City gambled on a touchdown and lost, heroically. The final score was Sarnia Imperials 26, Ottawa Rough Riders 20. It was widely considered one of the greatest gridiron spectacles in recent memory.

Standouts included Ottawa's Andy Tommy, who many must have thought was out for rest and recovery at the end of the half, what with torn shoulder ligaments and all. But after Tommy took his Novocain from Argonauts veteran doctor Smirle Lawson, he insisted on hitting the field again. Another gridiron gladiator was Sarnia's backfield star, Hugh Stirling, who kicked, broke up passing plays, tackled, threw forward passes, and basically did everything but serve up hot dogs in the stands.

# 5

## 1937–1944:
## WEARING TWO UNIFORMS

The Toronto Argonauts earned their berth in the Dominion Championship after defeating the ever-impressive Sarnia Imperials in the Eastern final in 1937.

The Winnipeg Blue Bombers — the Western Champions — arrived in Toronto by way of Ann Arbor, Michigan, the evening of Friday December 10. They brought with them Art Stevenson, whose eligibility wouldn't be decided until just before the game. The triple-threat Nebraskan had come to Canada within the last year to enroll as a medical student in Manitoba, and the Canadian Rugby Union rule called for a one-year residence. Following his talk with the running back Saturday morning, CRU president W.C. Foulds would cast the deciding vote.

The Blue Bombers were already considered to be at a disadvantage, having been out of competition for a month. What's more, they were heading into a game that would be played under a slightly different set of rules. They had won the Western Championship against the Calgary Bronks while being allowed to make forward passes from anywhere behind the line of scrimmage, and to create interference as far as 10 yards in advance of the line. It would be difficult for a team that played under one set of rules during the regular season to observe a different set of regulations in the gruelling post-season.

By kickoff time a bitter wind was sweeping the field at Varsity Stadium. The turf, though, was in fairly good condition. Workmen had scraped off as much snow as possible and smoothed over the frozen shags of earth. Regardless, the

Argos opted for running shoes over cleats. To aid visibility, the gridiron was marked with red instead of the customary white. About 12,000 spectators turned out to warm the seats and cheer on their leather-clad heroes. Following his meeting with W.C. Foulds, Art Stevenson was allowed to don his Winnipeg uniform and march onto the field with his teammates.

Argonaut coach Lew Hayman sat on the bench and throughout the game stole the occasional glance down at a rusty horseshoe positioned at his feet — his good-luck charm, acquired somehow after his team's Eastern final victory over the Ottawa Rough Riders. Ignoring superstition, the bookies had already favoured his squad 7–5 over the Bombers.

The Bombers were the first to score — a rouge from the foot of Steve Olander after two failed plunges. The Argos assumed the lead when Bill Bryers recovered a loose ball at the Winnipeg 20-yard line. From there, Earl Selkirk kicked three points. A second chance at a place kick was low and wide and Olander netted only a single point for the Bombers. The score was 3–2 at the half in favour of the Blue and Gold.

The incremental game continued in the third quarter when Bob Isbister increased the Argo lead by a point with a 70-yard punt. This was followed by a failed field goal from Winnipeg's Greg Kabat that resulted in a point for the Bombers. But it wasn't enough. The final score was Argonauts 4, Blue Bombers 3. Coach Hayman was observed raising his cold good-luck charm and pressing it to his lips. More satisfying was the taste of the champagne from Earl Grey's mug.

Tommy Munns, sports editor for the *Globe and Mail*, reported: "It was an exciting game with the thrills accentuated by the tenseness of the last period as Argos fought desperately to hang on to their precious one-point lead and the Bombers battled just as desperately to wipe it out. Yet it could not be called the best football of the season. Fumbles, attributed to hand-numbing cold and tactical errors by both teams entered into the struggle."

Differences in rules and styles of play explained away the defeat and salved some wounds. Still, the 25th Grey Cup marked a turning point in Canadian football because it reinforced the conviction formed in 1935 that there was now little difference in the skill sets of Eastern and Western players.

For Lew Hayman it was a fitting climax to a great season. He was now widely considered the best coach in Canada. After the game there was a civic banquet held in honour of players and officials. Blue Bombers' coach Bob Fritz spoke off the cuff and from the heart, confessing how he had seen the turning point for his team "not this afternoon, but one week ago, after watching Argonauts against Sarnia," and called the Argonauts the "best ball club he had ever seen." He then avowed that the West would be back next year to reclaim the Grey Cup, and received a rousing ovation.

• • •

Contrary to rumours that he might defect to Montreal, Lew Hayman returned the following season to coach the Argonauts, leading them to the Eastern final, where they once again conquered the troublesome Sarnia Imperials.

Meanwhile, in the West, the issue of a player's residence came up again. Winnipeg's Martin Gainor was suspended by the Canadian Rugby Union after being declared ineligible for the final for violating the continuous residence rule. There was evidence Gainor had been absent from Canada for several months in the previous year. Bombers manager Joe Ryan readily admitted Gainor's absence but maintained that the player had not violated the spirit of the rule as he was attending required classes at North Dakota University. Ryan appealed, citing the students' clause.

It was a record attendance at the 26th Grey Cup, with well over 18,000 packing the stands at Varsity Stadium. In a pre-game talk, Winnipeg coach Reg Threlfall declared that his team would either "win by a lot or get beaten by a lot."

By the end of the first half, his boys were leading narrowly 7–5. In the third quarter the Argos tightened the margin by a point but the Bombers still looked strong. The game could go either way. Unbeknownst to the Bombers — and the spectators — the defending Grey Cup champions were about to execute perhaps the most breathtaking offensive in the 17-year history of intersectional football.

The Argonauts began the fourth quarter on the Winnipeg 43-yard line with the way clear to unleash their secret weapon, Red Storey. A lateral sweep by Robert "Big Bob" Isbister and Art West put the ball on the 28-yard line; Storey swung wide to the right of the Toronto scrimmage line, ready to put into effect one of his coach's trademark extension plays. It was a cleverly designed manoeuvre that allowed Storey to cut sharply left and weave through the confounded Winnipeg lines. He finished his charge with a touchdown that gave the Argonauts a four-point lead. The Argos were neutralizing the Bombers.

Storey was good for two more touchdowns, and Bernie Thornton produced another. All together, the steamrolling Double Blue machine produced four touchdowns in the final quarter and all were converted, two by Annis Stukus and two by left-footed Bill Stukus.

Final score: Argonauts 30, Blue Bombers 7. With this game, the 1938 Argonauts ended their season the highest-scoring team in the history of Canadian football, having earned 220 points in just 10 games.

Winnipeg credit was given where Winnipeg credit was due. Standouts among that ensemble were Art Stevenson for his remarkable punting and sharp passing; Eddie James for his plunging; and fleet-footed linesmen Bill Ceretti and Martin Gainor (who just as swiftly had had his residency matter resolved).

After the game, the Bombers' Bud Marquardt shouldered his way into the Argonaut dressing room to trade jerseys with Red Storey. Amid the chaos of the Scullers' smoke-filled quarters, a small but impressive figure moved through, shaking hands and slapping backs. It was Sir Edward Beatty, president of the Canadian Pacific Railroad, under the escort of T.L. Church, member of Parliament. There were these high hats, and then there were the likes of eight-year Argo veteran Howard "Red" Vail. Not only was he finishing on top in his last game with the Argonauts, it was also his thirtieth birthday. He was presented with the gift of the game ball, which his teammates had rescued especially for him.

• • •

The Eastern final in 1939 was a hard lesson for a young and inexperienced squad of Sarnia Imperials. Many of them were fresh out of high school and no match for the larger, seasoned Ottawa Rough Riders, who went on to win the competition 23–1. The Riders would advance to play perennial threat the Winnipeg Blue Bombers at Lansdowne Park in Ottawa for the 27th Grey Cup.

Attendance reports varied, running up to 15,000. Regardless, it was a snow-covered field with a slippery turf that gave neither side a distinct advantage. Skill and strategy would be compromised. The winner might just be the team that made the most of their opponent's missteps.

Having said that, a solid Riders defence virtually eliminated any advantage the Bombers' famous forward passing might have given them: the Winnipeggers completed only one of eight. But the very dazzling proof of skill winning out over adverse conditions came in the last minute when the Bombers' Art Stevenson booted the pigskin for a point. Try as the Riders did with three subsequent but short-lived plays, the win went to Winnipeg. They defeated Ottawa 8–7 to take the Cup, their second in five years. Faithful Riders fans cheered as their combatants marched off the field at Lansdowne.

THE NAME "BLUE BOMBERS" GOES BACK TO 1936 WHEN, DURING AN EXHIBITION GAME AGAINST THE UNIVERSITY OF NORTH DAKOTA, *WINNIPEG TRIBUNE* SPORTSWRITER VINCE LEAH REFERRED TO THE TEAM AS "THE BLUE BOMBERS OF WESTERN FOOTBALL" — A REFERENCE TO THEN-HEAVYWEIGHT BOXING CHAMPION JOE LOUIS, AKA THE BROWN BOMBER.

A civic banquet was held later in the evening for both teams. Distinguished guests included officials from all levels of government, with mayors Stanley Lewis of Ottawa and John Queen of Winnipeg at the head table. A congratulatory telegram sent to Winnipeg coach Reg Threlfall from Prime Minister Mackenzie King was read aloud. Manitoba premier John Bracken told the attendees in his speech that he would like to see the Blue Bombers and the Rough Riders play in the final again next year. Back in Winnipeg, a welcoming committee was in the midst of grand preparations.

•  •  •

The following year, on November 25, 1940, J.P. McCaffrey, manager of the Ottawa Rough Riders, wired Canadian Rugby Union controller Fred Hamilton: "Sorry, regret it not possible to play Winnipeg at Toronto Dec. 14 as club feels they should disband after Balmy Beach game here Dec. 7. Regards."

That same day, Floyd Muirhead, sponsor of Toronto's Balmy Beach club also wired Hamilton, saying, "The powers that be have spoken. Due to the affiliations of the Balmy Beach Football Club with the ORFU and CRU, it is impossible for our club to participate in the game proposed. Kindly accept my personal and our club's congratulations for the very fine work you are performing through the Sports Service League for a most worthy cause."

Regarding the actual game of football, odds had the Balmy Beachers pinned as 2–1 underdogs.

Part one of the home-and-home Eastern final series between the Ottawa Rough Riders and Toronto's Balmy Beachers took place on Saturday November 30 at Varsity Stadium, in front of a modest crowd of about 5,000.

Conditions were less than ideal: blowing snow cut visibility and made play-making a challenge. The game was tied at two apiece when Rider Andy Tommy faked a run up the middle and threw a lateral pass to Dave Sprague, who then penetrated the Beachers' line for a touchdown. The final score was Rough Riders 8, Balmy Beachers 2.

The sequel to the Eastern final took place Saturday December 7. Ticket sales were admittedly soft. Sub-zero temperatures and heavy snowfall in the days leading up to the big game were making for less than promising conditions at Lansdowne Park. "Unless we get a break in the weather," said Rough Rider business manager Jim McCaffrey, "I don't look for a very large crowd."

The Riders were going into the game with a six-point lead in this total-points series, so the pressure was on the Beachers. Field conditions were not any better in Ottawa, but the points seemed to come faster. The Beachers grabbed a 5–0 lead in the first quarter, but only a few plays later Ottawa scored a touchdown on a three-yard run by Bobby Porter. Ottawa maintained the momentum and also capitalized on Toronto mistakes: a Rick Perley recovery translated into Tommy Daley touchdown. A trio of rouges from Sammy Sward in the final quarter sealed the game for the Rough Riders.

The final score was Ottawa 12, Balmy Beachers 5, which added up to a round score of 20–7 in favour of the Rough Riders.

Because of a rules dispute with the Canadian Rugby Union, the Western champions, the Winnipeg Blue Bombers, were refused participation in the 28th Grey Cup, and so title defaulted to the Eastern victors, the Ottawa Rough Riders.

• • •

Winnipeg Coach Reg Threlfall had the answers tucked in his jacket pocket. In the Winnipeg locker room after the 29th Grey Cup game, he told the press, "This scribbler" — and he waved it around — "I've had for two years. When we played Ottawa two years ago in the final I made diagrams of all their plays. This pad," — which he also held up — "has diagrams of the Ottawa plays noted by Bert Warwick when he scouted the Hamilton-Ottawa game last week. And this one," — a pad that he also flourished — "I drew myself in the first quarter of the game today. Compare them," he said, holding them out, "the plays are all the same."

And so the Bombers saw it all coming. They had a defence at the ready for every Ottawa play. Despite that, the final score indicated a much closer game. In front of a record Grey Cup audience of over 19,000 at Varsity Stadium, the Rough Riders went down 18–16 against the Blue Bombers.

The tearing down of the goal posts following a football game was a long-standing tradition — back in the days of wooden posts — and in 1941 the ritual was performed by the

18th Manitoba Reconnaissance Regiment, currently stationed at Camp Borden. Major Homer Robinson, a former Winnipeg sports official, had arranged tickets for more than 400 soldiers for Saturday's game. Early Sunday afternoon the unit paraded through downtown Toronto to the front door of the Royal York Hotel, where they presented the goal posts — as if they were presenting colours — to officials of the Winnipeg Blue Bombers club to be taken home as a memento.

• • •

The 30th Grey Cup was another East–West contest, but this time it was between a team combining players from the three services plus civilians (the Winnipeg RCAF Bombers) and a team consisting entirely of service personnel (the Toronto RCAF Hurricanes). That didn't mean that there weren't a few familiar names and faces. The only difference was that, off the field, they were wearing another uniform.

Included were the likes of Flying Officer Lew Hayman (coach, RCAF Hurricanes); Flight Lieutenant Eddie Thompson and Aircraftman 2 Bill Stukus (Hurricanes co-captains); Pilot Officer Bob Fritz (Hurricanes); and Ordinary Seaman Ches McCance (captain, RCAF Bombers).

More than 12,000 turned out to Varsity Stadium for the game. Fans were impressed with the way the players, who had chosen running shoes over cleats, manoeuvred through the minefield that was the gridiron — mud and turf dotted with patches of ice that were pooling water.

Despite the poor conditions, the Hurricanes managed to out-kick and even out-charge the Bombers. One analyst suggested that the Winnipeggers lost the game in the first quarter after a forward pass by Wayne Sheley on the Hurricanes' 12-yard line was intercepted by Eddie Thompson right on the Toronto goal line. The flight lieutenant then dodged and weaved all the way to the Winnipeg 44-yard line before finally being taken down.

The Hurricanes lost their 2–0 lead in the third quarter when some strong Bombers passing got Lloyd Boivin the ball, which he then ran for a touchdown. In the fourth quarter, Hayman's disciplined approach put the Hurricanes back on top. After a few fiery first downs, it was Pop Poplowski who hit over the middle from a scrimmage on the Bombers' three-yard line that produced Toronto's touchdown. They failed to convert but maintained their momentum and managed a rouge before the whistle. Final score: Hurricanes 8, Bombers 5. It was Lew Hayman's fourth Grey Cup in four tries, an impressive record.

*The RCAF Toronto Hurricanes following their victory in 1942 over the Winnipeg RCAF Bombers.*

Post-mortem discussions ran the gamut from field conditions to the month-long stretch between the Western final and the national final. It was politely suggested to the Canadian Rugby Union that they might solve both these problems by making the changes necessary to ensure that the Dominion Championship was always played in November.

• • •

In 1943, the Hamilton Flying Wildcats rescued an Eastern final championship against Montreal's RCAF Lachine in the dying minutes of the game. They may have saved Ontario's pride, but they would have to look a lot sharper if they expected to beat the Winnipeg RCAF Bombers at the 31st Grey Cup. The 1943 Bombers, with two exceptions, consisted entirely of Air Force personnel.

The train carrying the team from Winnipeg pulled into Toronto's Union Station on Friday November 26, and they held a practice at Varsity Stadium that very afternoon.

The Wildcats held their final workout in Hamilton on Thursday night and were scheduled to arrive in Toronto on Saturday morning by train. They had on their roster "eight members of the air force and two of the navy, the rest of the players being civilians, many of who work in war plants."

The teams were considered evenly matched. Analysts were calling a close game and bettors were looking for an edge. Experience can count for something: this would be Winnipeg coach Reg Threlfall's sixth trip to the East. Sometimes superstition counts, too: to date, no ORFU team had ever lost a Grey Cup game. Over 16,000 fans filed into Varsity Stadium, exceeding all expectations.

Trailing by seven points in the fourth quarter, the Bombers suddenly appeared fired up, like they actually wanted to win the game. But they proved no match for the Hamilton linemen, who put up an impenetrable wall.

Just minutes into the game, Wildcat Joe Krol sidestepped three Bombers to connect a 30-yard pass to Doug Smith, who all but fell across the line for a touchdown. The Bombers' first point came from Brian Quinn, and teammate Garney Smith provided a brief one-point lead as he darted around the end and ran 17 yards for a touchdown. Hamilton went on to score two touchdowns before the end of the quarter.

LEGEND HAS IT THAT "OSKEE-WEE-WEE," THE INFAMOUS HAMILTON FOOTBALL CHANT DATING BACK TO THE MID-1920S, WAS CARRIED INTO THE SECOND WORLD WAR BY LOCALLY-TRAINED RCAF PILOTS WHO USED IT TO IDENTIFY THEMSELVES WHILE FLYING OVER GERMANY IN ADVERSE WEATHER CONDITIONS.

After the break, Krol kicked a field goal to increase Hamilton's lead to 21–7. Winnipeg's offence finally kicked in at the end of the third quarter, with Quinn completing a pass to Jim Berry for a 42-yard touchdown. After a number of unsuccessful plays, Quinn eventually gained a single for the Bombers. Hamilton, however, managed to pad their lead with a couple of rouges before the whistle. The final score was Hamilton Flying Wildcats 23, Winnipeg RCAF Bombers 14.

It did not go unnoticed that on the Hamilton team were a couple of football veterans — coach Brian Timmis and captain Jimmy Simpson — both of whom were on the 1935 Hamilton squad that lost to the Winnipeg team that had brought the Grey Cup west for the first time. For these men it was a particularly sweet victory.

• • •

Though they lost the final game of a home-and-home series against Toronto's Balmy Beachers, the round score of 13–10 meant that the Hamilton Flying Wildcats would take the honours. It was 1944 and it would be the Wildcats' second consecutive ORFU championship and their third in four years. In the other home-and-home series — the all-Canadian Navy final between the Toronto HMCS York Bulldogs and a combined team from HMCS Donnacona–St. Hyacinthe — the Bulldogs soundly defeated the Montreal team 12–1. But as was the case in the other series, the round score meant that the title would go to HMCS Donnacona–St. Hyacinthe. All of this meant that the Donnacona would be meeting the Wildcats in the Dominion Championship.

Late in 1944, with the war seeming interminable, the decision not to hold an East versus West competition was made, and considering the way the various home-and-home series had played out so far, it wasn't feeling much like the Grey Cup. Fewer than 4,000 fans turned up at Civic Stadium in Hamilton — one of the smallest crowds on record. Also keeping the fans away was the fact that most of them were anticipating that Hamilton, perennial football champs at virtually every level, would have no problem defeating the Montrealers, who had shown little or no offence in their recent final against Toronto.

One of the *Globe and Mail* sports columnists admitted to not even tuning in on his radio. Montreal only sent down one sports journalist. He covered the NHL game in Toronto and then never bothered to continue on to Hamilton for the Grey Cup.

They all thought they had picked the winner, but they were all proved wrong. In one of the Grey Cup's biggest upsets, HMCS Donnacona–St. Hyacinth defeated Toronto's HMCS York Bulldogs by one point: final score 7–6.

Fans and players alike would have been relieved to know that this would be the last wartime Grey Cup game.

# 6

## 1945–1951: POST-WAR BOOM
## AND THE GREY CUP FESTIVAL

The Balmy Beachers hadn't been to a Dominion Championship final since the start of the war, and they hadn't won a Grey Cup since 1930 when they defeated the Regina Roughriders, then the East's tackle dummy. Ted Reeve's Beachers fought tooth and nail to get to the Eastern final in 1945, only to be overwhelmed by city rivals, the Toronto Argonauts.

The Double Blue Machine was in fighting form, having spent the season honing their skills battling much tougher squads than the Beachers or the current Grey Cup challengers, the Winnipeg Blue Bombers. It wasn't a question of ability. The Bombers hadn't played a game in three weeks, and only two games in their regular season were played under Canadian rules. All of their other games were played against minor U.S. colleges under a mixture of American and Canadian rules. Subsequently, odds were stacked 4–1 against them and the Winnipeggers were a little resentful, as they were coming east not for the ride but to play some serious football. Despite this, or because of it, tickets for the 33rd Grey Cup sold out in a matter of a few hours.

More than 9,000 huddled and bundled fans braved the December cold to watch East and West collide on an ice-covered field at Varsity Stadium. It became apparent early on in the game that the Westerners were fighting a losing battle. At halftime, bored spectators amused themselves with a snowball fight. When the traffic police that were retained as additional security took it upon themselves to clear the snow from the field, fans set their sights on them and opened fire.

The final score was Toronto Argonauts 35, Winnipeg Blue Bombers 0. To use an oft-repeated word in coverage of similarly lopsided sports matches, Bert Warwick's Blue Bombers were outclassed by the Argonaut team. The tally lifted the East's cumulative intersectional points total to 326 compared to 88 for the West. It was now widely accepted that if the West was to make any gains, they would have to start conforming to Eastern standards, forego the running guard, and become aligned with what former Bomber coach Reg Threlfall once described as "hot potato football." Bill Nairn, veteran of other Winnipeg clubs, admitted that it was time the West stressed more end runs and lateral passes. "We may as well accept it," he said. "We've got to play the type of ball they play in the East."

It can be easier to accept crushing defeat when the brilliance of your opponent is widely recognized: Winnipeg club president Art Chipman said he knew in the early minutes that the Bombers were in for a drubbing, but he "thrilled so much to the Toronto team's flawless play he lost interest in what score they might amass."

After the game there were the usual dressing-room graces. Jack Bracken, leader of the Progressive Conservative Party, confessed to Hamilton Flying Wildcats quarterback Joe Krol that he would much rather be able to do what Krol did on the field that day than be prime minister.

• • •

While covering the 1946 Grey Cup, Jim Coleman of the *Globe and Mail* wrote: "There is no single sports spectacle in this country which packs the oomph of a Grey Cup football final between the East and West. Even if Toronto possessed an arena capable of seating 50,000 customers, it is unlikely that it would be large enough to accommodate those who would like to buy tickets for this week's renewal of the annual schmozzle." This would be part two of this East versus West trilogy, and was witnessed by an audience of well over 19,000 at Varsity Stadium.

Teddy Morris was back at the helm as Argonauts coach and looking for a repeat of the last year's victory. His strategy was not to take anything for granted, even when it came to the Winnipeg Blue Bombers.

Jack West's Bombers did launch a powerful attack, but once the more experienced Eastern champs found their feet, the game changed. The game marked the debut of Toronto's so-called Gold Dust Twins: Joe "King" Krol and Royal Copeland. The two opened the scoring when Krol hit Copeland with a pass that he ran in for a touchdown. They repeated after a Copeland interception worked up to him receiving 30-yard pass from Krol, which he then hauled in, dodging would-be tacklers, for his second major of the game. Krol found another able receiver in Ron Smylie, who carried the ball down the sidelines and set up the Argos with a comfortable 16–0 lead at the break.

In the third, Krol's brilliant passing marched the Argos up field where, from the 25-yard line, he let fly a spiral to Copeland who, once more escaping Walt Dobler's clutches, ran it in for a touchdown. Krol was like a machine. Faking an end run, he connected with Leo Deadey on the Winnipeg 12-yard line. And on the very next play, Krol drilled a pass to Boris Tipoff in the end zone for a touchdown.

The Bombers managed their lone touchdown in the last few seconds as Dobler executed a plunge from the Argos' two-yard line. The final score was 28–6 for the Argonauts.

Quarterback Chuck Camelleri snatched the game ball and gave it to coach Teddy Morris as a souvenir of his second Grey Cup victory. Morris liked to point out that his Argonauts were "100 per cent Canadian." He strongly believed that homegrown Canadian talent could be developed to become every bit as competitive as the stars being brought up from the United States.

The playing field was levelling in every direction. This latest Grey Cup game provided real reason for optimism. It marked the first time that East and West played under rules that, with minor modifications, the Westerners had been advocating since their first Grey Cup victory in 1935. And meeting the East halfway, so to speak, the Blue Bombers dropped from their playbook their customary off-tackle offensives and made some use of the lateral pass.

As an aside, fans were apparently heard commenting on the condition of the Bombers' uniforms. According to an article in the *Globe and Mail*, "Their clothing was tattered and tear-worn, and every time that they were tackled the moths were knocked out of their kidney pads and went whirling though the autumn air." Former Bomber Lou Mogul was at the game and claimed to have recognized the pants he wore when Winnipeg defeated Hamilton back in 1935.

• • •

The 35th Grey Cup marked the sixth meeting between Winnipeg and Toronto, the Winnipeg team having lost all five of those previous matches. Bay Street was setting the odds at 5–1 in favour of the Argos.

Thursday afternoon, Coach West took his Winnipeg squad through practices on the half-frozen AAA Grounds in Hamilton, and on Friday, before heading to Toronto, the team took a quick sightseeing trip to Niagara Falls to see what all the fuss was about.

Several hundred Bombers fans were anticipated in the stands at Varsity, the majority being Winnipeggers relocated to the East, the balance arriving by train and plane.

"It had to be seen to be believed." So wrote Hal Walker in the *Globe and Mail* the following Monday. "It was large Joe Krol, Canada's greatest payoff football player, who snuffed out flaming Peggers' hopes of their first conquest of Toronto's famous double blue team which now has beaten the Bombers six times in the national final."

IN MARCH OF 1947, THE GREY CUP NARROWLY SURVIVED A HORRIFIC FIRE THAT GUTTED THE TORONTO ARGONAUT ROWING CLUB, DESTROYING DECADES OF TROPHIES AND MEMORABILIA. LEGEND HAS IT THAT IT WAS FOUND DANGLING BY A NAIL IN THE SMOULDERING REMAINS OF THE BUILDING.

It was a devastating loss for the Blue Bombers. Argos' coach Teddy Morris paid the Westerners sincere tribute after the game. His rival, Bombers coach Jack West, replied, "if we come down next year, brother, we will be a whole lot stronger, don't forget that."

The Winnipeg Blue Bombers did make the trip down again, but not the following year.

• • •

In 1948, the Calgary Stampeders and their fans rolled across the prairies like a Chinook, prepared to warm the hearts of any Easterner in their path. They rode a special CPR train, pausing at Winnipeg to stretch their legs in a square dance set to the music of their own travelling band.

But it wasn't all fun and games. On the Thursday before the game the team held a two-hour signal drill at Appleby College in Oakville, west of Toronto. Police officers enlisted to keep the crowd back had little to worry about as the stiff, bitter winds off Lake Ontario did most of the work for them.

The team and their entourage were scheduled to arrive in Toronto early Friday morning with their band, their horses, and their chuckwagons. They came to take Toronto. Sportswriters from all corners converged on the provincial capital to cover the game. The largest Canadian radio network ever assembled was set to broadcast the football final to millions of listeners from coast to coast.

Following a luncheon conference with Calgary alderman Don McKay at the Royal York, Toronto mayor Hiram McCallum greeted Calgary fans at the hotel and, decked out in gabardine pants, a "fancy" shirt, and a 10-gallon hat, confidently mounted his assigned mustang and rode up Bay Street to the steps of city hall, where he enjoyed a hearty breakfast of flapjacks and bacon. It was a little-known fact that McCallum was raised on a ranch in Alberta.

"It was quite a piece of mobile vaudeville by the time it hit Bloor St. One prairie schooner [covered wagon] even had a little prairie schooner tagging along behind. There were wagons

*Calgary Stampeders whooping it up in the now-legendary 1948 Grey Cup festivities.*

and trucks and cars and dogies and on them all were people, most of them peculiarly dressed in great big hats and great big boots and all of them shouting great big boasts." The supreme confidence, optimism, and gameness of the Stampeders — who had never won a Grey Cup, let alone made it to the final — was contagious. Even the Cabinet was talking football. In a media scrum, defence minister Brooke Claxton was offering 2–1 on the Ottawa Rough Riders.

Most of the faithful were there early, including the governor general. When Viscount Alexander arrived, the band played the national anthem, of course, and everybody started scrambling for their seats. This proved somewhat premature and, of course, the band played the national anthem all over again about 15 minutes later and the serious business started.

The governor general set the stage with a better-than-typical ceremonial kickoff. Rugger-style, he dug his own divot in the turf, situated the ball, then let fly with an impressive 25-yard boot.

During the first quarter, while attempting his second fake punt of the game, Ottawa's Howie Turner was swiftly brought down and five plays later the underdog Stampeders had their first touchdown. Calgary continued making progress with their sleeper play. While Norm Hill went unnoticed along the sideline, Keith Spaith hit him with him a neat pass for a touchdown.

In the final quarter, Ottawa's Pete Karpuk let loose a lateral pass that rolled around on the ground and, thinking the play was dead, he let it keep rolling. It did … until Calgary's Woody Strode picked it up and ran it all the way to the Ottawa 11-yard line before being taken down. Pete Thodos easily scored the winning touchdown, crossing the Ottawa goal line practically standing up. The final score was Calgary Stampeders 12, Ottawa Rough Riders 7.

Following tradition, the goal posts were immediately torn down. Their remains were carried by fans to the Royal York, where a bellhop fastened them to the mezzanine balcony railing. Shortly after, a couple of ragged-looking gentlemen made their way among the revellers with square pieces of wood in their hands, "genuine pieces of the goal posts," they said, "only a buck each." They were like street vendors in the Holy Land selling bits of relics from the Crusades. Some people were buying.

When players started coming through on their way to the civic reception, Woody Strode was immediately surrounded by autograph-seekers. Minutes later, Stampeder president Tom Brooks arrived with the Grey Cup and then no one could be heard over the ensuing cheers.

There was still the prevailing opinion that the Canadian Rugby Union was not making the most of this grassroots enthusiasm for the game and the Grey Cup. It was believed that a marginal increase in ticket prices could help pay for a larger, better facility and compensate the players and clubs properly for their work toward and support of the championship game.

Of course there was the money, but as pointed out in a *Globe and Mail* editorial from November 29, 1948, it was not going unnoticed that Grey Cup games "have a way of improving inter-provincial relations in a fashion that so far has eluded the political experts." The fall classic was clearly an investment that paid off in more than just financial dividends.

• • •

The last of the Calgary contingent arrived in Toronto the night before the 37th Grey Cup game, decked out in all the Western-style colour and pageantry people had come to expect following the 1948 spectacle.

It would be the Montreal Alouettes versus the Calgary Stampeders in 1949, and Lew Hayman's Larks were picked to win the game at 9–5 odds. The only variable as far as he was concerned was halfback Jack Harper who had dislocated his shoulder the previous weekend playing in the Eastern final against the Hamilton Tigers. His participation would remain in question until Saturday morning.

Attendance at Varsity Stadium for the game was just over 20,000. Weather conditions were less than ideal, but that didn't seem to slow the players down any.

An 85-yard drive in the opening quarter resulted in the Alouettes' Virgil Wagner scoring the first touchdown of the game. It was converted by Chester McCance. A second touchdown in the same span, this time from Bob Cunningham, gave plenty of indication what direction things were heading in (McCance also got the convert here). While Calgary quickly replied with a rouge and a Harry Hood touchdown, Montreal maintained their healthy lead going into the half after their third major, with Herb Trawick taking the credit. The score was Alouettes 17, Stampeders 7.

Montreal increased their lead in the third with another Virgil Wagner touchdown paired with a successful conversion by McCance, who contributed a field goal as well. Gains by Frank Filchock and Ralph Toohy set up Wagner nicely for his second touchdown of the game. Closing the scoring in the third was another McCance field goal, bringing the tally to 26–7 for the Alouettes.

But the Stampeders got back in the game in the fourth: Johnny Aguirre broke through the Montreal line and sacked Bob Cunningham for a safety; Sugarfoot Anderson snatched up a Wagner fumble and then returned it for a touchdown. But it wasn't enough. Montreal concluded the scoring with a point for a McCance missed field goal and a rouge by Fred

Kijek. The final score was Montreal 28, Calgary 15. It was a significant victory for Alouettes head coach Lew Hayman, as it was his fifth Grey Cup in five trips to the final.

The consensus seemed to be that the Alouettes and the Stampeders provided a great football game, and the only complaints heard were regarding the condition of Varsity Stadium. It was strongly felt that organizers, the hosts, and the CRU were neglecting their duties, to the point of it being an embarrassment and an abuse of paying spectators. *Globe and Mail* columnist Jim Coleman raised the hue and cry: "We don't deserve to have the Canadian Rugby Football Championship played in Toronto if we can't provide decent surroundings for the game."

Despite the fact that snow had been forecast as early as the Wednesday before the game, no attempt had been made to protect the field by laying tarpaulins, and although no snow had fallen for 36 hours, the snow hadn't been swept from the stands.

Coleman believed that conditions could not have possibly been any worse at CNE Stadium, but that would be like exchanging the devil you know for the devil you don't.

• • •

On their way to Toronto for the 38th Grey Cup, the Winnipeg Blue Bombers made their final stopover in London, Ontario. On the Thursday before the game they attended the NFL Thanksgiving Day match at Briggs Stadium in Detroit — Lions versus the New York Yanks. Bombers coach Frank Larson must have seen something in the action that impressed him, because less than an hour after they returned to the Forest City he had his team reviewing drills, running back kicks, and going through exercises under the floodlights at Labatt Park.

Following their bus trip to Toronto on Friday afternoon they held another practice at Varsity Stadium, scene of their upcoming battle with the Toronto Argonauts.

While it may not have been a sellout season for Canadian football across the board in 1950, demand for Grey Cup tickets was extremely high, with people who were not normally football fans clamouring for a seat at the stadium. The Grey Cup was apparently becoming a place to be seen.

The bookmakers were calling 7–5 odds for the Argos to win. And speaking of predictions, the weatherman was calling for upwards of 10 inches of snow to fall before the game. The forecast scared away some of these casual spectators, however, and Friday night they gave the scalpers some stiff competition as they hustled to trade in their seats.

By Saturday morning it was looking like the weatherman might get his way and a contingent of Toronto's street cleaning equipment was commandeered to clear the snow from the frozen Varsity gridiron. A couple hundred workmen were also brought in to shovel snow from the stands.

Some sharp criticism was once again lobbed toward the University of Toronto and the CRU for not providing better playing conditions for athletes and better conditions overall for paying spectators. The weather turned mild in the morning and the field was transformed into a mass of mud and puddle. For the cost of a tarpaulin and the proper handling of said tarpaulin, it was believed the quality of the game could have been vastly improved. Despite the conditions, 27,000 people filled the place.

The scoring began in the first quarter when a midfield punt from the Argos' Joe Krol sailed over Bomber Tom Casey's head for a rouge. Later in the second, a Krol mistake landed the ball on Winnipeg's 15-yard line and, failing to achieve a first down, Nick Volpe kicked a 21-yard field goal that put the Argos up 4–0. The score at the half was Argonauts 7, Bombers 0.

The only touchdown of this greasy game came in the third quarter following a drive that enabled Toronto's Teddy Toogood to force the ball to the Winnipeg one-yard line. On the third down, Al Dekdebrun slipped the leather across the Bombers' goal line. Nick Volpe failed in the conversion but Krol later kicked a single for the final point of the game. The score was Toronto Argonauts 13, Winnipeg Blue Bombers 0.

• • •

The 39th Grey Cup took place on November 24, 1951, and featured the Roughriders versus the Rough Riders for the first time in its history. Regina had earned the Western title after defeating their rivals of the era, the Calgary Stampeders. Several members of federal Parliament showed their support for the Westerners by donning white Stetsons in the House on the Thursday before the big game. That same afternoon in Toronto, Roughrider coach Harry "Blackjack" Smith threw a party for the press at the Sunnyside Motor Inn west of downtown. It was all in good fun.

Two 14-car special trains hauled the 10-gallon hat West-erners into Union Station on Friday and, determined to out-Stampede the Stampeders of 1948, Saskatchewan Roughrider fans stormed the Royal York in waves of green and white, raising the roof with their live bands, cowbells, and noise-makers. The annual dinner was held once again a couple blocks north at the King Edward Hotel, and the speeches were broadcast over the radio.

The parade commenced at 10:30 the next morning and wound its way up through the downtown area to the neigh-bourhood surrounding Varsity Stadium. Visitors from the Wheat Province tossed 15,000 miniature loaves of bread into the crowd along the parade route, as a gift to the citizens of Toronto. There was more food spilling out of the chuckwagons and, more symbolically, a float featuring a giant horn of plenty spilling not just grain but also an oil rig. The armed services were represented in army and navy floats and an RCAF cover of jets. There was also the now-customary procession of combines, cowboys, and square dancers. Rounding out the cast were the Misses — America, Canada, and Grey Cup. The festivities were now in full gear.

ROUGHRIDERS VERSUS ROUGH RIDERS: THE OTTAWA CLUB ADOPTED THEIR NAME IN 1898. IT WAS SAID TO DERIVE FROM LOGGING ON THE OTTAWA RIVER BUT THERE IS ALSO EVIDENCE SUPPORTING THE NOTION THAT THE NAME AND THE TEAM COLOURS — RED AND BLACK — WERE INSPIRED BY TEDDY ROOSEVELT'S REGIMENT IN THE SPANISH-AMERICAN WAR. THE REGINA RUGBY CLUB CHANGED THEIR NAME TO THE REGINA ROUGHRIDERS IN 1924, THEIR NAME REPUTEDLY DERIVED FROM THE NORTH WEST MOUNTED POLICE. IN 1948, THE REGINA-BASED TEAM BECAME KNOWN AS THE SASKATCHEWAN ROUGHRIDERS.

Ottawa Mayor Charlotte Whitton stole the show, however, wielding her ceremonial mace — a broadaxe with a 12-inch blade — and an equally sharp tongue on the steps of Toronto's City Hall. She predicted that her city's Rough Riders would win by seven points — "a touch and a goal." In a public exchange of gifts, Regina's mayor-elect Gordon Grant presented Toronto mayor Hiram McCallum with a six-foot loaf of bread. Whitton immediately swung back into action with her mace, bringing the blade down on the loaf of bread, declaring, "Half a loaf is better than none."

The ceremonial kickoff was delayed several minutes while groundskeepers at Varsity Stadium searched for an available football. A practice ball was eventually located in the Ottawa team's dressing room and Governor General Alexander got to make a rather impressive 30-yard punt. As game balls disappeared into the stands, eagerly sought after by souvenir-hunters, announcers were compelled to ask fans to kindly return any leather that happened to fly their way. At the time, a game ball ran about $32.50.

The first half of the contest was made up primarily of Ottawa Rough Rider touchdowns, capped off with a Mickey Maguire fumble that Virgil Wagner recovered. Tom O'Malley threw the subsequent touchdown pass to Al Baldwin and it was 12–2 for the Ottawa team at the break.

The third Ottawa touchdown came after as many quarters as O'Malley hit Pete Karpuk with a 40-yard pass. Karpuk out-ran Roughrider Del Wardien 25 yards to get the ball across the Saskatchewan goal line.

The Roughriders re-entered the game in the final quarter after an Ottawa fumble was recovered by Roy Wright on the Ottawa 30. Saskatchewan's Glenn Dobbs completed a pass to Jack Nix on the three-yard line that Nix then wrestled across the Ottawa goal for a touchdown. Minutes later, Saskatchewan once more gained possession, and a few plays later Sully Glasser capitalized on an opportunity to score the second touchdown for the Westerners.

But the clock ran out for the Roughriders, and Ottawa mayor Charlotte Whitton's prediction came true. The final score was Ottawa Rough Riders 21, Saskatchewan Roughriders 14. It was Rough Rider head coach Clem Crowe's first year in Canadian football, and his first Grey Cup victory.

# THIRD QUARTER:

## 1952–1982

# 7

## 1952–1962: COMING TO YOU LIVE FROM VARSITY STADIUM

The affair began on the evening of Tuesday, November 25, 1952, when the Edmonton Eskimos, team officials, and their entourage touched down at Malton airport outside of Toronto. Their TCA North Star had the word ESKIMOS painted on the side in gold and green. Media were waiting and the Westerners, stepping off the plane in their grey jackets and white Stetsons, obliged, waving for the photographers. The next morning, an advanced guard of Edmonton fans poured into Union Station. They came not just from Edmonton but from all points west of the Great Lakes, having received "warm receptions from mayors and citizens at every whistle stop." While fans continued converging on the city, Edmonton's coach, Frank Filchock, took his boys through a rigorous workout at Maple Leaf Stadium.

On Friday, the Grey Cup Special pulled into Union Station, packed with several hundred more Western rooters. During the 65-hour train trip, passengers kept entertained with live music and a baggage car converted into a dance hall and bar. When they disembarked they were greeted by the early birds from the West, a few hundred Torontonians, and mayor Allan Lamport. The football-crazed mob then paraded through the station concourse and went on to block traffic outside on Front Street. These unofficial celebrations carried on into the late afternoon at the Royal York, congesting the lobby — now decorated with oil derricks — hallways, and telephone switchboards. Grey Cup fever had taken hold.

Meanwhile, it was Argonauts coach Frank Clair's turn to take his team through a workout, this one on Trinity College's playing field, adjacent to Varsity Stadium. Later that evening, both teams headed down to the King Edward Hotel for the annual dinner.

Front and centre at the head table was trade minister C.D. Howe, standing in for prime minister Louis St. Laurent. The rest of the room was a who's who of Canadian football. In his speech, Regina old-timer Al Ritchie remarked that the Grey Cup was the "most important moulding influence of the last 100 years in bringing Eastern and Western Canada together." Another highlight of the evening was the Miss Grey Cup competition. Twenty-year-old Pat Hunter of Winnipeg, a stenographer from the Canadian Wheat Board office, was crowned princess.

Saturday morning, Edmonton fans were still arriving by train, bus, and auto. Identifiable by their sombreros, I LIKE ESKS buttons, and pins in the shape of oil derricks that would light up for a touchdown, they took over the city.

The parade commenced at 10:30, but it was difficult to figure out where it started and when it ended. It was made up of 88 floats — one of them carrying Miss Grey Cup — and wound its way through the streets of Toronto. The participants from Oil Country rode in convertibles and tractors, and on pintos and palominos, accompanied by three teams of northern huskies and innumerable pageant girls. They handed out Eskimo Pies and shares of stock in the "land of opportunity" to speechless Torontonians.

What followed was the crush into Varsity Stadium. A record 27,395 funnelled into the venue to witness the 40th Grey Cup. Anyone without a ticket resorted to radio or, for the first time, television. Fifteen years before the first NFL Super Bowl, the CBC was bringing the Grey Cup to the nation's living rooms. And if one wasn't able to view the game on the comfort of a chesterfield with feet firmly planted upon the hassock, there was always the option of watching the event at a local watering hole. The Paddock Tavern in downtown Toronto invited fans to come watch the game on their "giant TV screen." Over in Steeltown, about 25 television sets had been installed by Westinghouse in Hamilton Armouries, the city's largest assembly hall, for the company's employees and their friends. Several thousand football enthusiasts gathered there to watch the game. Cheat sheets were printed in the newspapers for novices, listing players' names and numbers for what O'Keefe Brewery marketers were referring to as "Canada's greatest single sports spectacle." Some 75 newspaper, radio, and TV reporters covered the event.

The Albertans had never won the national title and the Argonauts had never lost in nine tries. Odds averaged 8–5 in favour of the Argos, but the Eskimos were considered underrated — even in the Western final. Provisions were made for overtime and beyond: If there wasn't enough daylight for two additional 10-minute overtime periods, another game would be played Wednesday.

The weather office was promising a clear, cool afternoon with a high of about 2°C. The Varsity ground crew rolled the tarpaulin off the field. It was game time.

Acting prime minister C.D. Howe performed the ceremonial kickoff at 1:00 p.m.: Edmonton mayor William Hawrelak held the ball and Toronto mayor Allan Lamport watched.

Edmonton Eskimo Normie Kwong earned his team's and the game's first touchdown in an otherwise scoreless first quarter. The Argonauts inched ahead in the second after a Nobby Wirkowski touchdown that was converted by Red Ettinger, who later managed a field goal. About a minute before the break, Toronto made its second touchdown, also converted by Ettinger, ending the half at Toronto 15, Edmonton 5.

Kwong's second touchdown of the game and a Bill Snyder conversion narrowed the gap, but still left the Boatmen in the lead after three. The Eskimos ran out of offence in the final quarter and were kept scoreless. A touchdown from the Argos' Zeke O'Connor, followed by a conversion from Ettinger, closed the scoring in this Grey Cup contest. The final score was Toronto Argonauts 21, Edmonton Eskimos 11.

A Grey Cup celebration featuring Art Hallman and his orchestra took place in the Oak Room at Union Station after the game. Festivities carried on until midnight. By that time, the lobby of the Royal York resembled Times Square on New Year's Eve. A conga line of fans snaked around the pillars (the management had already taken the precaution of removing all plants and furniture). The noise and activity reached a crescendo at about 1:00 a.m., shortly before trains started leaving Union Station for the journey west. Members of the team had a little more time to recuperate: the Eskimos left the city on Monday the same way they came, on a chartered plane out of Malton. This time there were no photographers.

• • •

The next year, the battle for the Cup would be between Hamilton and Winnipeg. It wasn't the first time these two cities had met in the final, but it was the first time as the Tiger-Cats and the Blue Bombers.

But by 1953, it had become apparent that money was changing the game. In an anecdote covered by Jim Vipond in the *Globe and Mail*, Blue Bombers manager Scotty Kennedy recalled a casual meeting with past coach Reg Threlfall at his home in Fargo, North Dakota. They had been discussing a quarterback prospect, when Kennedy asked Threlfell how much he should offer the young man. Kennedy replied, "Six, eight, ten, or twelve thousand dollars." Kennedy answered, "Shucks, Reg, times have changed. The water boy gets more money now than what we paid you to coach."

Ticket buyers started assembling first thing Wednesday morning — a full 24 hours before they went on sale — outside the office at Hamilton's AAA Grounds. Their numbers swelled after shift change and the offices let out. By nighttime there were over 2,000 fans waiting outside the box office, braving the cold with their radios and portable record players, oil stoves, card tables, books, Thermoses, and food hampers.

Tickets were becoming scarce. Tiger-Cat and Bomber players were being hit up so hard they spent Thursday night in retreats outside of Hamilton and in Aurora, north of Toronto, respectively. If desperate fans could afford it, they were buying up television sets and consoles. This was an event to be experienced, or at least viewed on a tiny black-and-white screen. One local retailer in Toronto was advertising "Grey Cup TV Specials," and still had stock available of RCA's Winston 21-inch table model for $339, or $2,900 in today's dollars — roughly the cost equivalent of buying a 65-inch 3D plasma HDTV.

At the King Edward Hotel on the Friday night before the game, Ridley College held a pre-dinner reception honouring the grand old man of Canadian football, Dr. Henry Griffith, who had served as player, coach, and executive over a span of 50 years. Also in attendance were five members of the University of Toronto team he coached to victory in the inaugural Grey Cup match in 1909: Jack Newton, W.C. Foulds, Dr. Smirle Lawson, Pete German, and George Kingston.

Griffith was also honoured at the annual Grey Cup dinner afterward. The guest speaker was Secretary of State for External Affairs and future prime minister Lester B Pearson. In his speech he praised the U.S. contribution to Canadian football, remarking, "we owe American coaches and players a debt of gratitude for coming up here and playing the game in every respect." Other speakers included Toronto mayor Allan Lamport, Hamilton mayor Lloyd Jackson, Winnipeg alderman Jack Blumberg, CRU president Norm Perry, and Harry "Red" Foster.

Fans were coming to see the game from far and wide. Leonard Johnson of Vancouver had jokingly made the suggestion that he and his son Charles, based in Caracas, Venezuela, should meet up in Toronto for the next Grey Cup game. Charles took his suggestion seriously. When the schedule came down, he wired Toronto for tickets, then, after receiving confirmation, he contacted his father, who booked the next flight out of Vancouver. For Charles, it was an 8,000-kilometre journey from South America.

More locally, Toronto traffic authorities were issuing warnings against parking on lawns or obstructing driveways in the stadium area: "Persons attending the game should leave homes or hotels early, park their cars legally well away from the field of battle and walk or take a street car to the game."

For the first time in Grey Cup history, there would be six officials on the field. The sixth meant a pair of eyes that could rule on long passes and punts. Normally the two umpires would cover that, but to do so they often had to "relax their vigilance along the scrimmage line." Yes, there would be plenty of officials, and there would also be plenty of balls. The CRU had learned its lesson during the 1951 Grey Cup when 10 of the 11 game balls ended up in the stands, never to be seen again. This time there would be 18 available to the teams.

The only scoring in the first half of the game came in the form of a short touchdown run by Hamilton's Ed Songin, which was converted by Tip Logan in the opening quarter. Blue Bomber drives proved unsuccessful until the third quarter, when Gerry James was provided with the opportunity to run in a touchdown that was then converted by Bud Korchak. The Tiger-Cats replied swiftly, however, with a Vito Ragazzo reception that he ran for a touchdown. Logan was successful on the conversion, and the score after three was 12–6 for the Tiger-Cats. A 98-yard Winnipeg push engineered by Jack Jacobs could have been the game-changer, but it met with an abrupt end on Hamilton's two-yard line. Lou Kusserow's tackle forced Tom Casey to drop the ball as soon as his fingers touched Jacobs's pass. While the play is still being argued — was it interference or a clean tackle? — the victory went to Carl Voyles and his Tiger-Cats. The final score was Hamilton 12, Winnipeg 6.

It was Hamilton's first Grey Cup in 10 years, and it was a game that many critics consider to be one of the finest Cup matches ever played. Overall, it was a strong Ticats team, but singled out for praise was Vince Mazza. Gerry James was considered the Bombers' strongest player, and coach Trafton called Dick Huffman the best tackle in North America. James and Huffman both went on to become members of the Hall of Fame.

Evidently there is a long-standing tradition in Canada of rioting in the streets after a major sporting event. In downtown Hamilton, post-game celebrations carried on until the wee hours. Trashcans were set ablaze and rolled into the intersection of James and King Streets. Firemen were called out a number of times and threatened to turn their hoses on the crowds who surrounded them. Cars were rocked and trolleys were disconnected from their overhead wires. Police officers were placed on guard at a straw-filled Nativity scene that some revellers threatening to torch. Another group scaled a ledge to get to a 12-foot image of Santa Claus above a marquee, but police managed to tame them before they brought it down.

The following night the Bombers returned home to what was described as a hero's welcome. Despite below-freezing temperatures, several thousand fans greeted them at the airport. Team members mounted a flag-decked reception stand as coach Trafton introduced them. After a few words from Lieutenant Governor McDiarmid and Mayor Coulter, the team piled into cars that convoyed through Winnipeg in a parade that ended on the grounds of the provincial legislature.

• • •

The following year, 1954, saw a hard-fought, three-act Grey Cup drama played out by the Edmonton Eskimos and the Montreal Alouettes. Edmonton had already sent a squad three times to the Dominion Championship but had yet to bring home the trophy. They had one of the most injury-plagued teams in the Western Conference and were nearly the lowest-ranked statistically. What's more, late Wednesday rumours started swirling around the lobby of the Royal York Hotel in Toronto that quarterback Bernie Faloney had been fired. The team seemed to be unravelling right before the big game. Oddsmakers were posting 5–1 in favour of Montreal.

The television media were prepared to capture every scene as it unfolded. The CBC planned to broadcast live across Eastern Canada, with the signal travelling by cable to television sets in British Columbia. In Alberta there were reports of an Edmontonian who planned on cloistering himself in his bedroom, avoiding any radio or word-of-mouth updates until such time as the RCAF jet arrived with the film intended for local TV viewers. NBC would be broadcasting live coast-to-coast in the U.S. and so thousands of Manitoba football fans made plans to travel to Fargo, North Dakota, to watch the game on any available set.

Once again, football fans besieged quiet, staid Toronto. The first group of Westerners arrived Friday via the CPR before noon. They set up headquarters in a mock igloo in the lobby of the Royal York. Meanwhile, the CNR marshalled more than 100 coaches, parlour cars, sleepers, and diners to move the masses from Montreal. The first of 11 special trains brought the Alouette Band, majorettes, and team officials in on Friday night.

Television films of the 42nd Grey Cup final were shown in movie theatres for Canadian Armed Forces in Europe, Korea, and northern Canada. The CBC turned over to the Army and the RCAF kinescope recordings of the game for shipment to overseas bases.

Montreal's musical entertainment were enlisted to distract fans while the team was hustled out a back door at Union Station and transported by the Royal York freight elevator to their closely guarded rooms on the fourth floor. The band and majorettes were used similarly later on when the police directed them to the basement in order to draw the crowd away from the main doors as Governor General Massey arrived. When he was safely ensconced in his room, the pied pipers were allowed to draw the unruly crowd back into the lobby where they could resume the festivities.

Forecasters were predicting a storm from the West — and they weren't just talking about the Edmonton squad. In anticipation of the worst, crews worked electrical heat contraptions on Varsity Field all night, attempting to dry out the soggiest sectors on the grid. By 9:00 p.m., pillows of steam were rising into the cold night air. These handlers kept their devices running until 11:00 the next morning, just as the Grey Cup parade was making its way up University Avenue.

By noon, several thousand Alouettes supporters had converged upon the city, identifiable by their habitant toques, prop woodsmen's axes, and endless choruses of "Alouette." Newly elected mayor of Montreal Jean Drapeau announced, "I know the Alouettes are going to win. That is why I am the first mayor to come to a Grey Cup with our team. This will be a great victory for Montreal and we are going to have the Grey Cup game in our city within a few years."

Analyses of the contenders showed that for both teams the final quarter was consistently their strongest and that both had a knack for pulling through when the chips were down. But the vast majority were still predicting an Alouettes victory, either lopsided or by a close margin. In the end it was an upset — but by the slimmest of margins. The final score was Eskimos 26, Alouettes 25.

It was a thrilling sudden-death game, with two Eskie touchdowns in the last eight minutes. Standouts among the Westerners were Jackie Parker and Normie Kwong. It was a heartbreaker for Als supporters. A diehard fan from Montreal stood over his inconsolable compatriots in the Royal York

*Edmonton stars Jackie Parker and Normie Kwong clutch the Cup following their team's victory over the Montreal Alouettes in 1954.*

lobby afterward, playing "Taps" on his trumpet. He later switched to "Home on the Range" and soon had the crowd singing. Shortly after, the Edmonton team arrived in the hotel and was mobbed. One of their heroes, Eagle Keys, had to be carried through on the shoulders of teammates. He was soon placed in a taxi and taken to hospital. It turned out that he had played the last three quarters with a broken leg.

Montreal wasn't the only city vying to host the next year's Grey Cup. A movement to bring the final to Vancouver was spearheaded by *Vancouver Sun* sports editor Erwin Swangard. He was partly responsible for bringing the British Empire Games to Vancouver the previous year. For that purpose, Empire Stadium had been built — the biggest of its kind in the Dominion and the home of the B.C. Lions, freshman members of the Western Conference. The *Sun* created a four-page supplement that was distributed at the Grey Cup dinner and later slipped beneath the door of every room in the King Edward and the Royal York. Thousands more copies were distributed at the game. The headline read, "42,000 at Vancouver for 1955 Grey Cup Final." Their efforts paid off: the second act in this Edmonton-Montreal drama would be staged in the Pacific City.

• • •

Not to be outdone in the area of Grey Cup festivities, Vancouver pulled out all the stops in 1955 for the second consecutive Eskimos–Alouettes meeting. The city created a true Mardi Gras–type atmosphere, with streets decorated and brightly lit, bands roaming the downtown and invading hotel lobbies, and football-themed displays dominating every retail outlet. Thousands converged on the city's Chinatown as dragons danced and fireworks exploded long into the night.

Toronto's goodwill train was a great success and well-received by every community it passed through. It was reported that its ambassador, Mayor Nathan Phillips, had the time of his life. When questioned about the Ontario capital's lobby to host the next year's Grey Cup, Phillips declared that the important thing was the game, not where it was held. He credited the Grey Cup for being a "great factor in Canadian national unity."

Meanwhile, in the boardrooms, executives from Canada's two professional football leagues — the Big Four (Hamilton, Toronto, Ottawa, and Montreal) and the Western Interprovincial Football Union (Edmonton, Calgary, Vancouver, Regina, and Winnipeg) — met and made significant strides toward amalgamation under one Canadian Football League. Taking the lead in the initiative was Hamilton business executive Ralph Cooper, president of the Big Four. Reaction was very positive and boded well for the more formal discussions scheduled for the next January in Winnipeg.

*Alouettes cooling their heels along the sidelines at a regular season game at Molson Stadium in Montreal, 1955.*

It did not go unnoticed by the CRU or clubs in the East that Vancouver, a city without a team in the final, managed to sell more than 39,000 tickets — translating into gate receipts that far exceeded that of any other Grey Cup game in history. This would also be the first Grey Cup game to be broadcast in French. Montreal radio station CKAC was set to carry the play-by-play, and so would 12 other French-language stations in Quebec. All told, 234 press, radio, and television correspondents from Canada, the United States, and Europe would be covering the 40th Grey Cup.

Prior to kickoff, the talk was all about ticket shortages and the weather. Forecasters confirmed it would remain wet and foggy, so nine tons of straw had been dumped on the field at Empire Stadium to absorb the excess moisture. As an extra measure, a nylon tarpaulin was laid down to mitigate any further damage.

That year's edition of the Alouettes was already seen to be at a disadvantage. They were missing key players from the 1954 contest, with a few remaining players not performing as hoped, particularly after the beating they took from the Argos in the Big Four final. To add to their problems, an unexpected layover in Winnipeg hampered their practice schedule. There was no consensus among the oddsmakers. The widest margin had the Eskimos at 8–5, but bettors could also take a 7–5 chance on the Alouettes. "You can't go wrong with Kwong," became a popular mantra.

With his team down 1–0 in the opening quarter, Kwong capped a 57-yard drive with a one-yard plunge across the Alouettes' goal line converted by Bob Dean. The Eskimos' lead was short-lived, however, as Montreal responded with a long drive of their own that finished with Pat Abbruzzi carrying the ball across the Edmonton goal line and Bud Korchak good for the convert. The scoring duel continued with a 41-yard touchdown pass to Hal Patterson from Sam Etcheverry. The score at the end of the first quarter was Montreal 19, Edmonton 18. The action did not let up and there were three more touchdowns before the intermission, two for Edmonton and one for Montreal.

Normie Kwong's star continued to shine in the second half as he opened the play with a one-yard touchdown run. Edmonton offence went on to dominate the half, bringing their last touchdown courtesy of Johnny Bright, and a fourth quarter single and field goal, both from Bob Dean. The final score was 34–19 for the Edmonton Eskimos.

Stars from the winning squad included Rollie Miles, Earl Lindley, and quarterback Jackie Parker — with a little help from Normie Kwong and Johnny Bright, who each rolled in two touchdowns for a Grey Cup record 428 yards. The other record of note belonged to the Als' Etcheverry, who completed 30 passes for 508 yards. It was no wonder the New York Giants had their eye on him, and their chequebooks open.

• • •

In 1956, the circus rolled back into Toronto for the final act in the Edmonton–Montreal drama. The Eskimos had proved without a doubt that 1954 wasn't a fluke, but were they hungry enough for a three-peat? And Montreal had a lot of face-saving to do …

The executives met again, as well. The Canadian Football Council held scheduled contract talks, but now there were rumblings about the proposed amalgamation that only a year before looked to be at first and goal. Clubs were looking at line items such as travel costs and seeing little, if any, financial advantage to the proposed merger.

The Eskimos were camped in London, holding practices in a barn outside of town while the Alouettes remained in

Montreal. Both teams arrived in Toronto on the Friday before the game, in plenty of time for the dinner at the King Edward. There were the usual speeches and back-slapping, but more importantly further contributions were made to a fund that to-date had already disbursed more than $20,000 to players and families in financial difficulty.

Lew Hayman, managing director of the Argonauts, and John Fisher, executive director of the Canadian Tourist Association, each had their turn to address the audience after the politicos. Hayman, speaking to the exponential growth of football in Canada, admitted that at the executive level they were having "a little trouble keeping up with the game."

"The important thing," he affirmed, was to "think in terms of what is good for football, instead of what is good for us." Fisher reminded diners and the radio audience that of the eight major cities in Canada, four were west of the Great Lakes. "The West," he said, "is no longer way out there."

The Toronto constabulary was present at the Grey Cup parade the next morning to make sure that none of the estimated quarter-million spectators had too much fun. When a section of the parade decided to march along Bloor Street instead of turning toward Queen's Park, thousands in front of the Royal Ontario Museum broke police lines and swarmed onto the street, struggling for position. After the police put the parade back on track, a reverse crush occurred as thousands tried to recover their former positions. That's when the Hamilton Tiger-Cat majorettes, clad in leopard-skin outfits, began their cartwheels. A policeman stood beside the girls and pointed down the street, shouting, "Keep them moving!"

Sunday, November 24, kickoff time. All eyes were on Edmonton quarterback Don Getty. If he got the nod from coach Pop Ivy, he would be the first Canadian-born quarterback to work a Grey Cup game since 1947.

Scoring was tight, with Jackie Parker tying the game at 20–20 after a single in the third quarter. But after that, the Eskimos' offence really got rolling. Parker ended up tying the record for touchdowns scored in a Grey Cup game at three. And Johnny Bright and Don Getty — who was called on to play — each tallied a pair of touchdowns. Joe Mobra took credit for a field goal.

Though ultimately on the losing end, the Alouettes were not left out of the scoring bonanza. Sam Etcheverry set a new record for most interceptions with four and scored one of his team's touchdowns on a short running play. Hal Patterson scored a pair of touchdowns for the Als and Pat Abbruzzi scored one, as well. The final score was 50–27 in favour of Edmonton, a bit of a letdown to fans, who were expecting a much closer contest.

Immediately following the game, fans attended the civic reception, formed their own small parties, or toured the city's nightspots. The lobby of the Royal York Hotel was deserted except for a cluster of Montrealers defiantly singing "Alouette." But by 9:00 p.m. the Edmonton boosters were catching their second wind. Hundreds of them began to crowd the hotel lobby and the celebrations built and carried on until after midnight. So distracted were the revellers that Edmonton's Jackie Parker and Montreal's Tex Coulter weaved virtually unnoticed through the crowd.

• • •

It was 1957, and football fans had it on fairly good authority that the city fathers in Toronto were leaning toward converting the CNE grandstand into a football and soccer field with seating accommodation for 41,000. The projected cost stood at $1 million. There were arguments for and against the plan. One faction believed that such a financial commitment was foolish if the concept was not to include baseball. Another said that it was a folly when the current facility wasn't filling to capacity. Perhaps that group was not considering the possibility that seats weren't selling at Varsity Stadium the way they used to because spectators no longer found it enjoyable to watch a Grey Cup game there. The proposal was tabled for further discussion.

The Winnipeg Blue Bombers won the Western Conference title that year, upsetting the favoured Edmonton Eskimos. But were they truly the best in the West? Could the Bombers' momentum carry them through what would undoubtedly be a fierce gridiron battle with the best in the East, the Hamilton Tiger-Cats?

Hamilton's Grey Cup tickets were allotted on the basis of subscriber seniority. At the head of the line when the wicket opened was Argonaut executive Joe Wright. Tiger-Cats management had a chuckle. Wright was picking Hamilton by two touchdowns. While opinions aligned with allegiances, odds were set at 9–5 in favour of the Tabbies.

On the subject of tickets, a desperate Grey Cup fan posted an ad in the Friday edition of the *Globe and Mail.* He was willing to trade his four "excellent" tickets to the Maple Leafs-Bruins game scheduled for Saturday night at the Gardens for a pair of Grey Cup tickets. Apparently that was the going rate.

The weekend festivities kicked off with members of the Junior Board of Trade and the Ryerson Institute band welcoming visitors at Union Station on Friday morning. They handed out visitor gift bags containing cigarettes, magazines, chocolate bars, and headache pills.

A luncheon was held in the King Edward Hotel's Crystal Ballroom, where attendees were served by the likes of Metro Chairman Fred Gardiner, Mayor Nathan Phillips, and TTC Chairman Allan Lamport. The guest waiters were introduced by former mayor and chef-at-large Hiram McCallum. Later, the annual dinner was held in the same room and concurrently there was another dinner at the Queen Elizabeth Building at the CNE, where Miss Grey Cup was crowned. Carol Lucas, Miss B.C. Lions, received her winner's ribbon from Mrs. John Diefenbaker.

The Grey Cup had become a brand, and it was being used by businesses to sell everything from souvenir glasses to used cars. What was described as a "big league touch" was added to the field at Varsity Stadium when the words GREY CUP were painted on the turf in each end zone in 15-foot letters

There were legacies now. Two members of the Winnipeg squad that took the Cup back home with them in 1935 had sons on this 1957 team: Gerry James and Garry Roseborough. And manager Bill Boivin was a member of the squad that edged the Ottawa Rough Riders in the 1942 Grey Cup. There was more than enough room for nostalgia now.

A pre-game luncheon given by Mayor Phillips to all visiting dignitaries was held at the Lord Simcoe Hotel. Guests included mayor Lloyd Jackson of Hamilton, mayor Stephen Juba of Winnipeg, and prime minister John Diefenbaker.

The weatherman had changed the forecast from mild and dry to cold and wet. Officials mulled that over, as well as how to handle a deadlocked game. It was agreed once more to allow overtime, and under the new lights if necessary.

The Hamilton Tiger-Cats set the tone of the game after scoring two unanswered touchdowns inside of the first ten minutes of play. They scored three more in the final quarter, making it 32–0 before the Blue Bombers decided to enter the game, or ran out of turnovers for Hamilton.

But the game was perhaps most remarkable for an event that occurred along the margins. Hamilton's Ray Bawel intercepted a pass, and as Bawel ran down the sideline, a spectator, later revealed to be Toronto fan Dave Humphrey, tripped him. After much debate by the referees, the Bombers were penalized half the distance to the goal line. Hamilton capitalized on their first down on the Winnipeg 21-yard line, and two plays later Cookie Gilchrist ran 16 yards for a touchdown. The final score in this colourful chapter was Tiger-Cats 32, Blue Bombers 7.

It turned out to be an historic game for another reason: it was the last Grey Cup played at Varsity Stadium, a field that had played host to 29 of the 45 Grey Cup games.

The Blue Bombers' plane touched down in Winnipeg on Sunday afternoon and the team was immediately whisked off to Winnipeg Arena, where they were greeted by 6,000 cheering fans, despite the team having returned home empty-handed. The squad was introduced individually and paid a tribute.

There were festivities in Hamilton, too, of course. The Tiger-Cats' train pulled into town on Saturday night and, after being greeted by Mayor Jackson, they struggled to make their way through the mob that had assembled to welcome home the victors. It was bedlam. At Market Square, 25,000 awaited their arrival. Captain Steve Oneschuk introduced his players to the crowd, confessing, "rallies such as this and the one which you sent us off with last night, mean more to the players than I can tell you."

Several weeks later, after years of talk and negotiation, the Canadian Football League was founded.

• • •

The Grey Cup festival returned to Vancouver in 1958, coinciding with British Columbia's centennial celebrations. It was reported that the CBC's cameras and microphones would make this the most comprehensively covered Grey Cup game in history. In the East, that meant that festivities would begin with coverage of the parade, which would air at 12:30 p.m. Following that, to carry eastern viewers over until the pre-game telecast, there would be a couple of specials: *Football Fever*, a documentary narrated by Trent Frayne exploring the history of the game in Canada, and *Grey Cup Matinee*, which featured highlights of the current year's semi-finals and finals in the East and West, as well a clip from the last year's Grey Cup game.

*Ottawa Rough Rider Gerry Nesbitt taking down Hamilton's Bernie Faloney at Civic Stadium in Hamilton, 1958.*

Analysts were favouring the Tiger-Cats in this repeat of the 1957 matchup. Esteemed sportswriter and native Manitoban Scott Young was calling the final score Hamilton 30, Winnipeg 28, and hoped his ancestors would forgive him — especially if he was wrong.

Official attendance at Empire Stadium was just over 34,000, about 7,000 below capacity. Television was taking a bite out of gate receipts.

The first score of the game came on a successful 10-yard run by Tiger-Cats' Gerry McDougall. Halfback Ralph Goldston then picked up a Bomber fumble and ran the ball 65 yards for Hamilton's second touchdown of the game. Hamilton led 14–0 at the end of the first quarter.

A controversial decision followed: in the second quarter, Goldston tackled Bomber Leo Lewis. While under Lewis, Goldston reached up and slugged him. Goldston was ejected from the game. It was argued by Hamilton coach Jim Trimble at the half, but the official stood firmly by his decision. To date, it was only the second time a player had been ejected from a Grey Cup game. Meanwhile, Winnipeg had responded in the quarter with a touchdown and two field goals to draw within one. They then took the lead in the final seconds of the half when a Hamilton punt was blocked by Norm Rauhaus who recovered the ball in the end zone for a touchdown. It was now 20–14 Winnipeg. It seemed the tides had turned.

The Tiger-Cats regained the lead with two touchdowns in the second half, courtesy of Ron Howell. Winnipeg's Charlie Shepard responded with a touchdown of his own, putting them back ahead. But their lead was short-lived and the Ticats managed another major before the end of the quarter, which put them up by a single point.

But Hamilton could only pull out a single point in the final quarter. Winnipeg's Jim Van Pelt scored his second touchdown of the game and Shepard made sure his single counted. The Bombers hung on for the win, and Van Pelt's 22 points racked up during the game marked a new Grey Cup record. Final score: Winnipeg 35, Hamilton 28.

The Blue Bombers had made good on their promise made at the end of the previous year's final to bring home the Grey Cup the next year. After their plane touched down they were wedged into a motorcade that carried them to a rousing reception at Winnipeg Arena. The 10,000 fans in attendance erupted in ovations when, escorted by kilted pipers, co-captains Bud Tinsley and Herb Gray and coach Bud Grant walked in with the Grey Cup.

And there were speeches. Tinsley, a nine-year veteran of the squad, called it the "happiest moment" of his entire life. Halfback Ken Ploen thanked the crowd on behalf of the American players: "We thought Vancouver was very warm," he said, "but if there is a warmer town than Winnipeg, I haven't seen it."

• • •

It was 1959, and the competition for the Grey Cup between the Blue Bombers and the Tiger-Cats had become another one of the Canadian great football rivalries. It was the two teams' third consecutive year at the final. For the first time ever, Canada's gridiron gladiators would be doing battle at Toronto's CNE Stadium, but like a bad omen, there were already problems with the field.

Football commissioner Sydney Halter and Canadian Football League president Don McPherson visited the CNE grounds early Thursday morning. They learned that the tarpaulin had been lifted late, and so the field had not been able to dry properly. What they saw — with just over 48 hours to go before kickoff — was "sodden turf, soaked mud, and rutted areas." As the commissioner delicately put it, "It wasn't very good." The two men took turns coming down on their host city, which translated into stern orders being handed down by the CNE president and general managers to the groundskeepers. What followed was slow progress.

Slack attention to the venues only played into television's hand. Bruce West from the *Globe and Mail* had this to say: "Yes, sir, say what you like about television, but you have to give it full marks for bringing the Grey Cup game into the home." But apart from a cozy environment in which to view the game, television also gave spectators control over what they viewed and how long they chose to view it, that is, should the spectacle begin to lose its appeal.

Once more, Scott Young was picking Hamilton to win, this despite the fact that Western money was beginning to tilt the odds in favour of the Blue Bombers.

Winnipeggers in Toronto were invited to drop by the Oak Room at Union Station on Friday, the Blue Bombers' greeting spot for the trainloads of Winnipeggers due to arrive. Hot dogs and coffee would be served all day. Meanwhile across the street at the Royal York, police set up a temporary jail in one of the suites, insisting that it was meant more to "protect fans than prosecute them."

It was a slow start to the game with Winnipeg kicker Gerry James scoring the only points in the opening quarter — a 25-yarder that split the uprights. In the second, Bomber Charlie Shepard's punt was blocked by Hamilton's Vince Scott, but Scott was unable to recover. The Tiger-Cats dragged a single out of the affair and the score at the half was Winnipeg 3, Hamilton 1.

The Tiger-Cats tried to assemble a touchdown early in the third quarter but had to settle for a Steve Oneschuk field goal. Oneschuk repeated, and a single by Winnipeg's Shepard made it Hamilton 7, Winnipeg 4, at the end of the third.

Hamilton's Gerry McDougall took a hit from Roger Savoie in the final quarter, which caused him to lose the ball on the Tiger-Cats' 43-yard line. Bomber Bud Tinsley recovered, and after a couple of plays Shepard ran it in for a Winnipeg touchdown. Later, a 41-yard pass from Winnipeg's Ken Ploen was intercepted by Farrell Funston and carried to the Hamilton two-yard line. Shepard ran it over for the touchdown. With the wind at his back, Shepard went on to score three rouges.

Trailing by seven points, Hamilton failed on a third-down gamble. Ploen then made a successful 33-yard touchdown pass to Ernie Pitts in the dying seconds of the game and the final tally was Winnipeg Blue Bombers 21, Hamilton Tiger-Cats 7.

Post-game festivities in Toronto were subdued compared to recent years. Blue Bomber celebrations took place on one of the upper floors of the Park Plaza Hotel at Bloor and Avenue Road. In a somber moment, Bud Tinsley announced his retirement from football after 25 years, 10 of those years with the Winnipeg Blue Bombers. Robert "Bud" Tinsley, who had very nearly drowned in the infamous Mud Bowl at Varsity Stadium in 1950, was inducted into the Canadian Football Hall of Fame in 1982.

• • •

In mid-August, following an exhibition game between the Ottawa Rough Riders and the B.C. Lions, members of both teams cooled off with a late-night dip in Vancouver's English Bay and there was talk of a bet. More on that later.

A slippery field at Empire Stadium meant that defensive play dominated the 48th Grey Cup game between the Ottawa Rough Riders and the Edmonton Eskimos. Rider Gary Schreider opened the scoring with a 16-yard field goal. The first touchdown came in the second quarter in a Jackie Parker pass to Jim Letcavitz, who ran it unmolested into the end zone. The conversion was not successful. In the next series of plays, Ottawa's Russ Jackson faked a handoff, ducked to the weak side, and hit Bill Sowalski for a touchdown. Again there was no conversion and so at the end of the half, it was Ottawa 9, Edmonton 6.

There were no marks on the board in the third quarter, but in the fourth, Edmonton's Joe Bob Smith fumbled on his own two-yard line after getting knocked by Lou Bruce. Bruce's teammate, Kaye Vaughan, recovered the ball as it tumbled into the Edmonton end zone. The touchdown was successfully converted by Schreider. In the last minute, Rough Rider Doug Daigneault intercepted an Edmonton pass, quashing any hopes of an Eskimo comeback.

With the teams distracted in their huddles, and little or no security at the sidelines, fans rushed the end zones, eager to carry out the annual tradition of tearing down the goal posts. One fan got so caught up in the moment he actually made off with the ball. More spectators invaded the field, surrounding the two teams as they scrimmaged at Ottawa's 33-yard line. With 41 seconds still left on the official clock, Commissioner Sydney Halter had no choice but to call it a game. The final score was Ottawa Rough Riders 16, Edmonton Eskimos 6.

GREY CUP TELEVISION VIEWERS IN 1960 INCLUDED DINNER PARTY GUESTS ALONG TORONTO'S FASHIONABLE AVENUE ROAD AS WELL AS MEMBERS OF POSH CLUBS AND HOTEL GUESTS DOWNTOWN: BOTH THE CARLTON CLUB AND THE TORONTO LAWN TENNIS CLUB BROUGHT IN GIANT-SCREEN TELEVISIONS AND WERE OFFERING BUFFET DINNER AND DANCING FOLLOWING THE GAME, WHILE UNIVERSITY OF MANITOBA GRADUATES HOSTED A GREY CUP DAY REUNION AT THE LORD SIMCOE HOTEL.

It was Ottawa's first Grey Cup victory in nine years and the fans back home turned the place upside-down. The hundreds that converged onto the intersection of Sparks and Banks Streets quickly swelled to several thousand. Ottawa police closed off a couple of blocks in the core, but in doing so trapped a number of cars and buses. For drivers there were some tense moments as fans rocked their vehicles, threatening to overturn them. Outside the epicentre, in the blocked traffic, children caught up in the frenzy jumped from car roof to car roof.

Getting back to English Bay, the bet was that if the Riders made it to the Grey Cup and won, there would have to be a second plunge into English Bay. The bet had been made between Rider Bobby Simpson and Gary Schreider's next-door neighbour. And so on the Sunday following their victory, Simpson, Schreider, and three of their teammates took a bath in the chilly 9°C waters. The swim got Schreider off the hook for $10.

• • •

The Grey Cups of 1961 and 1962 were notable for a number of reasons. For starters, they would be the fifth and sixth meetings between the Hamilton Tiger-Cats and the Winnipeg Blue Bombers in a decade. Each had won two of those previous engagements.

On the Saturday morning before the 1961 game, the parade, consisting of 25 floats and 18 bands, wound its way through the streets of downtown Toronto.

In the afternoon, while the game was on, the streets downtown were quiet and there was little sign that Toronto was host city to the 49th Grey Cup. Everyone was either at Exhibition Stadium or watching the game on television at one of the hotels, bars, or at home.

The game got off to a powerful start after Hamilton quarterback Bernie Faloney hit Paul Dekker with a short pass deep in their territory. Dekker went on to outrun six Winnipeg defenders for 90 yards to score the first touchdown of the game. In the final play of the first half, the Tiger-Cats were sitting pretty with a first down on the Winnipeg one-yard line. Coach

Trimble opted for a touchdown rather than a field goal but the ball was fumbled at the snap and Winnipeg got the single. The score after two periods was Hamilton 7, Winnipeg 1.

But the Bombers were hungry, aggressive, and Trimble knew his boys would have to be hungrier if they were going to maintain any kind of a lead and pull out a victory; at that point he was not convinced. But after Ralph Goldston caught a pass from Faloney, broke a tackle by Bomber Nick Miller, and reached the end zone after a 23-yard gallop to put the Cats up 14–4, Trimble was starting to believe. However, Winnipeg was turning on the offence: after a long drive from their own 23-yard line, the Bombers put three more points on the board with a Gerry James field goal. Late in the fourth quarter, Winnipeg's Farrell Funston caught one from Kenny Ploen and made a 34-yard gain that put the Bombers on the Tiger-Cats' five-yard line. James plunged for a dramatic touchdown, tying the game at 14 at the end of regulation play.

After a scoreless first overtime period, it was a Ploen touchdown in the second that won the day. He dodged a number of Tiger-Cat defenders while running the 18-yard game-winning touchdown. Gerry James got the convert and the final score was Winnipeg Blue Bombers 21, Hamilton Tiger-Cats 14.

If there was a consensus it was that it was a tough game. Both sides had the sprains and bruises to prove it. It was the first overtime win in Grey Cup history, and for Hamilton it was an historical two overtime games played in the span of a week (the first game being the Eastern final against the Toronto Argonauts — the second game of a home-and-home series). To quote Tiger-Cat lineman John Barrow, "I'm tired."

There were the customary wild celebrations in the lobby of the Royal York, complete with music, crowds, people in wild costumes, and conga lines. The police were there to make sure no one burned the place down. At 1:00 a.m., the hotel was closed to all but registered guests. Anyone who didn't have a key, or hadn't made friends with anyone with a key, took to the streets.

Several hundred revellers — some of whom may have actually been Grey Cup enthusiasts — gathered at the intersection of Yonge and Dundas Streets, hooting and hollering and setting fire to a couple of dozen trashcans. Firefighters turned their hoses on the cans as well as the firebugs.

The victorious Blue Bombers flew home Sunday. Upon landing, they piled into their 45-car motorcade and were escorted along a parade route to Winnipeg Arena, where they were greeted by several thousand waiting fans. The fans cheered as the players were introduced and walked onto a miniature canvas football field at centre ice. First man out was co-captain Steve Patrick, who was also carrying the Grey Cup. He spoke for the team, saying, "With the ballplayers we have on this club, we'll bring home this Grey Cup ... for quite a few years." Quarterback Kenny Ploen received a standing ovation. The biggest cheer, however, was given to head coach Bud Grant. "Some people," he said "were surprised when our coaching staff said this was our finest team. But they proved they are the finest team that ever played in Canada."

Back home, the defeated Hamilton Tiger-Cats assembled on a temporary grandstand in front of the Royal Connaught Hotel. They still appeared shattered. Master of ceremonies Norman Marshall opened by saying, "This was a game in which no one lost anything," and went on to point out that while the Westerners had won the Grey Cup, Miss Tiger-Cat had won Miss Grey Cup, Bernie Faloney had won the MVP, and the team had won the hearts of fans everywhere. Cheers rose from the crowd.

When it was Mayor Lloyd Jackson's turn to speak, he shared with the crowd that while in Toronto he was told repeatedly that no other city in Canada supported its football club like Hamilton. Three months later, Lloyd Jackson's bid to have the city be home to the Canadian Football Hall of Fame was accepted.

• • •

At an event held the Thursday before the 50th Grey Cup, Canadian Football League president Jake Gaudaur announced the names of the first three inductees into the Canadian Football Hall of Fame: Hamilton Tigers' lineman Brian Timmis; former Big Four and Intercollegiate player, coach, and referee Joseph Breen; and the late D. Wes Brown of Ottawa, a long-time football executive. They were chosen by a committee of eight to which Timmis and Breen were then added.

At that time there was some ink in the papers about the ratio of U.S.- to Canadian-trained players. Certain numbers indicated that in Saturday's game it might be 37 Yanks to 23 Canucks, depending on the exact shade of one's passport, with Hamilton enjoying a perceived edge over the Blue Bombers. That was a game for bookies and patriots. And speaking of bookies, Hamilton coach Jim Trimble was predicting a 24–12 victory for his Tiger-Cats. All of this in spite of the fact that Canadian football fans were still experiencing what had to be called a Winnipeg Blue Bombers dynasty.

Balmy weather was forecast for the December 1 game, with temperatures expected to reach 12°C in Toronto. As the cold smoke rolled in off Lake Ontario, the Vancouver delegates pitching hard for 1963 pointed at the windows of the meeting room in one of the downtown towers. It was agreed that the next Grey Cup would be contested at Empire Stadium.

But the fog was becoming a real concern. Kickoff was scheduled for 1:00 p.m., but if there was a delay past 4:00, the game might have to be postponed until Sunday. It would be unprecedented. There were Winnipeg fans that welcomed the idea: the Bombers had just come out of a tough three-game series against the Calgary Stampeders in the Western championship. The players, however, didn't see it that way. To them, 24 hours wasn't going to make a difference. There were the out-of-towners to consider, too. And the media — not just the press that came to cover the game, but the American broadcast, which was now in jeopardy. If the game was indeed postponed, the CFL would lose an opportunity to bring the Grey Cup to an audience of 40 million via ABC. CFL president Jake Gaudaur saw the broadcast as a marketing tool to leverage a more lucrative U.S. television deal and a way to showcase the Canadian product to potential recruits at American colleges.

Cutting it a bit close, at 10:50 Saturday morning, following an inspection of the field at Exhibition Stadium, Sydney Halter, president of the CRU, declared that the show must go on. Fans, however, were asked to retain their ticket stubs, just in case.

*The Fog Bowl of 1962: The Winnipeg Blue Bombers and Hamilton Tiger-Cats were each looking for an edge.*

There were almost 33,000 spectators in the stands, but very few of them saw any of the plays. Visibility, never greater than 80 yards, dropped below 40 yards at one point. Players could no longer follow punts or long passes, and it was a passing game — though Hamilton was having some trouble in that department.

With the Winnipeg Blue Bombers leading the Hamilton Tiger-Cats 28–27, the game was stopped with nine minutes and 29 seconds left to play. After a 15-minute wait and a huddle among executives and officials, it was decided that the game should be finished the next day.

With less than half the original spectators turning out for the conclusion, the teams picked up where they left off: the Bombers with possession, second down and 10 to go on the Hamilton 54-yard line. On the injury list were Winnipeg's Charlie Shepard and Hamilton's Ron Ray and Tommy Grant (four cracked ribs). Most noticeably absent, however, was Hamilton's quarterback, Joe Zuger, out with an ankle injury. Some said the result would have been different had he been on the field.

The consensus was that Hamilton outplayed Winnipeg in Sunday's denouement, and the stats support it — however, the score never changed. The stars were not in line for Hamilton and in those brief minutes they saw their efforts crumble in incomplete passes and penalties.

For their efforts in Saturday's play, laurels went to the Bombers' Charlie Shepard, who caught his first touchdown pass in six years, putting the Bombers ahead 14–5; Hal Ledyard, whose passing gave the Bombers so much momentum in the second quarter; and Leo Lewis who, playing in his fifth Grey Cup, scored two touchdowns and passed for a third. And on the Hamilton team, halfback Garney Henley was singled out for his touchdown runs of 74 and 18 yards and catches that were good for 118 yards. Hamilton coach Jim Trimble praised the Bombers' Bud Grant, and Grant returned the compliment.

In the days that followed, the 50th Grey Cup game became known as the Fog Bowl.

# 8

## 1963–1976: GROWING PAINS, PROFESSIONALLY SPEAKING

Grey Cup celebrations in 1963 began in a relatively subdued manner, perhaps owing to the state of international affairs after events of the previous week. Only days prior to the 51st Grey Cup, to take place in Vancouver, U.S. president John F. Kennedy was assassinated in Dallas.

But the game would go on. And there would be the scheduled revelry as well as the usual board meetings. There was talk of moving CFL headquarters from Winnipeg to Toronto, the country's commercial centre. There was also talk that Commissioner Halter then may have to step down, as he had a law practice in the prairie city. The item was tabled for the annual meeting, which was to take place in February in Edmonton.

On the Thursday before the big game, this time around between the Ticats and the hometown Lions, groundskeepers began to prepare the field at Empire Stadium. After a month of steady rain, the surface more or less resembled a swamp. But with the sun finally breaking through, it was time to let the more game-friendly elements — and about 20 huge blowers — take control. Plywood siding and tarpaulins were removed from the field, allowing a potential frost to take the last bite out of any remaining moisture. At sundown on Friday, the tarpaulin was quickly re-placed to prevent any new moisture from gaining ground.

That same day had seen the first wave of fans pour into Vancouver, the standouts being the several thousand who arrived by train from Calgary, hooting and hollering, clutching bottles and tumblers, and sporting cowboy hats and red-and-white rosettes. In contrast were the Toronto fans, who arrived wearing bowlers with haloes wobbling above them and hatbands that read "Toronto the Good." The festival had arrived and hearts were lifted.

Vancouverites had the most reason to celebrate: not only were they the host city, but for the first time in Grey Cup history they had a team in the final. Emotions may have been running high for the Lions, but people's money rested on the Tiger-Cats. About 36,500 packed Empire Stadium and the weather looked like it was going to co-operate for a change, with the sun cutting the haze and making a beautiful backdrop out of Grouse Mountain. Prior to kickoff, a silent tribute was held for the fallen American president.

In the end it was Hamilton Tiger-Cats 21, B.C. Lions 10. Hamilton quarterback Bernie Faloney's running and passing made him the undisputed hero of the game, completing 13 of 20 passes for a total of 261 yards. Two of his throws, to Hal Patterson and Willie Bethea, made for touchdowns. It was Hamilton's first victory in their last five Grey Cup tries and the champagne flowed freely in the dressing room. Tributes were paid to rookie coach Ralph Sazio.

But the game was not without its controversy, and Hamilton tackle Angelo Mosca's style of play came under fire. Mosca was booed as the players made their way off the field. Unfazed, the two-way tackle later ambled into the Lions' dressing room and offered a hand to his recent combatants. He was refused at every turn. His rivals didn't care for his aggressiveness and the results of that aggression that had ended with halfback Willie Fleming being led off the field late in the second quarter with a concussion that benched him for the rest of the conflict.

Ticat lineman John Barrow perhaps summed it up best when he agreed that Mosca was "tough and aggressive," but respected him as a player who could take it just as well as he could deliver it. B.C. coach Dave Sckrien conceded that his Lions were perhaps "not as hungry as you have to [be to] win a Grey Cup game." He sent the Lions' champagne back to the equipment room with a note scrawled on the case: "Grey Cup in 1964."

The game was indeed changing, both on and off the field. ABC television had carried the game through 123 U.S. affiliates between Boston and Los Angeles. If the ratings demonstrated the venture to be a success, then the broadcaster would consider carrying the entire CFL season the next year.

• • •

In 1964 the venue shifted back east to CNE Stadium in Toronto. Friday's festivities included the coronation of Miss Grey Cup — Miss Montreal Alouette, Susan Browne. While Ms. Browne may have won the beauty contest, her hometown lost the other competition — the one to host the Grey Cup the following year.

The proposed football stadium at Ville d'Anjou was not to go through as planned, and so the date had to be forfeited. It was decided that the championship would remain in the East, but hosting duties fell to Toronto. Sensing blood in the water, sports media asked the owners of the Alouettes if this meant the team might be up for sale. Replying in the negative, Alouettes spokespersons said they would reopen the agreement that they'd had running with McGill since 1931. Promises were made regarding the revitalization of the long-standing football tradition in Montreal, but it was obvious that serious work needed to be done.

Following the meetings was the annual dinner at the Royal York Hotel. Ralph Sazio, head coach of the Hamilton Tiger-Cats, was chosen Coach of the Year by his colleagues.

Would he lead his team to victory the next day? Only a year after their loss to the Cats, the opportunity for the Lions to exact revenge had come swiftly.

Going into the game, the Tiger-Cats were rated as eight-point favourites. CNE Stadium officials promised that conditions would be good regardless of what the meteorological prognosticators had to say, but those still in possession of their five senses were giving them the same credence they afforded the analysts and bookmakers: very little.

The 52nd Grey Cup was played through rain and on the mud-slicked field at CNE Stadium. Over 32,500 were in attendance.

The only scoring in the first quarter was a Lions touchdown from Bob Swift that was converted by Pete Kempf. Their second touchdown came in the next quarter courtesy of Jim Carphin, but B.C. failed to convert. Hamilton got on the scoreboard with a single from Joe Zuger. The Lions increased their lead with another touchdown, this time from Willie Fleming. This time Kempf made the conversion, and the score going into the half was B.C. Lions 20, Hamilton Tiger-Cats 1.

Hamilton opened the third with their first touchdown of the game, from Johnny Counts, that was successfully converted by Don Sutherin. The Lions responded with two more touchdowns, both from Bill Munsey and both converted by Kempf. Munsey was replacing injured running back Bob Swift, and they were his only two touchdowns of the season. The first came after a handoff from quarterback Joe Kapp that Munsey ran for 18 yards. The second was the result of a Johnny Counts fumble that Munsey picked up and ran back for 71 yards. The score after three was B.C. Lions 34, Hamilton Tiger-Cats 8. The Cats held the Lions scoreless in the final quarter, while they themselves tallied another 16 points on a touchdown by Tommy Grant, a single by Zuger, a safety, and a touchdown by Stan Crisson that was successfully converted by Don Sutherin.

Later, in the Lions' dressing room the champagne flowed. Commissioner Halter made his way through the mob with the Grey Cup hoisted above him and then handed it to Kapp. The Cup caught some of the bubbly and it was passed around like a communal chalice for all to drink from.

• • •

According to reports, the Royal York Hotel's lobby the Friday night before the 53rd Grey Cup game was "livelier than Yorkville on a summer's night" — and this was 1965, the era of Neil Young, Joni Mitchell, and Gordon Lightfoot playing coffee houses and clubs on that strip. At the annual dinner, the Annis Stukus Trophy for coach of the year was presented to Winnipeg's Harry Grant in front of a capacity audience of 1,200. Toronto mayor Ralph Givens declared it "a night when you can feel unity in Canada."

It was going to be the Hamilton Tiger-Cats against the Winnipeg Blue Bombers for the sixth time in 10 seasons, and once again the weather was the big story. On the Friday night before the game, the forecasters were predicting north-westerly gales of 70 kilometres per hour, with gusts of up to 90 kilometres. The Wind Bowl was blowing into town. Memories of the Fog Bowl still lingered, and after what was undoubtedly a sleepless night, Grey Cup coordinator Harry McBrien was speeding up a ramp on the Gardiner Expressway early Saturday morning, trying to work in a last-minute inspection of the field at CNE Stadium, when he was pulled over by a traffic cop. Grinning silently in the backseat were CFL commissioner Sydney Halter (also a member of the bar in Manitoba) and magistrate Tupper Bigelow. At least the field was in fine condition.

The parade started at 9:30 a.m. Saturday morning, and included 30 floats, 20 bands, and 15 majorette groups, as well as a couple of added attractions: a gold-coloured elephant and a championship steer from the Royal Winter Fair, the latter of which was to be presented to the winning team. Stiff breezes prevailed, bringing temperatures down to just above the freezing mark. The Most-Chilled Award went to a bathing-suit-clad girl on water skis who was perched on a float advertising a local marina. She was also wearing a fur coat, but witnesses reported that it wasn't being used to its full effect.

The other sideshow to that year's game had been an altercation on the Thursday morning between Jim Trimble and a sportswriter from the *Montreal Star* that ended with the scribe being sent to Toronto's Western Hospital. A contrite Trimble later publicly apologized and shook hands with his opponent, Iain MacDonald. Toronto police questioned both men but no statements were filed. It was apparently just an argument between friends.

Better prepared for weather at the game than our bathing-suit-wearing model was sportswriter Scott Young, who reportedly donned "short underwear, a sleeveless woollen sweater over the underwear top, then a shirt, flannel slacks, white turtle-necked woollen sweater, eider-filled hunting jacket, thick woolen socks, shoes, overshoes, woolen scarf, thick Harris Tweed overcoat, and a woollen toque." When the cab driver asked Mr. Young if he was off to the North Pole, he replied, "Exhibition Stadium."

A capacity crowd of more than 32,000 were on hand for the game. Spectators had to find ways of dealing with the strong winds off Lake Ontario, as did the officials. Before the game started, the officials and coaches agreed to expand the rules a little: it was decided that short punts into the wind would be ruled dead as soon as the receiver touched the ball.

During the game, while it may have seemed that the wind was with the Blue Bombers, they were continuously met by an intractable Tiger-Cats defence. That, along with a few failed gambles, cost the Bombers the game.

Already leading by a point in the first quarter, the Tiger-Cats' Frank Cosentino hit Dick Cohee with a pass that Cohee hauled in for a seven-yard touchdown. After a couple of failed advances, Winnipeg conceded a safety touch to close the quarter at 10–0 for the Tiger-Cats. In the second quarter the Blue Bombers' Art Perkins broke tackles in an eight-yard touchdown run that got Winnipeg into the game. Before the whistle, Leo Lewis took a handoff from Kenny Ploen and ran it in along the left side for a touchdown, converted by Norm Winston. Winnipeg was leading at the half, 13–10.

Hamilton regained control of the game after the break when quarterback Joe Zuger hit Willie Bethea for a 69-yard passing touchdown that Don Sutherin converted. It was 17–13 for Hamilton but the Tiger-Cats quickly accumulated five more points after a couple of safety touches were conceded by Winnipeg and a high snap recovered by Zuger on his own 30-yard line was kicked to Billy Cooper into the Bombers' end zone. The scoring was rounded out by a Winnipeg field goal from Norm Winston. The final score was Hamilton Tiger-Cats 22, Winnipeg Blue Bombers 16.

The cold, windy weather persisted into the evening, keeping most of the celebrants indoors. Subsequently, in the major hotels it was mayhem. A guest at the Royal York, perhaps after losing money on the Blue Bombers, was charged with malicious damage after hurling bureau drawers, chairs, and a mattress out the window of his room on the 17th floor. More contained was the giant party held by the Junior Board of Trade in the hotel's convention rooms. There were three bands and, fitting for 1965, go-go dancers. But things got quiet around 11:00 p.m., when the first wave of departing Westerners marched across the street to board their special train back to Winnipeg.

• • •

In 1966, the Grey Cup spectacle made its fifth trip to Vancouver and was set to feature a contest between the Saskatchewan Roughriders and the Ottawa Rough Riders at Empire Stadium. Almost 37,000 fans would pack the stands in this, the 54th Grey Cup.

The Ottawa Riders leapt out of the gate when Whit Tucker dodged Dale West to receive Russ Jackson's pass for a 61-yard touchdown. Moe Racine failed to make the convert, and Saskatchewan bounced back after intercepting Jackson midfield, returning the ball 51 yards. Ron Lancaster then hit Jim Worden for a nine-yard touchdown and Jack Abendschan was good for the convert.

Saskatchewan turned that momentum into a lead in the second quarter when Al Ford caught a touchdown pass that Ottawa's Bill O'Billovich couldn't steal away. The Eastern Riders came close, however, with a passing play where Tucker caught a smart pass for an 85-yard touchdown. Bill Cline's 51-yard punt tied the game at 14 before the intermission.

The match remained in a stalemate after a scoreless third quarter. The earth moved in the fourth, though, when Lancaster threw a bullet to Hugh Campbell from the Rough Riders' five-yard line and Campbell ran the touchdown; not surprising, considering he set a league record with 17 touchdowns in the 1966 season. Minutes later, George Reed shot 31 yards up the middle of the field for another Saskatchewan touchdown. A Roughrider single brought the final score to Saskatchewan 29, Ottawa 14.

In the post-game ritual, fans assaulted the goalposts but were confronted for the first time by aluminum crossbars and uprights welded to a thick, gooseneck-shaped pole that reached out toward the goal line. Try as they might, they were unable to bring the 600 pounds of metal crashing down on their heads and had to content themselves with tearing up sod and pitching it at one another.

Over 6,000 fans packed the Regina Armouries the Sunday following the big game awaiting the arrival of their Roughrider heroes and history's first Grey Cup for Saskatchewan. After 56 long years, which included nine Grey Cup battles — five of them consecutive — the Green and White had finally brought the trophy home to Regina.

• • •

In 1967, the Hamilton Tiger-Cats and Saskatchewan Roughriders took turns holding final workouts on the slick practice field at Lansdowne Park in Ottawa on the Friday before the game.

Meanwhile, in a fourth-floor boardroom of the Château Laurier, event strategies were being discussed. Harry McBrien, the CFL's indefatigable Grey Cup coordinator, had suffered a heart attack a few months before, and coming to the rescue were a trio of veteran organizers of Grey Cup festivals in Toronto. It was like pulling together a 48-hour Expo 67. Apart from the usual myriad details that kept the phone ringing off the hook, there were a handful of other matters that needed to be dealt with — additional stands were required at Lansdowne to bring the seating up to the Grey Cup minimum of 31,000; it was discovered at the last minute that the contractor did not paint the numbers on the seats; and there was no heat in the stadium washrooms. Come game day, Harry McBrien would be at home, quietly enjoying the game on television.

Friday night the annual Grey Cup fundraising dinner was held, with over 1,000 people in attendance. Head table luminaries included Rich Little, Lorne Green, and Peter

Jennings. Awards were presented for contributions to the history of the game in Canada, and one of them was to honour Harry McBrien.

It was a different party later in the evening, with high school and college students parading up and down Sparks Street Mall. Ottawans, the majority it seemed, were adopting the Saskatchewan Roughriders as their own.

*The official program for the Centennial year's Grey Cup spectacular.*

More than 31,000 spectators crowded into Lansdowne Park the following afternoon. Hamilton's Joe Zuger got the scoring started with a quarterback run from the Saskatchewan three-yard line. Zuger continued to put himself to work in the second quarter, drilling the ball to Ted Watkins for a 72-yard passing play. An unsuccessful field goal attempt by Tommy Joe Coffey and two Zuger singles gave Hamilton a healthy 17–1 lead by the time the half was done.

The remainder of the scoring action occurred in the latter part of the fourth quarter, first with another single from Zuger and then a touchdown from Billy Ray Locklin, the result of a fumble return. The final score in this Centennial year rout was Hamilton Tiger-Cats 24, Saskatchewan Roughriders 1.

• • •

The generation gap made itself evident in the lobby of the Royal York the Friday night before the 56th Grey Cup game. It was 1968, and the younger set was on the main floor, while the over-35s watched grimly from the mezzanine railings, having forgotten that a mere generation ago it was them down there whooping it up and embarrassing themselves. For most of the evening, police security looked on, just smiling and nodding, but at midnight it was time to close the doors and seal off Front Street between York and Bay.

There were broken bottles and toilet paper streamers decorating the boulevard. Traffic in the area got a bit thick, made all that much worse along King Street, where as many as a dozen horses, many carrying a couple of riders — often men in business suits and women in similar attire — dodged cars and ignored the blaring horns. Surprisingly enough, the evening's festivities ended with no major incidents.

The state of the field was on many minds the morning of the game. Early reports indicated that the marshy field at

CNE Stadium was more suited to cranberry cultivation than football. Groundskeepers were called out to try and rectify the situation with a platoon of portable hairdryers. Nearly 33,000 spectators would be there to witness Prime Minister Trudeau kickoff the game at 1:00 p.m.

Rough Rider Don Sutherin's single in the first quarter was bettered by his 27-yard field goal in the second. Calgary smothered that effort with a pair of majors before the half, both converted by Larry Robinson. The first was a quarterback sneak by Peter Liske, and the latter was a Terry Evanshen reception. The score at the break was Calgary 14, Ottawa Rough Riders 4.

But the Riders stormed back in the third quarter, bringing down Calgary's Ron Stewart who was attempting a punt return. This put Ottawa midfield. Rookie halfback Vic Washington made an impressive 14-yard gain that set up Russ Jackson's goal-line touchdown run. It was now 14–11 for the Stampeders.

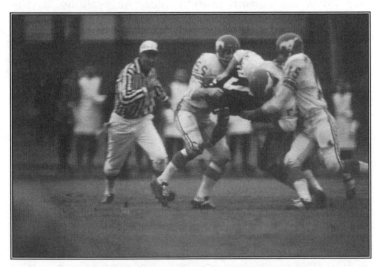

*It took three Stampeders to bring down Ottawa Rough Rider Vic Washington in the 1968 Grey Cup.*

Early in the fourth quarter, Washington caught from Jackson but dropped the ball, retrieving it quickly. He rounded the Calgary defenders and went on to run an amazing 80 yards for a touchdown. Later in the quarter, Jackson coordinated a 70-yard passing play with Margene Adkins for another touchdown. Calgary re-entered the game in the dying minutes when Dick Suderman recovered Rider Bo Scott's fumble on the Ottawa 14. Liske found Evanshen in the end zone, but it would not be enough to catch them up with the Rough Riders. The final score was Ottawa 24, Calgary 21.

Vic Washington ended the game with 128 yards on 13 carries. He was named Most Valuable Player. For Calgary, it was a fitting end to a bad week, with key players coming down with the flu after having arrived in Toronto and other players either benched or playing injured. Many felt that victory had been within their grasp but was lost to costly errors. It would be a long trip home for the boys from Wild Rose Country.

• • •

The Roughriders and the Rough Riders arrived in Montreal on Friday November 28, for what was the 60th anniversary of the first Grey Cup game in 1909. The Regina team checked into the Sonesta Hotel while the Ottawa team settled into Ruby Foo's, located west of downtown. Coach Eagle Keys and his Prairie 'Riders held a workout on a field adjoining the Autostade, the site of Sunday's game. Ottawa coach Frank Clair, meanwhile, had his team go through their calisthenics on the nearby Loyola College Athletic Field.

There was good reason for Ottawa boosters to be concerned: To begin with, the last time these two teams met, in 1966, the Westerners had taken the Cup home. And several weeks before, the Regina ruffians had beat Clair's squad 38–21. The Green and White were also undefeated in their last nine games.

Ottawa's hopes hinged on an outstanding performance by their star quarterback, Russ Jackson. During the Schenley Awards ceremony that was held at the Odeon Theatre the Friday night before the game, Jackson had received double honours: He was named Canada's Outstanding Professional Football Player as well as Best Canadian. It was the third time the Hamilton native was named Outstanding Player, the fourth time he was Best Canadian, and the third time he was a double winner. Numbers-wise, in the course of the 14-game schedule, Jackson passed for 33 touchdowns. He threw the ball 358 times, completing 193 passes for 3,641 yards. He also impressed with his running record, picking up 578 yards on 64 carries. When asked about his duties Monday morning as vice-principal of Sir John A. MacDonald High School in Ottawa, Jackson said that, regardless of the outcome of Sunday's game, he would be taking Monday off. "There's no problem," he said. "The kids behave themselves." As it turned out, this would be his last game as a professional football player. When pressed about his future plans, he replied by saying that his football would be "limited to any occasional help I may be able to give the kids at school."

On the subject of honours, that year four players were selected for the Hall of Fame: Abe Eliowitz of an earlier vintage Ottawa Rough Riders (1933–35) and the Montreal Indians (1936–37); Art Stevenson of the Winnipeg Blue Bombers (1937–41); the Alouettes' Sam Etcheverry (1952–60); and "China Clipper" Normie Kwong of the Calgary Stampeders (1948–50) and Edmonton Eskimos (1951–60).

There seemed to be a more pronounced East versus West feel to the match that year. Perhaps it was the political climate — or maybe it was just football. "I hope Ottawa wins," said Leo Cahill, coach of the Toronto Argonauts, "but that's strictly for personal reasons." Calgary coach Jim Duncan predicted that

Saskatchewan would win the game: "Sure, it's a sentimental pick. I'm from the West but really I'm not a sentimental guy."

Autostade, built for Expo 67, was filled to capacity that day with 33,172 spectators. But because the stadium had been constructed especially for the Expo, the builders likely hadn't taken into consideration the possibility of hosting events in the dead of winter, and the gridiron that weekend was frozen, with ice lacing the field.

Saskatchewan took an early 9–0 lead in the first quarter, largely because of Alan Ford's reception of a 27-yard pass from quarterback Ron Lancaster. Their other two points came after Bill Van Burkleo conceded a safety. But after a three-game drought in which Ottawa quarterback Russ Jackson was unable to throw a scoring pass, he finally had some success, and Ron Stewart caught two of his passes for touchdowns, one coming from an 80-yard play that put the Rough Riders in the lead 14–9 at the end of the second quarter.

Saskatchewan pulled a couple of singles in the third, the first from a field goal attempt that went wide and rolled to the dead line and the second following a kick that was conceded by Ottawa's Barry Ardern. The Green Riders continued to create opportunities for their opponents: Dan Dever recovered a ball for Ottawa, setting up his team on the Saskatchewan 27-yard line. On the following play, Jackson dodged a tackle and reached Jim Mankins who was just beyond the goal line for another touchdown.

The only scoring in the final quarter was done by the East Riders. Following a single by Don Sutherin, Russ Jackson made the final dramatic play of the game, and his career: just prior to being dragged down by Cliff Shaw, Jackson flipped the ball to Stewart, who then ran 32 yards for his second touchdown of the game. The final score was Ottawa Rough Riders 29, Saskatchewan Roughriders 11.

Tensions, whether real or perceived, seemed to be running high that day, and minutes before the end of the game, a few hundred Montreal police in full riot gear marched into the Autostade. Outperforming the Ottawa majorettes, they went on to upstage the post-game presentations as well.

Jackson was chosen the game's Most Valuable Player, capping off a stellar career. He came out of retirement briefly the following year to play in an Ottawa versus CFL All-Stars game. He has been called the best Canadian-born quarterback to play in the CFL and is a member not only of the Canadian Football Hall of Fame and Canada's Sports Hall of Fame, but the Order or Canada.

• • •

In the lead-up to the 1970 Grey Cup, the Miss Grey Cup award went to a teary-eyed, near-speechless Nancy Durrell, Miss Alouette. The 21-year-old McGill University student was presented with a bouquet of roses, as well as a handkerchief, by Saskatchewan Roughrider quarterback Ron Lancaster. When asked about her political stance, the young woman claimed to agree with much of what the Women's Lib movement stood for, "but not all," she added, "or I wouldn't be standing here tonight."

The weather had been mild and rainy, and there was little indication that the precipitation would let up before game time. The field at CNE Stadium had been thoroughly soaked before it could be covered with tarpaulins, and whenever they would try to remove the covers, the puddling rain would drain into the turf. The groundskeepers were already tiptoeing around numerous loose patches of sod that littered the field. Stadium manager Ken Twigg affirmed that things had indeed "taken a turn for the worst."

"I didn't want to steal any glory from the Alouettes." That was the reason given by Prime Minister Trudeau for falling

15 yards short of his ceremonial kickoff of the previous year. Trudeaumania was still in evidence in 1970, though, and spectators sought autographs, kisses, and handshakes from the popular leader. Twelve-year-old Linda Hembruff daringly asked the prime minister for the red carnation in his lapel and he happily obliged.

But Trudeau wasn't the only one with that certain flare. Larry Lawrence, Calgary's backup quarterback, styled a thick blonde coif and could often be seen wearing a "mod" tan two-piece accented with a Sherlock Holmes–style cape. But the Stamps would need much more than just style if they were going to beat the Montreal Alouettes that year.

In the first quarter, Calgary found themselves midfield after intercepting a Frank Andruski pass. Montreal's defence, however, fell into action and forced a punt from the Stampeders that bounced off of Bob Storey's chest and was subsequently recovered 15 yards from Montreal's end zone. It only took two plays for Calgary's Hugh McInnis to plunge it across the line and give the Stamps the lead. Larry Robinson made the conversion. The Alouettes then managed to turn a play that could have been a loss into a significant gain: before being taken down by Calgary's Terry Wilson, Moses Denson tossed the ball to Ted Alfien who was free and easy in the Stampeder end zone. While George Springate did not make the convert, he did, however, make good on a field goal, leaving it Montreal 9, Calgary 7 at the break.

The Stampeders took the lead in the third after a high snap on a Montreal punt attempt let Dick Suderman recover the ball on the Alouettes' 34-yard line. Larry Robinson's subsequent field goal made it 10–9 for the Calgary squad. Later in the same quarter, Al Phaneuf intercepted Jerry Keeling and returned the ball to the Calgary 27-yard line. Als quarterback Sonny Wade faded back for what looked like a throw but instead handed off to Tom Pullen, who ran it in for a touchdown. In the final quarter, Wade found Garry Lefebvre for a touchdown pass. The final score was Montreal Alouettes 23, Calgary Stampeders 10.

*Prime minister Pierre Elliott Trudeau presents the Grey Cup to the Montreal Alouettes in 1970.*

After the game, it was reported that progress on the Canadian Football Hall of Fame in Hamilton was moving along nicely. Mayor Victor Copps told the media that the $400,000, 20,000-square-foot facility was on schedule to open in 1971, and would be the "world's first electronic sports museum." The opening was to coincide with the city of Hamilton's 125th anniversary celebrations.

• • •

"This is a first," exclaimed CFL commissioner Jake Gaudaur. "Someone from the licensing department in Vancouver's city hall phoned my suite and said we'd have to get a permit before the game can go on Sunday. We didn't have $25 in our petty cash, but I took up a collection in the room and scraped up enough to buy the licence."

Remembering Grey Cup events of the past, the Hotel Vancouver posted notices in the lobby that year, stating "No service will be provided at this bar to any Calgarian on a horse." Barring horses, the attendance at Empire Stadium was still a respectable 34,000.

Calgary's Herm Harrison's single-handed reception of a Jerry Keeling pass in the Toronto end zone got things off to a spectacular start. The Argonauts attempted to put together an equally big play in the second quarter but ended up settling for an Ivan McMillan field goal. Before the end of the half, Stampeder Jesse Mims added another touchdown to the board, making the score Calgary 14, Toronto, 3.

The Argonauts' one and only touchdown came in the third quarter when Calgary punt-returner Jim Silye dropped a kick. It was promptly recovered by Joe Vijuk, who passed to Roger Scales who then ran 33 yards for a Toronto touchdown. Later in the fourth quarter, and with only two minutes remaining on the clock, Argonaut Dick Thornton intercepted a pass and dodged and weaved his way 54 yards up to the Calgary 11-yard line. A field goal would tie the game; a touchdown would win it. A rattled Joe Theismann pulled himself off the Toronto bench to lead the offensive. Leon McQuay carried the ball for three short yards and fumbled on the second down. The Stamps' Frank Andruski recovered it. The Argos defence, consistent throughout the game, halted the Calgary advance, and the Westerners chose to punt on the third down. The errant ball was kicked out of bounds by Harry Abofs; Calgary retained possession and ran out the clock.

Final score: Calgary Stampeders 14, Toronto Argonauts 11.

It was Calgary's first Grey Cup since 1948. The only one smiling in the Argonauts dressing room after the game was Roger Scales, who scored his first-ever touchdown in the third quarter. After what was for the most part a fairly unremarkable game, judges were at a loss as to whom they ought to be selecting as its stars. In the end it was decided that Outstanding Player should go to Calgary's middle linebacker Wayne Harris, and Best Canadian should go to defensive end Dick Suderman.

That year the CFL was discussing expansion. New York had just applied for a franchise and their application was just one of two being examined by executives, the other being from a Chicago group. Things were definitely getting interesting. Gaudaur made it clear that he was opposed to expansion into the United States — he saw it as "the first step in the collapse of the Canadian league as we know it" — but his bosses were aware of the revenue being generated by the NHL franchises and saw nothing but dollar signs.

• • •

The Schenley Award for outstanding player was believed to carry a sort of jinx with it, in that no player who won it would in the same year be a member of the Grey Cup–winning team. Russ Jackson managed to break the curse in 1969, and in 1972, Hamilton Tiger-Cat Garney Henley hoped to do the same in his team's battle against their Saskatchewan adversaries.

The 60th Grey Cup was to be played at Ivor Wynne (formerly Civic) Stadium in Hamilton in front of a crowd of 34,000. The artificial turf was nicely broken in, the Ticats were healthy, and confidence was being expressed in the ability and cool-headedness of rookie-of-the-year quarterback Chuck Ealey. The Hamilton team was also going into the game with a six-point spread over the Saskatchewan Roughriders.

FORMER MONTREAL ALOUETTE DEWITT "TEX" COULTER
PAINTED PORTRAITS OF THE SCHENLEY AWARD-
WINNERS AS PART OF THEIR PRIZE. COULTER ALSO
PAINTED PORTRAITS OF MAJOR NHL STARS AND WAS
OFTEN REFERRED TO AS THE NORMAN ROCKWELL OF
CANADIAN SPORTS.

It was a more tumultuous story in the backrooms and hallways of the league, however, where talk ranged from expansion into the United States to simply selling the larger CFL franchises to the NFL. It was all about television money, and it was common knowledge that each NFL team made as much from that one revenue stream alone as all nine CFL teams combined — about $1 million a year. Rumours abounded, and anything and everything seemed

*Hamilton Tiger-Cats star Angelo Mosca raises the Cup toward the crowd at Ivor Wynne Stadium, 1972.*

to be on the table. Whether they knew it or not, the ground seemed to be shifting beneath the feet of the players. It may have only been a tremor at the time, but it was an indication of things to come.

The game began with a little controversy: A 16-yard touchdown pass by Hamilton's Chuck Ealey to Dave Fleming was declared legal despite the fact that replays clearly indicated that Fleming was out of bounds when he caught the ball. Later in the opening quarter, a Bob Krouse punt was blocked but Hamilton recovered and Ian Sunter made good with a 27-yard field goal. Saskatchewan tied the game at 10 in the second following Lancaster's eight-yard touchdown pass to Tom Campana, and a 20-yard field goal from Jack Abendschan.

A scoreless third quarter followed and the drama held until the final two minutes of the fourth when, from their own 15-yard line, Ealey threw 27 yards to Tony Gabriel. Ealey went back to Gabriel for another 12 yards. A third toss to Gabriel got Hamilton to the Saskatchewan 41-yard line with less than a minute on the clock. With time on their side and a field goal within range, Ian Sunter managed to put it between the uprights for three points and the win. The final score was Hamilton Tiger-Cats 13, Saskatchewan Roughriders 10.

• • •

It was November 1973, and another Grey Cup weekend was being celebrated in Toronto. The lobby of the Royal York Hotel once again resembled a grownup version of a bouncy castle at a child's birthday party, complete with a cowbell and siren accompaniment. Uniformed officers watched and plainclothesmen mingled, eyeing the staggering denizens decked out in "pink pant-suits and silver-glittered black frocks under those special-occasion mink stoles." A veteran of Grey Cups past, a 57-year man with the CPR stated that it was actually "a lot quieter than other times. Other years the riff-raff got in."

A new tradition of giving the media the opportunity to simultaneously grill the coaches of both Grey Cup teams provided an added sideshow that year, and featured Jack Gotta, the Ottawa Rough Riders coach, and Raymond Jauch of the Edmonton Eskimos. It was a curious dance: the media would pry and the coaches would, for obvious reasons, disclose nothing in each other's presence, and so it would become like a vaudeville act, with the more entertaining coach gaining favour.

Edmonton's Roy Bell got things off to a dramatic start with a 38-yard touchdown run in the first quarter. But the Rough Riders didn't sit back and quarterback Rick Cassata quickly answered with a 38-yard touchdown pass-and-run to Rhome Nixon. After a rib injury to Tom Wilkinson, Edmonton's backup quarterback, Bruce Lemmerman, stepped in and managed to bring the Eskimos close enough for a Dave Cutler field goal. The score at the end of the first quarter was Edmonton 10, Ottawa 7.

Less than a minute into the second quarter, following a low and awkward snap, Edmonton punter Garry Lefebvre was tackled by Rough Rider Wayne Tosh in the end zone for a safety. At the close of the half, Gerry Organ kicked a field goal to make it 12–10 Ottawa.

The Rough Riders were looking to pad their lead early in the second half, and in the third they did just that with an 18-yard touchdown run by Jim Evenson. In the fourth quarter, Lemmerman left the field with an arm injury and Wilkinson, with his rib injury now frozen, marched back out onto the gridiron. There were no immediate results as Tyrone Walls fumbled a Wilkinson pass on their own 47-yard line. Ottawa's Wayne Tosh made the recovery and Organ kicked another field goal to make it 22–10 for the Rough Riders. An Edmonton touchdown with just seven seconds remaining proved to be too little, too late. The final score was Ottawa Rough Riders 22, Edmonton Eskimos 18.

In meetings over the weekend, Calgary presented a bid for the 1975 Grey Cup. Included in their bid was a commitment to expand the seating at McMahon Stadium from 27,000 to at least 32,000.

• • •

The days immediately leading up to the 62nd Grey Cup were more subdued than in years past. Vancouver was host city once again, with 34,450 prepared to watch four-point favourites the Edmonton Eskimos take on the Montreal Alouettes at Empire Stadium. The two teams appeared evenly matched: the one time they met in the regular season, the game ended in a draw, 28–28; no one team was suffering from an unusual amount of serious injuries; both quarterbacks were in fine form; and the weather bureau was predicting a particularly soggy field, which would give neither any advantage. The reasoning, though, for giving Edmonton the nod, was that they had more experience with Empire Stadium's artificial turf and Montreal had had dismal showings against Western teams all season.

SHIPPED BY RAIL FROM LONDON, ONTARIO, THE SO-CALLED "GAME SAVER" WAS A FOUR-WHEELED ZAMBONI-LIKE CONTRAPTION PURCHASED BY THE PACIFIC NATIONAL EXHIBITION FOR $20,000 TO SQUEEGEE AND SUCK ANY EXCESS MOISTURE OFF THE FIELD AT EMPIRE STADIUM. GROUNDSKEEPERS CHEERED UPON ITS DELIVERY.

During the game, it poured down with rain, making for poor visibility and a ball as slippery as a bar of soap. Edmonton fumbled twice and lost the ball on both occasions; Montreal fumbled thrice but once managed to regain control. The Als took some solace in the fact that if this Grey Cup were being played back home, they'd be running through knee-deep snow.

When it became clear to coach Marv Levy that quarterback Jimmy Jones wasn't going to be generating the much-needed offence, he called Sonny Wade off the bench. Wade immediately got to work with some excellent passing.

The only thing better than Wade's arm was Don Sweet's foot, and the kicker scored on four out of five attempts, breaking George Fraser's Grey Cup record set back in 1941. The Als held on to take the victory, final score Montreal 20, Edmonton 7.

It was the Alouettes' second Grey Cup victory in five years. Quarterback Wade was selected as Top Offensive Player; defensive end Junior Ah You was chosen Top Defensive Player; and Don Sweet was named Top Canadian. There was hope that these achievements might make the Montreal fans stand up and take some notice of their team: empty seats at the Autostade the last few seasons were translating into annual losses in the area of $100,000.

• • •

Calgary's chance to host the Grey Cup finally came in 1975, and it was a game that no one in attendance would soon forget — but not because there was any particularly good football being played.

More than 32,000 spectators braved temperatures of -10°C at McMahon Stadium. Apart from the frigid conditions, it was a game characterized by overthrown and dropped passes, fumbles, interceptions, and some questionable refereeing.

The 63rd Grey Cup did, however, produce some interesting trivia. The final score was Edmonton Eskimos 9, Montreal Alouettes 8. It was the first Grey Cup game not to produce a touchdown since 1937, when the Argonauts had beaten the Blue Bombers 4–3, and the first time since 1945 that all the points were scored by Canadians. That game, coincidentally, was also played between the Argos and the Bombers.

The heroes of the game were the kickers (discounting the blonde dressed in nothing but a cheesecloth skirt who frolicked around the field during "O Canada"). Montreal's Don Sweet started off the duel in the first quarter with a 35-yard field goal, and then went on to kick a record 47-yard field goal. Dave Cutler later broke that record with his own 52-yarder through the uprights. Cutler scored every one of the Eskimo's points and was named the Outstanding Canadian of the game.

• • •

In numbers, it was the ninth championship final to be played at CNE Stadium; the 39th time Toronto had hosted the event; and the 64th Grey Cup. The year was 1976, and people were beginning to wonder if it wasn't all getting a bit tired.

There would be the usual chaos at the Royal York on Friday night; the parade on Saturday morning; negotiations with the scalpers outside the stadium; the victory celebrations in the hotels; the drinking and carousing in the streets — made more interesting now by the flavour of a certain stretch of Yonge Street where all the lights seemed to be red — followed by the hangover Sunday morning and the mad rush to catch planes and trains and automobiles and leave the mess for someone else to clean up.

There were those who were nostalgic for the days prior to 1948, before it became a so-called festival. Cynics were viewing the Grey Cup game now as nothing more than an excuse for several thousand people to go berserk in downtown Toronto. Had the shine come off the Cup? Where did the actual game of football fit in this picture?

The first indication that fans were still interested in the game was the record crowd of 53,467. It was an interesting matchup: the Saskatchewan Roughriders and the Ottawa Rough Riders, two teams that had been defying the odds since the start of the season. Neither was favoured to win their division and it had been a few years since either team had made the trip to the Grey Cup. Saskatchewan had also lost its great fullback George Reed early in the season, and Ottawa was supposed to have gotten steamrolled by the Alouettes. But both teams had respectable offences: the Westerners scored 427 points for a total of 5,800 yards; the Easterners scored 411 points with a total of 5,873 yards.

Ottawa took an early 10-point lead in the first quarter after a Gerry Organ field goal followed by a CFL record 79-yard punt return for a touchdown. But Saskatchewan stormed back in the second quarter as Ron Lancaster passed to both Steve Mazurak and Rob Richardson, who each came through with touchdown receptions. Bob Macoritti contributed a field goal and, after an unsuccessful play following an interception by Saskatchewan's Ted Provost, the score at the half was Ottawa 17, Saskatchewan 10.

The teams shared a pair of field goals in the third quarter, leaving Saskatchewan still within striking distance. Ottawa was on the move with their next possession but were halted by the Green and White at the goal line. The Riders regained the ball, and with a half-minute on the clock found themselves on the Saskatchewan 24-yard line.

It was a split-second decision. Ottawa quarterback Tom Clements waved off the play being signalled to him. Reading Clements, Tony Gabriel ran the ball toward the end zone, faking a post pattern and rounding the corner. Provost fell for it and Gabriel caught Clements's 24-yard pass for the winning touchdown. It was a brilliant play, executed perfectly. In Grey Cup lore, it has become known as "The Catch." Final score: Ottawa Rough Riders 23, Saskatchewan Roughriders 20.

The 64th Grey Cup is notable for a couple of reasons other than The Catch: All of the scoring in the game was done by Canadian-born players. It was also the last Grey Cup win for the Ottawa Rough Riders before the club folded in 1996.

## 9

## 1977–1982:
## THE EDMONTON ESKIMOS DYNASTY

They were nicknamed the "Alberta Crude" — the Edmonton Eskimos' powerful defensive line consisting of Ron Estay, David Boone, Bill Stevenson, and Dave Fennell. And they came thundering onto the field in front of a record 68,000-plus crowd at Olympic Stadium in Montreal in 1977. There had been a lot of talk from them in the days previous, a great deal of bravado. But in the end it was a disciplined and well-prepared Alouettes team that routed the Edmonton squad 41–6.

The 65th Grey Cup was dubbed the "Ice Bowl." After crews had removed the protective tarpaulin, a storm piled 25 centimetres of snow onto the field. Then, 15,000 halftime show participants held a rehearsal on the field, packing the snow and melting the bottom layer. Try as they might, the field workers' efforts to remove the ice only turned it into a slippery mess. On game day it was -8°C. One of the Alouettes had the bright idea of using one of the worker's staple guns to stud their shoes. The team passed it around and the staples gave them a little traction, perhaps just what they needed.

Coach Marv Levy's Alouettes proved as solid as the frozen ground on which they played and were by all accounts the superior squad. This was the Als' third victory in four Grey Cup appearances since 1970 and their second against the Eskimos. Montreal quarterback Sonny Wade collected the Outstanding Offensive Player award after a stellar performance. He completed 22 of 40 passes for a total of 340 yards, and threw three touchdown passes and only one interception. Also outstanding was Don Sweet's kicking: he kicked six field goals and had two singles, and converted all three Montreal touchdowns. The game saw 25 Grey Cup records either set or tied.

Eskimo quarterback Tom Wilkinson and others on his team commented that their opponents' familiarity with the artificial turf may have given them a certain advantage. The Als knew how to work it; the Esks didn't.

The media weren't kind to the losers and many made jokes about the Eskimos' earlier bragging remarks. Their time was coming; they just needed to dial down the attitude and focus on their game.

• • •

Under executive manager Norm Kimball the Eskimos spent the following season getting their house in order and becoming not just the wealthiest club but also the tightest organization in the Western Conference. Halfway through the 1978 season they relocated from 28,000-seat Clarke Stadium to the 43,000-seat Commonwealth Stadium. On the players' side, the Alberta Crude were solid and consistent and had allowed only 301 points, the fewest in the high-scoring Western Conference that season. They also allowed only 1,599 yards rushing — the third-best in the league. Dave Fennell was selected Most Outstanding Defensive Player and in Dave Cutler they had the best kicker in the West. The Esks finished their season with 10 wins and two ties in 16 games, and were injury-free. They were a mature, focused team now. At the final they appeared calm, but simmering just below the surface was the belief that they could not go home this year without the Cup.

It was the Grey Cup's 40th trip to Toronto and its 10th trip to CNE Stadium. The scalpers were having a heyday. On the Saturday night before the game, a first-year business student from Ryerson claimed to have made about $700 in two nights by scalping seven pairs of tickets. He was working the downtown hotels.

> TWO ALBERTA PREMIERS PREVIOUSLY PLAYED FOR THE EDMONTON ESKIMOS. PETER LOUGHEED (1971–85) PLAYED WHILE STUDYING LAW AT THE UNIVERSITY OF ALBERTA IN 1949 AND 1950, AND HIS SUCCESSOR IN OFFICE, DON GETTY (1985–92), QUARTERBACKED THE 1956 GREY CUP VICTORS.

Coach Campbell said the Eskimos game would be a passing one, with quarterback Tom Wilkinson fitted with excellent targets Tom Scott and Waddell Smith. The Als, on the other hand, were expected to work more of a running attack. Sunday afternoon it was time for the analysts to put away their microscopes and the bookies to close their books and get on with the business of watching the game.

The Alouettes were outscored 10–0 in the first quarter after a faked field goal and a three-yard touchdown from Jim Germany, and Wilkinson just kept chipping away with a steady barrage of short passes. The other strategy of the Eskimos was to shut down Alouettes quarterback Joe Barnes and halfback David Green, which they did.

There were seven provincial premiers sitting in the covered portion of the stands. Apparently, Alberta's Peter Lougheed and Quebec's Rene Levesque wagered $15 on the outcome. Levesque lost. The Edmonton Eskimos beat the Montreal Alouettes 20–13.

The Big Green Machine was on a roll now.

• • •

During training camp the following season, Alouettes running back David Green set three goals for himself: to make at least 1,600 yards rushing; win the Schenley Award; and help make sure the his Als brought home the Grey Cup in 1979. He ended the season rushing for 1,678 yards and won the award for Outstanding Player of the Year. While his agent started lobbying for a four-year, $1-million contract, Green started focusing on the Cup. But he would have to contend with the Eskimo juggernaut featuring the likes of outstanding defensive end Dave Fennell, rookie of the year receiver Brian Kelly, and outstanding offensive lineman Mike Wilson.

In the annual boardroom meetings held on the Friday before Sunday's game, the league adopted unanimously a fully interlocked schedule — replacing the partial interlocking schedule adopted in 1961 — and fast-tracked implementation for 1981. "At Grey Cup time we don't usually make major decisions," commented commissioner Jake Gaudaur, "but this was an important step to becoming one league. This new schedule will give the fans in all cities an opportunity to see all players in their home park in one season and will stimulate new rivalries."

The teams were back at the "Big Owe" in Montreal on November 25, with 65,000 fans packing the place, no doubt most looking for a repeat of 1977 rather than 1978. But there would be no ice this time around; the weather was unseasonably mild.

David Green did his part: he carried 21 times for 142 yards and broke several tackles when his team most needed tackles to be broken. He was named Outstanding Offensive Player of the Game. But the Alouettes ended up giving the Cup away in penalties — 16 times in 145 yards compared to the Esks' four times in 25 yards — the most tragic call being at the tail end of the game when Gerry Dattilio got the red hanky for clipping Pete Lavorato, who was about to take down Keith Baker in an 85-yard punt return. It would have been the Als' only touchdown and might have turned things around for them. Might have. The final score was 17–9, all of Montreal's points coming from the foot of field goal master Don Sweet.

The Eskimos demonstrated that a Grey Cup can sometimes be won with simple poise and class.

• • •

In 1980, the Grey Cup bounced back to CNE Stadium in Toronto, but instead of another rematch between the Eskimos and the Alouettes, the Eskimos were this time being challenged by the Hamilton Tiger-Cats, who hadn't taken home the trophy since 1972.

The broadcast started at 1:00 p.m. EST, a half-hour before kickoff. The viewing audience was projected to be between 5.5 and 6 million according to the people in charge of the CBC telecast. And for that, sponsors were paying up to $14,000 for a minute of air time. The colour commentary was being handled by Mike Wadsworth, Frank Rigney, and Russ Jackson.

This would be Eskimo place kicker Dave Cutler's seventh trip to the Grey Cup. At the time, he was second in three categories for Cup records: second in most points scored (40); second in most Cup field goals (11); and second in most goals in a Cup game (4). He was top in the league in most career points (1,542), most career field goals (357), most points in a single season (195), and most field goals in a season (50). He had come a long way after being Edmonton's first draft pick in 1969.

The final score was 48–10, the widest margin of victory since Queen's University crushed the Regina Rugby Club 54–0 back in 1923 — in the bad old amateur days. These Edmonton Eskimos were now only the second team to win three consecutive championships in the modern Grey Cup era.

There were other stars in the game. Eskimo quarterback Warren Moon completed 21 of 33 passes for 398 yards. He threw three touchdown passes and was named Outstanding Offensive Player. It was his third Grey Cup ring in three years. Slotback Tom Scott caught two of Moon's throws and one of Tom Wilkinson's for a total of three touchdowns — tying Jackie Parker (1956), Red Storey (1938, Toronto), and Ross Craig (1913, Hamilton Alerts). All told, 21 records were set or extended and five were tied.

The irony is that the talent gap between the East and West now favoured the West, and many felt that the Western Conference final between the Edmonton Eskimos and the Winnipeg Blue Bombers was the true championship game. In numbers, the Eskimos put together 606 yards in total offence compared to the Tiger-Cats' 201. A great day for the winners, but perhaps not such a great day for the league.

The Grey Cup presentations were made at one of the far ends of the field. Drunken spectators crashed the snow fencing and poured onto the field. At one point David Boone lost the trophy to a fan but quickly recovered it.

In December 1980, the 10-year veteran of the Eskimos, wingback Don Warrington, was killed in a car accident. Long-time friend Dave Cutler remembered him fondly, and when it came time for the Esks to enter the Grey Cup for the fourth consecutive year, coach Hugh Campbell took the opportunity to pay Warrington another tribute, saying that Warrington typified the Eskimo dynasty: he wasn't overly talented but was capable and exhibited a relentless effort.

• • •

In 1981, the Edmonton team was being challenged by the Ottawa Rough Riders, the 1976 Grey Cup champions, with Olympic Stadium in Montreal as host venue once more.

Bookies in the city pegged Ottawa as 22-point underdogs. Indeed, the Eskimos' greatest enemy might be their own over-confidence. Ottawa finished their season with a 5–11 record. Edmonton finished 14–1–1. In their two engagements in the regular season, Edmonton had beaten Ottawa 47–21 and 24–6. The only thing that might give the Riders an advantage was the weather forecast. They performed well in adverse conditions and it was said that such conditions always worked for the poorer team. At this point, the Riders would probably have taken any advantage given them.

THE EDMONTON FANS MIGHT BE THE BIGGEST HEROES OF THE FABLED ESKIMOS DYNASTY. IN 1979 THEY SET A WESTERN CONFERENCE ATTENDANCE RECORD OF 340,239 (COMMONWEALTH STADIUM HAS A CAPACITY OF OVER 63,000). ATTENDANCE HAS RARELY IF EVER FLAGGED SINCE THEN, AND THEY HAVE LED THE LEAGUE IN ATTENDANCE SINCE 2001.

But it was no cakewalk. Ottawa's rookie quarterback Julius Caesar Watts clearly had the Edmonton defence, and his Riders were leading 20–1 by the break. Late in the first half, Warren Moon had been called off and was replaced by Tom Wilkinson. Obviously refreshed and with a new perspective, Moon marched back out onto the field in the second half and went on to score on two touchdown plunges. He handed off to Jim Germany for a third touchdown and passed to Marco Cyncar for a two-point convert that tied the game with less than five minutes remaining. And then, with just three seconds left in the game, Cutler attempted a 27-yard field goal. It was good.

The final score was 26–23. The Eskimos were the first team in league history to win four consecutive national titles. Tom Wilkinson went out on top after confirming his retirement in the post-game locker room scrum.

• • •

The year was 1982, and the Toronto Argonauts had not won a Grey Cup in 30 years. In fact, the team had failed to make an appearance at the national final in 11 seasons. The Argos had finished the previous season with two victories and 14 losses — historically their worst performance — and failed to make the playoffs for the fourth consecutive year. Rookie head coach Bob O'Billovich turned things around in 1982, however, and the Double Blue finished the regular season 9–6–1, with quarterback Condredge Holloway taking the Schenley Award. They were going into the match against the reigning champs as 6½-point underdogs.

Those damn Edmonton Eskimos. Kicker Dave Cutler, the team's 14-year veteran, remembered growing up hating the New York Yankees because they always won. "People are sick of us," said fullback Neil Lumsden. "Most people recognize excellence, but they want us to give someone else a break." But they were off to a shaky start in the regular season, losing five of their first eight games. In fact, by midseason they were in last place in the Western Conference. It had been looking grim but there was a return to form after Labour Day and in the second half of the season they achieved a perfect record, ultimately defeating the Blue Bombers in the Western playoffs to earn their berth at the Grey Cup.

On the Saturday night before the game the Eskimos didn't get much sleep: the alarm system at their Toronto hotel sounded most of the night, and Warren Moon was battling the flu and was already feeling sleep-deprived.

*Edmonton Eskimos coach Hugh Campbell poses with the Grey Cup in November 1982, following the team's fifth consecutive victory.*

There were almost 55,000 spectators at CNE Stadium in Toronto. Wet snow followed by a driving rain made for a slippery artificial turf, but that didn't seem to put off Moon. Though the Grey Cup defenders were not off to a spectacular start, they eventually managed to pull it together.

The Eskimos opened the scoring with a Dave Cutler field goal, but the Argos responded with a touchdown pass hauled an impressive 84 yards by Emanuel Tolbert. At the end of the first quarter it was Argos 7, Eskimos 3. The first play of the next quarter saw the Eskimos' Brian Kelly nab a 16-yard toss from Warren Moon for their first touchdown of the game. But the Argos regained the lead following a 10-yard reception by Terry Greer. Another Moon pass to Kelly yielded a touchdown for Edmonton, while an Argos safety brought the score at the intermission to Eskimos 20, Argonauts 12.

The final score was 32–16, and Moon was the named Outstanding Player, having completed 21 of 33 passes for 319 yards.

Police took to the field at the end of the game, and one senior officer remarked how easy his job was that year: "Everyone just seems to want to get out of this place. They're wet and they're cold. Geez, this is a rotten stadium for a football game. Unless they dome it, I guess they won't be playing any more Grey Cup games here, will they?" And they didn't. Soon after, the 70th Grey Cup became known as the Rain Bowl.

A few weeks later, Hugh Campbell departed Edmonton to assume coaching duties for the Los Angeles Express of the fledgling United States Football League. Achieving a 70–21–5 record, he had led the Eskimos to the Grey Cup in each of his six years as coach. At the conclusion of the 70th Grey Cup, he had the best record of any coach in the history of the CFL. He was inducted into the Canadian Football Hall of Fame in 2000.

# FOURTH QUARTER:

## 1983–2011

# 10

## 1983–1992:
## A DECADE OF UNCERTAINTY

The 1983 Grey Cup game would be the first played indoors, and under the white, billowing ceiling of the new B.C. Place Stadium. The CFL seemed to be entering a new modern age: commissioner Jake Gaudaur was talking retirement; a committee was finally being set up to study the quality of the officiating in the league; and there were teams that appeared to be emerging from their own Dark Ages.

*Q: If you lived in a ground-floor apartment, what would you look down on?*

*A: The Toronto Argonauts.*

After years, if not decades of being the league's punch line, and losing games, fans, and money, the storied Argonauts were a force again, albeit one still struggling to forge itself a new identity, something other than the "Bottomless Boatmen." They finished the best in the league in 1983 with a 12–4 record, scoring 452 points and allowing only 328. No one in the East could touch them.

Their Grey Cup opponents would be the B.C. Lions, who also performed strongly that season, finishing 11–5 and racking up the most points in their conference (477) while allowing the least (326).

The two teams had never met in the final. What's more, in the previous three decades the Argos and the Lions had each only made it twice to the championship — each team winning one and losing one. This would be new territory for both organizations.

Kickoff was scheduled for 3:00 p.m. PST. There were just under 60,000 paying attendees.

At the start of the second half, the Argonauts were trailing 17–7 and seemed to be sleepwalking the gridiron. Toronto head coach Bob O'Billovich called their much-touted quarterback, Condredge Holloway, off the field and sent in his reserve, Joe Barnes. The first thing Barnes needed to do was wake up his teammates: his first two passes, drilled perfectly to Paul Pearson and Geoff Townsend, were both dropped, and kicker Hank Ilesic missed three easy field goals.

It took them a while, but the Argos eventually found their feet — or foot. In the fourth quarter, kicker Henry "Hank" Ilesic scored one from 43 yards out and with still nine minutes left to play. Barnes felt they were finally within striking distance and made sure his team kept up the pace.

THE TELEVISION AUDIENCE FOR THE 71ST GREY CUP, HELD ON NOVEMBER 27, 1983, WAS REPORTED TO BE 8.1 MILLION, OR ONE-THIRD OF THE POPULATION OF CANADA AT THE TIME.

With four minutes remaining, Barnes fired another pass to Pearson, who caught it on the Lions' 45-yard line but was tackled and lost control of the ball. Argo wide receiver Emanuel Tolbert found himself at the right place at the right time and recovered the ball. The Argo drive was still alive. Barnes passed to Tolbert who was on the Lions' 25, and then to Pearson on the three. The Argos were closing in.

With only a couple of minutes left on the clock, Barnes flipped the ball to Cedric Minter in the end zone. Though they failed at the two-point convert, the Argos were now ahead. Successfully defending their one-point margin until the bitter end, they tamed the B.C. Lions 18–17 to take the Grey Cup.

For the first time since the Fog Bowl in 1962, the winner was decided by a single point.

Back in Toronto, thousands took to the streets, racking up their own Grey Cup statistics: 90 extra officers from six divisions were summoned downtown to help curb the violence and general mayhem; three patrol wagons were called to the scene; and by midnight at least 20 arrests had been made. Yonge and Dundas Streets appeared to be ground zero, with stores being broken into and garbage cans set ablaze. One officer said, "We're just here because we want to make sure there is a Yonge Street when people come to work tomorrow."

But they weren't all bad. In the words of one celebrant, "It's a long time since Toronto has had something like this to cheer about," and to quote another, "Thank God for Joe Barnes!"

And while there was talk of a new Argos dynasty, two of the game's stars, Minter and Ilesic, were already in talks with NFL clubs. This would be a common theme this decade: stagnant CFL pay versus lucrative NFL contracts. There would be no dynasty if the team couldn't hold itself together. Even O'Billovich's contract was up and, although he was expressing interest in staying on as coach in Toronto, there was nothing yet in writing.

• • •

It was 1984, and the city of Edmonton's first time hosting the Grey Cup. They were ready to show Canada a good time — Edmonton-style. The manager of the Westin Hotel, a veteran of Grey Cup festivities in Toronto and Hamilton, oversaw the transformation of its elegant interior. Out with the potted palms and cushy loveseats, and in with the souvenir stands and tradeshow-style booths hawking outdoor survival gear. Even the courtyard bar was given a gingham-inspired makeover. On

Jasper Avenue, girls wandered around in Klondike costumes while men dressed as miners pulled a mule behind them.

The head of Edmonton's Grey Cup organization said that his city's bash was going to be bigger and more elaborate than anything that came before it. It was reported that the game ball, along with the competing teams' colours, were to descend from the skies in the arms of four parachutists, and that Canadian astronaut Marc Garneau was to lead the annual Grey Cup parade.

Edmonton area bars ordered 30,000 souvenir shooter glasses and there was a contest to come up with an official Grey Cup shooter. The winner was a concoction named Illegal Procedure: hot chocolate, steamed milk, cherry brandy, Swiss chocolate almond liqueur, Praline Pecan liqueur, topped with whipped cream and sprinkled with shaved chocolate. Forget the shooter glass; this cocktail needed a vessel the size of the Grey Cup to hold it.

But let's not lose sight of the football game. The brawl that year was between the Winnipeg Blue Bombers and the Hamilton Tiger-Cats. The Bombers hadn't won since 1962 and the Ticats since 1972, and it would be their first meeting at the Grey Cup since 1965. Both looked hungry, but the Bombers were heavily favoured. They had finished the regular season 11–4–1 versus the Ticats' 6–9–1 record.

Being the most northerly city on the CFL's map, naturally there were concerns about the weather. No one wanted a replay of the -10°C environment in Calgary in 1975. So far the forecast was good: no snow, few clouds, and a high near 2°C.

Early Sunday morning the overnight train arrived from Winnipeg and dropped off the last of the 1,000 or so blue-and-gold-bedecked Bombers fans that had been invading the city since Wednesday. For some it had been a long and boozy ride on the Panorama train. Any Hamilton fans present kept a low profile.

The CBC was commemorating the 50th anniversary of its first Grey Cup radio broadcast. Things had come a long way since then: this Grey Cup would be carried not only by the CBC and CTV in Canada, but by ESPN in the United States. No doubt those who were enjoying the view from the living room had some sympathy for those in the stands. By kickoff time the temperature had dropped to -17°C. The grass surface has completely frozen over and was more suited for hockey. The crowd, which started off at just over 60,000, started thinning at halftime. By the final quarter there was a gradual retreat from the walk-in freezer that was Commonwealth Stadium. Spectators knew they weren't going to be missing anything. The final score, for anyone who was still interested, was Blue Bombers 47, Tiger-Cats 17.

Hamilton had had an impressive start, leading in the first quarter 14–3 and scoring another three points in the second. But then the Bombers exploded, accumulating 27 points before the half was up — a Grey Cup record for most points in a quarter. By the final gun, Winnipeg had racked up 44 consecutive points, thoroughly humiliating their Eastern opponents.

Chosen as the game's Outstanding Player was Winnipeg quarterback Tom Clements, who completed 20 of 29 passes for 281 yards, including two touchdowns. Ironically, it was Tiger-Cats quarterback Dieter Brock who had been traded by Winnipeg for Clements the previous year. (Brock could claim the first touchdown of the game.)

For catching five passes for 47 yards, two punts for 31 yards, and rushing 12 times for 89 yards, Winnipeg fullback Sean Kehoe was named Outstanding Canadian. As a former Edmonton Eskimo, he knew how to work the Commonwealth playing surface. And kudos went to the diminutive Trevor Kennerd, who was good for four field goals and five converts, but perhaps more importantly always gave his team something to work with in his spectacular kickoffs.

The Winnipeg fans still braving the elements took to parading around the stadium, cheering and hollering. "Forget that Loserpeg stuff," exclaimed one fan. "From now on, you can call us Winnerpeg!"

Press and VIPs invaded the Hamilton locker room after the game. Some of the players were already drowning their sorrows in champagne. Quarterback Dieter Brock came out of the showers and spotted the Great One, Wayne Gretzky, sipping a beer. Brock introduced himself.

"I really enjoy your work," he said.

"Thanks," replied Gretzky. "I'm sorry you had such a bad day."

• • •

The excitement seen the previous year in Edmonton was not evident in Montreal in 1985. Media were reporting a thoroughly underwhelmed city and one very sedate Cup headquarters at the Sheraton. There was no fever.

It was a reflection of the season the Montreal Concordes had experienced — lacklustre attendance at Olympic Stadium and financial losses amounting to $3 million that year (a total of $13 million over the past four). Interested parties were looking for excuses. Was the league not marketing itself effectively enough? Did lopsided Grey Cup victories like the one witnessed the previous year in Edmonton hurt the game? Was Canadian football losing its audience to baseball? It was even suggested in Montreal's case that the increasing linguistic and cultural divide in that city might be playing a part.

The new era that had begun a few years before following the first indoor game and the resurrection of the Toronto Argonauts seemed to be losing yardage. Overall attendance among the nine teams had fallen 10 percent in 1984 and 3 percent in 1985. There was also increasing instability among the franchises — two prime examples being Montreal, which had just received a renewed commitment from their owners, and the Calgary Stampeders, who were now working on a refinancing scheme.

The league was looking for a Hamilton Tiger-Cats win this year — for the underdogs to take the Grey Cup and not only rekindle interest in Canadian football, but inspire other struggling franchises. It was a heavy burden, but Hamilton actually had a chance in their rookie quarterback, Ken Hobart, who was being likened to both Russ Jackson and Bernie Faloney. What's more, he was a fan favourite: hard-working and down-to-earth, he seemed to personify Steeltown.

On the other hand, the Lions had not won the Cup since 1964, and despite an attendance record that was the envy of most every other club in the land, fans on the West Coast were getting a little impatient for a victory.

The league — and Hamilton — didn't get their wish. The B.C. Lions defeated the Tiger-Cats 37–24.

The truth is that, while emotions might run high, statistically speaking it was a long shot to begin with. The Tiger-Cats had finished the regular season 8–8, while the Lions finished 13–3. The Lions had been picked to finish first in their division, which they did, handily defeating the previous year's Grey Cup victors, the Winnipeg Blue Bombers, in the Western final.

The Lions began their charge early in the game with an 84-yard touchdown — quarterback Roy Dewalt to Ned Armour. Hamilton's Less Browne tried to steal it away from Armour, but the wide receiver wouldn't have any of it. Coach Don Matthews' Lions were playing not only like they had to have the Cup, but like they had something to prove — and they more than succeeded.

"We've been knocked around all year," said Dewalt after the game. "But the fact we're here as winners says something." Dewalt completed 14 of 28 passes for 394 yards and was responsible for three touchdowns. He was chosen Offensive Player of the Game.

A similar sentiment was expressed by Lions kicker Lui Passaglia: "I don't want to hear any more about the Winnipeg Blue Bombers or the Hamilton Tiger-Cats. The best team in Canada is the B.C. Lions." The Vancouver-born Passaglia managed five field goals.

Hamilton hopeful Ken Hobart played most of the game with two injured shoulders. In the dressing room afterward he said his left shoulder "went on the second play of the game" after a brief encounter with B.C. defensive end James Parker. It was during a second-quarter play, he said, that they got his throwing shoulder.

Paid attendance at Olympic Stadium was 56,723, but there were thousands of empty seats. The actual crowd was estimated to be less than 50,000. Meanwhile, on the other side of the "Land of the CFL," proactive Vancouver police quickly sealed off the portion of Georgia Street in front of the art gallery and rerouted traffic. The celebrants, however, did not even come close to resembling those post–Grey Cup hooligans in Toronto in 1983. There was only a minor amount of mischief and the crowd dispersed after a couple of hours.

• • •

A poll taken in 1986 indicated that 49 percent of Canadians planned to watch the Grey Cup — but only 28 percent regularly followed the league.

"In order for a sporting event to have this kind of popularity," claimed Richard Gruneau, a sports sociologist at the

University of British Columbia, "it has to be seen as something that surpasses sport, like the Olympics in a way. The Grey Cup is about a lot of things. It's about history, politics, national identity, and East–West tensions, if only for the moment. People see it as an institution."

The 74th Grey Cup would be played between the Hamilton Tiger-Cats and the Edmonton Eskimos at B.C. Place Stadium. The Eskimos were coming off a brilliant season. They won the Western Conference title by defeating the B.C. Lions 41–5, and finished with a 13–4–1 record. The Tiger-Cats finished their season 9–8–1, a worse record than four of the Western teams. It is for reasons like this that football purists were calling for an end to the East–West format and wanted to see the two best teams in the country compete for the Grey Cup. The CFL actually gave it some consideration, but commissioner Doug Mitchell believed the format was an integral part of the institution, and so it remained.

This is not to ignore the fact that the Eastern Conference teams were in a bit of disarray, with all four owners talking about jettisoning their money-losing clubs. Carling O'Keefe had recently announced it was interested in selling its Toronto Argonauts, an organization now carrying an $8-million debt. A group of investors was reported to be interested. Bill Brick, former assistant general manager of the Calgary Stampeders, was brought aboard to investigate the Argos' viability. His first comments were about how to better position a team within a market of three million people.

Meanwhile, at the executive level, former Ontario premier Bill Davis was appointed chairman of the CFL's board of governors.

"We thought the position Bill Davis has," explained Mitchell, "and the relationship he has with the business community in Toronto, would assist the league."

At that moment, the B.C. market was looking reasonably healthy. About 60,000 paying customers came to B.C. Place Stadium, probably expecting to see the 10-point underdog Tiger-Cats get trounced by the more dominant Edmonton Eskimos. Instead they got something else for their money.

Less than two minutes into the game, Hamilton's Grover Covington knocked the ball out of the hands of Edmonton quarterback Matt Dunigan. Hamilton defensive lineman Mitchell Price recovered. On the next play, Hamilton quarterback Mike Kerrigan connected with wide receiver Steve Stapler for a 35-yard touchdown. Paul Osbaldiston kicked the convert at 1:35 and suddenly it was Hamilton 7, Edmonton 0.

The Tiger-Cats continued their relentless drive in the second quarter and by halftime the score was 29–0. Many thought it to be over, and for all intents and purposes, it was.

THE 74TH GREY CUP WAS THE LAST TO USE DUAL CBC/ CTV COMMENTATOR SETS, A BROADCAST TRADITION SINCE 1962 WHEN STEVE DOUGLAS HANDLED THE PRE-GAME SHOW, FUTURE HALL OF FAMER BERNIE FALONEY OFFERED HIS PRE-GAME ANALYSIS, AND JOHNNY ESAW COVERED THE PLAY-BY-PLAY.

Edmonton didn't register on the scoreboard until well into the third quarter. With possession on the Hamilton 37-yard line, Matt Dunigan managed to drive the Eskimos further to the Hamilton six-yard line, where Damon Allen took over as quarterback and ran the ball in on the first play for a touchdown. Tom Dixon kicked the convert to make it 36–7.

But people were already leaving their seats, and before long about a third of the place was empty. Outside, scalpers were practically giving away their tickets. Souvenir hawkers, on the other hand, were suddenly doing a brisk business with fickle fans interested in Tiger-Cats paraphernalia.

Those who left early missed Hamilton's Osbaldiston tie a Grey Cup record with his sixth field goal of the game, a 47-yarder at 14:36. When the final gun mercifully went off, the score was Hamilton Tiger-Cats 39, Edmonton Eskimos 15.

The win gave Harold Ballard his first championship win as an owner (at the time, he also owned the Toronto Maple Leafs).

• • •

League commissioner Doug Mitchell was calling 1987 a survival season. At the beginning of the season the Montreal Alouettes folded and other franchises had had their share of troubles. Aside from the CFL's Grey Cup Extravaganza that was held at the Vancouver Convention Centre, festivities surrounding the 75th Grey Cup were noticeably subdued. Newly elected to the Canadian Football Hall of Fame in the Football Reporters of Canada section, Trent Frayne remarked that the Grey Cup had become "just another day at the office."

League diagnostics aside, that year's matchup was garnering some genuine interest from football fans. In league play, the Edmonton Eskimos had become the first CFL team to score more than 600 points. At the other end of the field would be the Toronto Argonauts, who exhibited a near-impenetrable defence. It had the potential to be a tense, hard-fought battle.

CBC was anticipating a stronger television viewership in this Grey Cup, considering the season's ratings were up 10 percent over the previous year. New to the airwaves was a CFL radio network, an assembly of 75 stations across Canada prepared to cover the Grey Cup event.

It would be a near-full house at B.C. Place in Vancouver — 58,478 seats sold to fans who probably spent the entire time on their feet. The game started spectacularly: a missed field goal try by Lance Chomyc of the Argos was carried for a record 115-yard return by Henry "Gizmo" Williams for a touchdown, giving the Esks a 7–0 lead. After that it was one thrill after another, a game full of big plays.

In the second quarter, Toronto tailback Gill Fenerty caught a pass from quarterback Gilbert Renfroe that he then carried 61 yards for a touchdown, tying the game 10–10. In the same quarter, Argo middle linebacker Doug Landry scored a 54-yard touchdown on a fumble return, giving Toronto a 24–10 lead. And finally, just before the half, after replacing an injured Matt Dunigan, Damon Allen drilled an eight-yard scoring pass to Marco Cyncar, narrowing Toronto's lead to 24–17.

And that's when everyone on and off the field took the opportunity to catch their breath.

Renfroe injured his knee in the final quarter and was replaced by Danny Barrett, who ran the ball 25 yards up the middle on a draw for a major. They missed the two-point conversion, but the Double Blue were still sitting with a 36–35 lead.

Last but not least, with only 45 seconds left on the clock, rookie Jerry Kauric booted a picture-perfect 49-yard field goal that lifted the Edmonton Eskimos to a 38–36 victory over the Argonauts.

In the words of Edmonton coach Joe Faragalli, "Never in my life have I seen a Grey Cup game like that. If you didn't like that game, you're brain-dead."

It was just what the ailing league needed; some were calling it the best football they had ever seen. And if that didn't work, there were always the provincial governments. Having already called on the mayors of the eight CFL cities, all of whom pledged their undefined support, commissioner

Doug Mitchell was now calling on the provincial premiers for assistance. Lines of credit had already been extended to clubs by British Columbia, Alberta, and Saskatchewan. It was unclear what else could or should be done by these government bodies. It was a risky business on many fronts.

• • •

Following the collapse of the Montreal franchise at the beginning of the previous season, the Winnipeg Blue Bombers were moved to the Eastern Division. That year, when they met with the B.C. Lions at Lansdowne Park in Ottawa, it would be the first time in history that — geographically speaking — two Western teams would be playing for Lord Grey's Cup.

Now that some fans and players — and owners with an eye on gate receipts — had tasted from a Grey Cup played indoors, and more would with the debut of the domed stadium in Toronto the next year, a serious debate grew around the idea of only holding the Cup in enclosed venues. Opposed were the three other Western cities — Edmonton, Calgary, and Regina. Also opposed was Commissioner Mitchell and soon-to-be commissioner Bill Baker, who both argued that it was a national event and that all eight cities should have the opportunity of hosting. It also gave every host cities an economic boost and helped spread interest in the game. Average attendance at Lansdowne during the 1988 season, for example, went up from 18,000 in 1987 to 23,000. Most of that was attributed to a significant increase in season ticket sales; buyers were promised their same seats for the Grey Cup.

The Western fans rolled into Ottawa, bringing all of their colour and unbridled enthusiasm — and their travel budgets — to the capital. The city of Calgary hosted its pancake breakfast on the Sparks Street Mall on the Thursday. Klondike Kate, a veteran of many a Grey Cup festival, provided musical entertainment in the lobby of a downtown hotel. The CFL hosted its own little get-together at the Ottawa Civic Centre. Several thousand guests were entertained by music legend Ronnie Hawkins as well as others.

The Schenley Award ceremony was held on Friday night at the National Arts Centre. Ex-Chicago Bear and now-B.C. Lion David Williams was named Outstanding Player of the Year. In his acceptance speech, he thanked Edmonton for trading Matt Dunigan to Vancouver. "He's a great quarterback," said Williams. "We wouldn't be here without him."

Elsewhere, Dunigan was being credited with tilting the oddsmakers' numbers six points in the Lions' favour. The Lions and Bombers were considered fairly evenly matched and so it might come down to a duel between the quarterbacks, with Dunigan having the possible edge over the Bombers' Sean Salisbury.

Proving the weather wasn't always a factor in the financial success of a Grey Cup, with a forecast of a high of 3°C and a chance of showers, the Ottawa event still managed to sell 50,604 tickets.

But the forecasters aren't always right. In fact, sometimes they're dead wrong. The sun shone and it was an unseasonably mild 14°C. And the Winnipeg Blue Bombers became the first team in Grey Cup history to win the game going in with a .500 record, nine wins and nine losses in their league season. It was another jaw-dropping, down-to-the-last-minute championship.

The jaw-dropping part came early in the third quarter. The Lions were leading 18–14 and had possession on their 20-yard line at third and one. Dunigan, to the surprise of many sitting in the stands and at home in their living rooms, attempted a quarterback sneak. He was stopped cold by Winnipeg's Mike

Gray. Bomber Trevor Kennerd was brought out for a kick and sent it sailing through the uprights.

The last-minute excitement was fast and furious. A Trevor Kennerd 30-yard field goal put the Bombers up 22–19. With only 2:55 left in the game, the Blue and Gold were leading for the first time. Next came the kickoff, and the Lions carried for 75 yards, all the way to the Bombers seven-yard line. Dunigan rifled a pass but it got swatted out of the air and intercepted by Gray, halting what might have been the Lions winning drive.

There was now 1:26 remaining. It was decision time: rather than have Bob Cameron punt from his own end zone, Winnipeg coach Mike Riley chose to give up a safety touch, narrowing his team's lead to 22–21.

With one minute left to play, Riley elected to use the kickoff to send the ball deep into Lions territory. However, a 36-yard return by Anthony Drawhorn gave the Lions the ball on their own 45-yard line. More jaw-dropping action: a rough-play penalty to B.C. running back Anthony Cherry dragged the ball back to the 30-yard line. It was over.

There was some blame-storming in the Lion's dressing room afterward, while champagne flowed freely across the hall in the Blue Bombers'.

"I think it's about time the Grey Cup came back east," quipped head coach Mike Riley.

• • •

The first Grey Cup game played in Toronto's SkyDome facility took place in 1989. It was nice not to be playing in a blizzard … or fog, freezing cold, or under a torrential downpour. However, the artificial turf apparently still left something to be desired. The Argos had already been expressing their dissatisfaction with it, making it sound like nothing more than a rug stretched over a baseball diamond, with soft and protruding areas and barely visible yard lines.

All of that aside, there was some real excitement mounting for the game, and new reasons for optimism in the league. The 77th Grey Cup would be contested between two franchises whose continued existence until recently was very much in question: the Hamilton Tiger-Cats and the Saskatchewan Roughriders.

At the same time last year, after an argument with the city of Hamilton about the rent, owner Harold Ballard was having the team's equipment packed up and hauled out of Ivor Wynne Stadium and put into cold storage. He was threatening to either move or fold the club. For about four months there were no Hamilton Tiger-Cats. The club's outlook brightened in the spring when it learned it had been sold — for $2 — to Hamilton businessman David Braley. He also wiped out their $1-million debt.

One of the first things Braley did was draw up a proper marketing budget. When defensive tackle Mike Walker left home in Seattle for training camp that May, he couldn't believe what he was seeing: "There were these commercials on TV for the Ti-Cats.... Then I saw all these billboards — 'Buy a Ticket and Feed the Cats,' and 'It's Feeding Time.'" Season ticket sales in 1989 jumped from 3,800 to 7,000, and average attendance rose from 14,756 to 17,233.

"We're well on our way now to putting the team on its feet financially," said Braley. What's more, these Tiger-Cats, who only a year before were threatened with extinction, were playing at the Grey Cup. They were playing good football.

There were comparable stories coming out of Regina. Three years before when then-CFL president Bill Baker was hired to save the Roughriders, he became a man on a mission. His word was "football is your heritage," and he brought it to anyone who would listen. In some ways, though, Baker was in a tougher spot than Braley. For one, the Roughriders hadn't earned a playoff berth in 10 years. They were also lacking talent on the field. So it would take more than just money (of which they had none); it would also take some real team-building.

Baker hired John Gregory as coach, and together they came up with a three-year plan. During that slow team-building period they would have to get the Rider Nation to keep believing. There were fundraisers, ticket-a-thons, and volunteer committees organized. The players pitched in, too. Attendance in 1986 was as low as 18,000; in the 1989 season it rose to 24,000. The club managed to add $1.2 million in revenue even after trimming the budget by $800,000. Everyone had something to cheer about, because after all that effort, the lowly Saskatchewan Roughriders had finally made it to the Grey Cup.

They held their pep rally in Maple Leaf Gardens on the Sunday morning. Present were Rider mascot Gainer the Gopher; the Pride of the Lions marching band; Saskatchewan premier Grant Devine; Maple Leaf and Saskatchewanian Wendel Clark; and Ron Lancaster and George Reed, two Rider greats from the past.

Sometime after the pep rally, the throngs in green and white likely ran into the throngs in black and gold on the streets of Toronto as they converged on SkyDome. Over 54,000 fans filled the concrete bowl. Later, many were to call it the most exciting game in Grey Cup history.

A hush fell over the sections full of Saskatchewan fans after Paul Osbaldiston gave Hamilton an early 6–0 lead with two field goals. The 'Riders came back to life along with their team's offence midway through the second quarter, when their quarterback, Kent Austin, completed three touchdown passes. The Ticats, however, continued to claw away.

Wanting to close the gap a little before the end of the half, Saskatchewan's Dave Ridgway was called out. Ridgway had moved to Canada from the United Kingdom, where he had played soccer as a teenager, and so he knew a thing or two about kicking a ball. Unfortunately, he missed his first try of the game and Hamilton led 27–22 after two quarters.

Ridgway was brought out again at the end of the third, and this time he made good, contributing to a renewed 'Riders offensive that included a Tim McCray touchdown, giving them a 34–30 lead. The 'Riders maintained their momentum, and with less than two minutes in the final quarter, moved ahead once more, with Ridgway kicking his third field goal of the game.

The Tiger-Cats then got their second wind and Mike Kerrigan began an aggressive drive, marching his team down the field. A pass to Tony Champion — which he caught in a spectacular backward diving catch — resulted in a touchdown. The game was now tied 40–40 with only 44 seconds left to play.

But Saskatchewan refused to let up and quarterback Kent Austin starting putting together his final push. He completed three passes for 48 yards, positioning his team for a winning field goal from Hamilton's 26-yard line. Ridgway was called out. All week long he kept talking about not wanting to have to kick the winning field goal in the last seconds of the game. There were seven seconds left on the clock.

It was a breathless moment. Bob Poley snapped the ball to Glen Suitor's hands and Ridgway drilled it through the uprights with just two seconds left on the clock. The crowd, probably standing for most of the final quarter, went completely berserk. Final score: Saskatchewan Roughriders 43, Hamilton Tiger-Cats 40.

It had been a long and sometimes painful 23-year drought for the Roughriders, but "The Kick" was finally sending the Grey Cup home to Saskatchewan.

"They played a great football game," said Ridgway, referring to his teammates, "and it comes down to a skinny little guy in a clean uniform. But that's what they pay me for." Ridgway was named Most Valuable Canadian.

Kent Austin threw for a remarkable 474 yards and three touchdowns and was named the game's Most Valuable Player. Hamilton's Mike Kerrigan completed 23 of 35 passes for 303 yards. Both quarterbacks had only one interception. The record books had to be reopened that year, as well, as 15 Grey Cup records had been set, including most points scored by both teams in one game.

• • •

It was Vancouver's turn to host the Grey Cup, their fourth time in eight years, and ticket sales were alarmingly soft: just 46,968. On the previous three occasions, sales were consistently just under 60,000. The 1990 figure actually represented the lowest Grey Cup attendance in 14 years. Theories for the sharp decline in sales abounded, and ran from the recession to the CFL simply taking football fans for granted.

There were indications, though, that the Cup was still garnering strong television ratings. In 1989, it had ranked first among sports events, and fourth among all television shows. It was a televised Canadian cultural event. Also, the last three Grey Cups had been exciting to watch, a thrill to the end. And it looked like that might be the case again that year.

The Edmonton Eskimos were still considered a force to be reckoned with, and entertaining to watch. And the Winnipeg Blue Bombers had just won the Grey Cup in 1988, although there was some concern about their offence. This season they became the first team in CFL history to finish with the league's best overall record (12–6) while scoring the fewest points of any team. What's more, their quarterback, Tom Burgess, was the only quarterback in the league to have more interceptions (27) than touchdown passes (25). Of course, one could drill deeper into stats such as these and find other ways of looking at them, but on the surface it wasn't all that impressive.

But sometimes the best offence is a good defence. The Bombers managed to defuse the Eskimo offence early in the game when Edmonton quarterback Tracy Ham's pass was intercepted by Greg Battle on the one-yard line and returned to the Edmonton 43. That one move seemed to rob Edmonton of their drive and momentum. After that, the Bombers defence pretty much put the Edmonton team on lockdown.

At halftime the score was Winnipeg 10, Edmonton 4.

Battle made his second interception at the start of the second half and returned it 34 yards for a touchdown. This is when the scoring juggernaut started to roll. In the third quarter alone, the Winnipeg Blue Bombers scored 28 points — a Grey Cup record for points in a quarter.

Edmonton scored their touchdown at the beginning of the fourth quarter with a Tracy Ham pass to Larry Willis that almost didn't make it past Less Browne. But Winnipeg wasn't finished. There was a safety, a field goal by Kennard, and one last touchdown — a two-yard plunge by Warren Hudson that was converted by Kennerd. The final score was Winnipeg 50, Edmonton 11.

It was only the third time that a team had scored 50 or more points in a Grey Cup game.

Many agreed that the Eskimos lost it on the turnovers. Said coach Faragalli, "You just can't turn the ball over seven times and expect to win. You just can't do it."

It was no coincidence that at the awards dinner the previous Thursday, Battle was named the CFL's top defensive player in 1990.

• • •

The Vegas oddsmakers were calling the Argos by five over the Stamps, but there were injuries: Raghib "Rocket" Ismail was still nursing a slight concussion, his second of the season, which he received the previous weekend in the Eastern final against the Blue Bombers. And Matt Dunigan's lingering shoulder injury likely meant that Rickey Foggie, who had yet to start in a pro game, might be starting for Toronto in the 79th Grey Cup. Things could get interesting.

It seems as if some festival traditions never die: Itsy, the Calgary horse that gallops up and down the sidelines after Stampeder touchdowns, made it to Winnipeg for the Grey Cup, and would be making an appearance in the lobby of the Cup's hub hotel Saturday evening for pictures and souvenirs.

Also following tradition, the game would be fought on a frozen field. Winnipeg was hosting its very first Grey Cup. Despite the weather forecast, there was no problem selling 52,000 tickets to the event. Fans arrived early for the tailgate parties and the drinking and cavorting in the stands. The temperature on the field at Winnipeg Stadium was about -18°C, but football die-hards came prepared in balaclavas, parkas, sleeping bags, and snowsuits.

Arriving on the scene were the new Argonauts owners, Bruce McNall, John Candy, and Wayne Gretzky. There was some friendly booing.

And just in time, it looked like Argo quarterback Matt Dunigan was going to get to play after all: team doctors injected his shoulder with Novocain. And Rocket Ismail, seemingly recovered from his head-banging episode, would play too.

The game got off to an exciting start with Argo defensive back Ed Barry intercepting Calgary quarterback Danny Barrett's first pass attempt. Barry returned it 50 yards for a touchdown. Barrett made up for it, though, with a one-yard run over the goal line that left the score 8–7 at the end of the first quarter.

Scoring in the second quarter was limited to one field goal each, and so Toronto carried their one point lead into the second half.

Calgary managed to take the lead in the third quarter, but couldn't hold it. Before his Novocain wore off, Dunigan got busy again and threw a 48-yard bullet to Darrell Smith, making it 19–14 for Toronto.

Not giving up, Calgary narrowed the gap again in the fourth quarter with a 12-yard touchdown reception by Allen Pitts, making it 22–21. Then came Raghib "Rocket" Ismail's spectacular 87–yard kickoff return for a touchdown, breaking Roughrider Alan Ford's Grey Cup record from 1969 and stunning the largely Calgary-supporting crowd. The Argonauts were now leading 29–21.

The Stamps' Keyvan Jenkins fumbled on the ensuing kickoff, and Keith Castello covered the ball to set up a 36-yard touchdown from Dunigan to Paul Masotti. It was all over for the Calgary crowd.

Final score: Toronto Argonauts 36, Calgary Stampeders 21.

Raghib Ismail broke another Grey Cup record: most yards on kick returns by a running back with 183 yards, breaking Roughrider Tim McCray's record by 14 yards, which he set in 1989. And for that and many other reasons, the man called "Rocket" was the 79th Grey Cup's Most Valuable Player.

Sitting on a bench in the locker room and nursing his shoulder after the game, Dunigan remarked, "Half these tears are joy and half are pain."

Back in Toronto, several hundred fans took to the streets, but it was nothing like it was in 1983 when the Argos defeated the B.C. Lions. The police were prepared this time, and closed off sections of Yonge Street. They already had 200 officers in place along the strip and on adjacent downtown streets.

When McNall, Candy, and Gretzky had purchased the Toronto Argonauts, Candy felt his role should not be limited to just signing the occasional cheque. He invented and gladly assumed the role of number one promoter, not just of the Argos, but of the Canadian Football League.

"If you're going to continue," he said, "you're going to have to think in a bigger sense."

Wading into the U.S. expansion debate, he was unequivocally for it. Addressing the concerns of some cultural nationalists, he said, "We're not getting rid of the Canadian identity. We're building it up. The league is still the *Canadian* Football League. It's the Canadian game.... People should be proud of what we have to offer. To knock it is to knock yourself."

The debate continued over the next year.

• • •

"I think they have a tendency up here to downgrade a lot of things that are Canadian," said Doug Flutie, quarterback for the Calgary Stampeders. "The Canadians need to take more pride than they have. For some reason, they've grown up with the mentality of trying to compare themselves with things that go on in the U.S. all the time, almost an inferiority-type thing. There's no need for it."

His comments were coming on the eve of the 80th Grey Cup.

Another hot topic in 1992 was CFL expansion into the United States, and Flutie was being looked upon as either a possible pitchman, or at least the poster boy for the proposed venture. A few of the expansion cities that commissioner Larry Smith was considering were San Antonio, Sacramento, and St. Petersburg. The idea had its opponents — Winnipeg MP Lloyd Axworthy for one: "Expansion into the U.S. will destroy the league in terms of its character, its intent and its soul." He went as far as presenting a private members bill that would prevent the move.

Potential investors from a number of American cities and from Montreal were in Toronto to take in the big game. Upon arriving, they were somewhat taken aback by how little Grey Cup atmosphere there was in the city. They were expecting a little more enthusiasm from Torontonians, perhaps even a welcome wagon or two for the out-of-towners. But Torontonians apparently weren't interested. The city of Calgary put on their free pancake breakfast, which attracted few people, and the CFL's Fanbowl theme park at the Metro Toronto Convention Centre was launched with little fanfare. And there was no parade of any kind. The fact was that the Grey Cup had become a very tough sell in the larger markets and was performing better and more consistently in the smaller ones.

What's more, when McNall, Gretzky, and Candy purchased the Argos, part of the deal was that Toronto would play Grey Cup host in 1992 and 1993. Ticket sales for that weekend's game, however, were so poor that Argo chief operating officer Brian Cooper had no choice but to sell the 1993 option. His potential buyer was the Calgary club whose Stampeders would be meeting the Winnipeg Blue Bombers on the field at SkyDome the next day.

The previous year, when Winnipeg — with their outdoor stadium — played host to the Cup, they sold out 52,000 tickets in September. With only two days to go before the big game in Toronto, there were still 8,600 tickets available. (The attendance turned out to be 45,863, the lowest Grey Cup turnout since 1975.)

There was always hope that the game itself would spur interest, as it had sometimes in the past, but it was looking like it might have all the makings of another romp, the Stampeders with 24 points holding the Blue Bombers scoreless until the fourth quarter. The Bombers finally got on the board with a 46-yard field goal by Troy Westwood, and then Danny McManus reached Gerald Alphin with a 27-yard pass for a touchdown. But by then it was too late.

The final score was Calgary Stampeders 24, Winnipeg Blue Bombers 10.

It had been Dave Sapunjis that hauled in Calgary's first touchdown pass, a 35-yard catch from Flutie that put Calgary up 10–0 at the end of the first quarter. Sapunjis finished the game with 85 yards on seven passes and took the honours as Outstanding Canadian.

Flutie passed for 480 yards, only 28 yards shy of the Grey Cup record set by Montreal's Sam Etcheverry in 1955. He systematically picked apart the Bombers defence and got the Stampeders within scoring range on four of Calgary's first five offensive series. Flutie was named game MVP.

In the locker room afterward, Stamps owner Ryckman referred to Flutie as the "Wayne Gretzky of football." There was a new star in Canada's football firmament.

## 11

1993–1999:
THE AMERICAN EXPERIMENT

In 1993, Calgary Stampeders quarterback Doug Flutie became the first CFL player to be chosen as the league's Most Outstanding Player for the third consecutive year. In doing so, he joined a small group of quarterbacks in the CFL pantheon that included legends Jackie Parker and Russ Jackson, both of whom were present at the ceremony. Accepting the honour, Flutie called the 1993 season the most enjoyable of his career. Unfortunately, his team was defeated by the Edmonton Eskimos in the Western Division final, so he didn't get to compete in the championship.

It was a disappointment, not just for Flutie and his organization, but for Calgary supporters in general, as the city was set to play host to the 81st Grey Cup. Management at McMahon Stadium had the seating capacity temporarily increased by 11,000 just for the occasion. And they must have sold every ticket at the wicket, because attendance was estimated to be in the neighbourhood of 50,000.

Las Vegas oddsmakers favoured Edmonton over the Bombers by four points. The other oddsmakers, Environment Canada, were calling for clear skies and a high of 2°C. It turned out to be a balmy 6°C, leaving the prognosticators on shaky ground.

Early mistakes by the Blue Bombers seemed to spell their doom. In the first 10 minutes the Eskimos took advantage of a blocked punt, a fumbled kickoff return, and an interception. Running back Lucius Floyd scored on a four-yard carry, and wide receiver Jim Sandusky caught a two-yard pass from quarterback Damon Allen. Sean Fleming made the convert and was also good for a field goal before the close of the first quarter, making it 17–0 for Edmonton. It was looking not so much a battle as a rout.

In the second quarter, Edmonton continued its rampage with a single and another field goal from Fleming. Before the Blue Bombers even got on the board, it was already 21–0. After a three-yard run, Winnipeg's Michael Richardson finally scored a touchdown and Troy Westwood made the convert. After trading off a pair of field goals, it was 24–10 going into the half.

Winnipeg turned up the heat in the third quarter with a one-yard run from Sam Garza followed by a 32-yard Westwood field goal. Now the Blue Bombers were only trailing by four points. After that, Sean Fleming put it to the boot, scoring two more field goals for the Esks — tying the record of six in a Grey Cup game. Westwood then added another three points to the Bombers' tally. But Damon Allen was looking to close it up, and at the end of a long drive, with 44 seconds remaining, set up Fleming for his last field goal of the day. The final score was Edmonton 33, Winnipeg, 23.

Allen was named Most Valuable Player and Sean Fleming was selected Most Valuable Canadian. It was Edmonton's first Grey Cup since 1987.

Following Grey Cup weekend, the press area was to be converted into a baker's dozen of luxury boxes. It became increasingly obvious that in this era, that was one way that a club could pay the bills.

On the subject of the expansion into the United States, in the past year there had been the announcement of two expansion teams — the Sacramento Surge and San Antonio Raiders — the folding of one of those teams — San Antonio — a couple of weeks later, and the first regular-season CFL games played in the United States.

• • •

The Canadian quota guidelines set out by the CFL were very explicit: of the 37 players allowed per team, 20 had to be "non-imports," a non-import being "a player who has spent a total of five of his first 15 years in Canada, or who has never played football outside of Canada." The yin to that yang, an import, was defined as "a player who played football outside of Canada and who did not play football in Canada prior to his 17th birthday" (the CFL's age of majority). Understandably, there were those who took issue with the fact that the U.S. expansion teams were exempt from these rules.

While Baltimore sent a complement of media-types to the game, by some reports no journalists were sent from the other U.S. expansion cities: Sacramento, Las Vegas, and Shreveport.

It's virtually impossible to look back on the 82nd Grey Cup and not think of it as the year that, for the first time in history, an American team, the Baltimore Football Club, was competing for Lord Grey's silver chalice. This remarkable 82nd Grey Cup drama was played out at B.C. Place Stadium in Vancouver in front of a somewhat tense crowd of 55,000, most there to cheer on the hometown team.

The Lions took an early lead in the first quarter. Quarter-back Kent Austin moved his players downfield and set up Lui Passaglia for a 47-yard field goal. Baltimore responded swiftly in the second quarter with a pair of touchdowns, the first being a one-yard run from quarterback Tracy Ham. The second came after Baltimore safety Alvin Walton nabbed an Austin throw and passed to Karl Anthony, who bolted 36 yards before crossing the goal line.

The game was won by a 38-yard field goal courtesy of Lui Passaglia in the last second of official time. The moment the ball sailed through the uprights, Passaglia was mobbed by players and fans. The final score was Lions 26, Stallions, 23. It was the Lions' first victory in nine years, and their third lifetime Grey Cup. The pandaemonium on the field continued as fans festooned in maple leafs and proudly wearing their red and white crowded the field, forcing the Grey Cup to be awarded in the safety of a room under the stands.

After settling some confusion around the ballots, Vancouver native Passaglia was named Most Valuable Canadian and Karl Anthony the game's Most Valuable Player.

For the time being, at least, the Cup would remain north of the border.

• • •

At the beginning of the American experiment, there were many confident nationalists that said the game would never change, that Canada was exporting a unique product and that that's what would always give it a certain appeal and make it successful. However, there was a meeting scheduled for the owners of the eight Canadian and five U.S. teams following the 1995 Grey Cup where everything from the league name to the size of the field and the rule book appeared to be on the table. It was a divisive issue, even among the Canadian owners.

Patriotic sentiment aside, the truth was that, rather than being any kind of a saviour, the U.S. teams were becoming a financial burden on the league, dragging it down even farther. Baltimore, the most successful by far, saw its crowds shrink in its second season and would likely see them shrink more upon the arrival of an NFL team. The other four teams — the Birmingham Barracudas, Memphis Mad Dogs, Shreveport Pirates, and San Antonio Texans (previously Sacramento Gold Miners) — were faring poorly as well. In an effort to salvage the club, the Pirates were organizing a move to Virginia. It was anticipated that the Barracudas would also move, or perhaps even fold.

Only time would tell.

• • •

Taylor Field in Regina expanded overnight for the 83rd Grey Cup as temporary bleachers were erected at either end of the field, bringing the capacity to 55,000 for the battle scheduled to take place between the Calgary Stampeders and the Baltimore Stallions. Nearly every seat in the house was sold for this, the first Grey Cup hosted by Regina.

The teams were well-matched — to the extent that both finished the regular season 15-3, with 8-1 records at home and 7-2 records on the road. And both teams were free of any major injuries. The Stallions led the U.S. Southern Division and the Stampeders had taken the Northern Division title. It was just another way of saying Canada versus the U.S.

Being Regina, and being November, all week the weather was a concern. As spectators settled into the stands, what had started earlier as a stiff autumn breeze was becoming a gale-force wind, with gusts of up to 80 kilometres per hour — a mere 10 kilometres per hour less that the safety maximum allowed for the temporary stands holding about half the crowd. By kickoff there was a wind chill of -20°C, and the temperature continued to drop as the afternoon became evening.

Facing the wind, the Stallions charged first, just two minutes in, with an 82-yard punt return by Chris Wright — a Grey Cup record. Calgary responded with two Mark McLoughlin field goals before the end of the quarter, bringing themselves to within a point of the Stallions.

The Stampeders' first touchdown came in the second — a three-yard pass from Doug Flutie that Marvin Pope delivered, making it 13-7 Calgary.

But before the break, the ever-impressive Baltimore squad — their special teams in particular — managed an Alvin Walton five-yard fumble return for a touchdown and three Carlos Huerta field goals for a total of 16 points, making it 23–13 for the Stallions. The longest of Huerta's field goals was for a Grey Cup record 53 yards.

Baltimore opened the third quarter with a single. After that, Calgary managed to put together one more touchdown — a Doug Flutie one-yard plunge followed by a McLoughlin convert. Flutie seemed to be back on his game, but it would be the last time Calgary added to the board. Capping a 92-yard drive, Baltimore answered with another touchdown in the form of a 13-yard run from Tracy Ham.

The fourth quarter saw two more Huerta field goals, making it a total of five for the kicker. The crowd held their breath in anticipation of a classic Flutie-style comeback, but Baltimore, lead by Pringle, played keep-away and skillfully managed to run down the clock. The final score of the "Wind Bowl" was Baltimore Stallions 37, Calgary Stampeders 20. The Cup, for the first time, was heading south of the border.

Tracy Ham, 17-for-30 for 211 yards, was the game's Most Valuable Player. Flutie finished 23-for-49 with 287 yards. For the third time in as many Grey Cup appearances, Calgary's Dave Sapunjis was voted Most Valuable Canadian.

• • •

There was a great deal of Grey Cup nostalgia going around in 1996. Perhaps it was because it was the first time since 1972 that Hamilton was hosting. Perhaps it was the hangover of the loss of the Cup to Baltimore the previous year. Maybe it was the folding of the Ottawa Rough Riders club, one of the oldest football organizations in Canada, at the end of the regular season. There was no denying that it felt like the league was at a turning point, or on the edge of a precipice.

> THE ORIGINAL ALOUETTES FRANCHISE FOLDED IN 1982 AND FOLLOWING A FINANCIAL RESCUE A NEW TEAM WAS FOUNDED: THE MONTREAL CONCORDES. THE CONCORDES FEATURED THE ONLY QUEBECOIS-BORN QUARTERBACK TO START A CFL GAME IN LUC TOUSIGNANT. THE TEAM MADE IT AS FAR AS THE EASTERN FINAL IN 1985 BEFORE UNSUCCESSFULLY RE-BRANDING ITSELF AS THE "NEW" MONTREAL ALOUETTES IN 1986. THE TEAM FOLDED ONCE MORE, ONLY A DAY BEFORE THE 1987 SEASON GOT UNDERWAY. IN 1994 THE BALTIMORE FOOTBALL CLUB WAS GRANTED A FRANCHISE, OFFICIALLY BECOMING THE STALLIONS IN 1995. THIS MOST SUCCESSFUL OF U.S. EXPANSION TEAMS FOLDED IN 1996, THEREBY ENABLING THE CFL'S RETURN TO MONTREAL AND THE REBIRTH OF THE ALOUETTES.

At any rate, keeping the hope alive in the East was Hamilton. Grey Cup weekend there would include plenty of live entertainment, a charity casino, and a street party. There would also be a parade. Hamilton opened its doors, and the people came, not in the numbers seen in years and Grey Cups gone by, but they did come.

About 38,500 of them would fill the stands at Ivor Wynne Stadium to see the Toronto Argonauts compete with the Edmonton Eskimos for Canadian football supremacy.

The Eskimos were rated the underdogs. There to support the underdog Eskimos was the cheerleading team that almost didn't make it. When it was learned that the organization couldn't afford to send them, their cause was taken up by the local media and mayor Bill Smith and $12,000 was raised to get the girls to Hamilton.

Fitting the nostalgia of the weekend, the conditions were cold and windy, and heavy snow was falling. It started Friday afternoon and carried with it all of the elements of a classic Grey Cup game.

Scoring began with a one-point safety conceded by Toronto quarterback Doug Flutie. Edmonton scored the first touchdown — a 64-yard pass from Danny McManus that found Eddie Brown. It was a spectacular shoestring catch.

The second quarter featured a scoring barrage that saw a combined total of 41 points from the teams. It started with Argos kicker Mike Vanderjagt clearing a field goal, then Jimmy Cunningham returning a punt 80 yards through the blowing snow for a touchdown. Vanderjagt pulled off one more field goal, making it 13–9 for the Argos. After that, the teams spent the rest of the half trading touchdowns. The first, a 75-yard pass and run from McManus to Jim Sandusky, allowed Edmonton to regain the lead. They lost it again when Toronto's Robert Drummond plunged from the one-yard line. The see-saw tilted yet again when the Eskimos' Henry "Gizmo" Williams returned the kickoff 91 yards — a new Grey Cup record. He skipped his trademark touchdown flip because of the treacherous snow-covered field, settling instead for a bow to the crowd. Flutie closed the scoring bonanza after marching his team to the Edmonton 10 and running the touchdown in himself. The score at the end of the half was 27–23 for the Argos. By that time, so much snow had accumulated on the field that they had to bring in tractors to remove it.

The snow removers got back to it at halftime with power sweepers and push brooms, but they were fighting a losing battle as the weather system continued blowing in off of Burlington Bay.

There was another Vanderjagt field goal relatively early in the third, and another in the final quarter. Edmonton managed to trim Toronto's lead after Eric Blount's five-yard touchdown. But in the dying minutes came the usual flurry of activity Grey Cup fans had become accustomed to. A 71-yard drive by Flutie led to a 27-yard field goal, what would be Vanderjagt's last of the game. The score was now 36–30 for the Argonauts.

Another Toronto touchdown and a successful convert by Vanderjagt in the last two minutes pretty much sealed it for the Boatmen, but the Eskimos weren't going to roll over so easily, and with 10 seconds left on the clock, McManus found Marc Tolbert with a seven-yard pass, ending the scoring at the "Snow Bowl." Final score: Toronto Argonauts 43, Edmonton Eskimos 37.

Doug Flutie was chosen Most Valuable Player of the game, finishing with 302 yards passing and 98 yards rushing. The previous week he had been selected the league's outstanding player for the fifth out of six years. He was the CFL's rushing leader with 1,403 yards and a passing efficiency rating of 64.1 percent — the best in the league. His numbers spoke volumes.

In the dressing rooms after the game, with the season now officially concluded, questions about the league and whether or not there would be a next season were tossed around. Obviously growing impatient with all of the talk and speculation, Argos coach Don Matthews simply said, "The game will survive in spite of everyone."

• • •

The Argos had the best regular season record in 1997. They also had at the helm the league's most outstanding player in quarterback Doug Flutie and the most successful coach in CFL history in Don Matthews.

While oddsmakers favoured the Argonauts by a couple of touchdowns, the Roughriders were looking for an upset (linebacker Dan Rashovich in particular). It seemed like all of the pressure was on the Argonauts to repeat rather than the underdog Roughriders to come through.

Flutie was still raising the bar in Canada as far as quarterbacking was concerned. He passed for 5,505 yards and 47 touchdowns that season. He took an almost forensic interest in his game.

None of this is to say people were writing off the Roughriders, These were two very different teams, and each would be approaching the game in their own way.

It was a full house at Commonwealth Stadium in Edmonton, with over 60,000 rabid football fans, mostly from the Western provinces, who had come to see what the 'Riders had left after their remarkable season. They had finished third overall but then defeated the Edmonton Eskimos 31–30 in the playoff to take the Western title.

The game started impressively enough for the men in green, with Shannon Baker returning the opening kick 74 yards, deep into Argonaut territory. The drive concluded with a 28-yard Paul McCallum field goal. The Argos got on the board after skillfully engineering a 32-yard drive that ended with a touchdown strike from Flutie to CFL rookie of the year Derrell Mitchell.

The second quarter opened with Flutie marching his troops down the field once more. He hit Robert Drummond with a six-yard touchdown pass, widening the gap to 14–3. Saskatchewan narrowed it with a three-yard plunge courtesy of Shawn Daniels. They missed the convert, however. The first half closed with a pair of field goals from Mike Vanderjagt, extending the Argo lead to 20–9.

*Doug Flutie hoists the Cup following the Argonauts win over the Saskatchewan Roughriders at Commonwealth Stadium in Edmonton in 1997.*

The movements of the Argonaut team in the third quarter must have been nothing short of breathtaking for the fans, regardless of their stripe. Toronto kick returner Adrion Smith caught the ball on his own 15-yard line and ran for a record 95 yards for a touchdown. Following an interception, Flutie orchestrated a 73-yard drive, at the end of which he called his own number from 10 yards out for another touchdown. Lastly, Flutie found Mike "Pinball" Clemens wide open in the end zone to make it 41–9 going into the final quarter.

Saskatchewan got back in the game when quarterback Reggie Slack passed 51 yards to Mike Saunders, who hauled it in for a touchdown. Vanderjagt worked in another couple of field goals, and the Roughriders rounded out the scoring with a one-yard plunge from Slack. The final score was Toronto Argonauts 47, Saskatchewan Roughriders 23.

In the end, 'Rider Pride could not overcome a superior and masterful Argonaut team led by Doug Flutie, the game's Most Valuable Player.

• • •

The attendance at Winnipeg Stadium in 1998 was a mere 34,157, the lowest turnout for a Grey Cup game in almost a quarter-century. Several thousand short of a sellout, come game time, volunteers were enlisted to hand out free tickets to make it more visually appealing for television viewers.

The contest for the 86th Grey Cup was between the Calgary Stampeders and the Hamilton Tiger-Cats. At least it wasn't snowing, and temperatures were hovering around a comfortable 10°C under clear skies.

It was all about the kicking in the first quarter. It began with Calgary's Mark McLoughlin missing a 48-yard field goal attempt and the Stamps settling for the point. Hamilton's Paul Osbaldiston succeeded in his 24-yard attempt, bringing the score to 3–1 for the Tiger-Cats. Shortly thereafter, McLoughlin made amends with a 34-yard field goal.

In the second quarter, Calgary came out and scored the first touchdown of the game after a charge from Kevin Anderson. The second also saw Hamilton's first touchdown of the game — Danny McManus hit Ron Williams with a 34-yard pass, putting the Tiger-Cats up 13–10 halfway through the quarter. After a penalty against Calgary, and with no time on the clock, Osbaldiston made his third field goal of the game — Hamilton 16, Calgary 10. It looked like Hamilton's return to form in 1998 was going to result in a Grey Cup victory.

Osbaldiston opened up his team's lead even farther in the third quarter after scoring a couple of singles. However, Calgary quarterback Jeff Garcia's 75-yard drive and concluding one-yard plunge once again made it a one-point game — Hamilton 18, Calgary 17.

In this era of rebuilding, the Calgary Stampeders' return to form began with three consecutive 15–3 seasons from 1993 to 1995. Dave Sapunjis was named CFL's Top Canadian twice in this span. In 1996, Kelvin Anderson became the second Calgary player to earn CFL Top Rookie honours. Their first-place finish in the Western Division was iced with a Grey Cup victory in 1998.

The game-changer came about halfway through the fourth quarter when an interception by Stampeders defensive back Aldi Henry translated into a Mark McLoughlin 22-yard field goal that put Calgary back in the lead. McLoughlin soon padded that lead with another field goal. The Stamps were still charging.

Hamilton's Danny McManus hit running back Archie Amerson with a pass up the middle and Amerson, dodging three successive tacklers, travelled 47 yards to Calgary's two-yard line. Ron Williams plunged in for the touchdown, but they failed on the two-point convert. Again, it was a one-point game — 24–23 in favour of Hamilton.

With no time left on the clock, Mark McLoughlin cleared the ball through the uprights in a 35-yard field goal. A dramatic end to a hard-fought game. Final score: Calgary Stampeders 26, Hamilton Tiger-Cats 24.

The Calgary players standing on the sidelines cheered and threw their helmets into the air. Running onto the field, they were joined by hundreds of fans. The victory was sweetest for Jeff Garcia, who proved after living in Doug Flutie's shadow that he could win the big game. Garcia was named Most Valuable Player of the game.

• • •

The rumours of the CFL's death had apparently been greatly exaggerated. Hamilton Tiger-Cats coach Ron Lancaster admitted that, as recently as three or four years before, when he was coaching Edmonton, he was thinking that the best thing for the league to do would be just to shutter its doors. But at that time, with regards to the health of the league and overall interest in the game, he thought that they were "in the process of turning a corner." Tiger-Cats quarterback Danny McManus concurred, saying that the "tradition that this league has had means the people of Canada would not just let this thing fold."

Indeed, in 1998 and 1999, TSN viewership rose 50 percent and CBC ratings increased 20 percent. In the same span,

*The quintessential "Pinball" move: Michael Clemens prepares to dart up the grid at Ivor Wynne Stadium as the Argos faced the Tiger-Cats in another Labour Day Classic, 1999.*

overall attendance at the games increased by 15 percent. It was an indication that the CFL had never really lost its core audience. The fans were coming back.

But because the league and its teams had been ailing for so long, the cooler heads understood that some of the remaining problems would not be going away. There were still financial concerns regarding some of the teams. It was expected that only two of the eight teams — Calgary and Edmonton — would actually turn a profit in 1999. The teams in the three largest markets — B.C., Toronto, and Montreal — would not. Hamilton was expected to break even. Most worrisome were the Saskatchewan and Winnipeg organizations; both were anticipating heavy losses.

With spending under control, salaries addressed, and the American experiment more or less behind them, what they had to focus on was just staying the course and not backsliding. In that regard, CFL commissioner John Tory definitely seemed like the right man at the right time.

The Grey Cup was making its sixth trip to B.C. Place Stadium in Vancouver. Attendance was expected to be just over 45,000. It was to be a rematch between the Hamilton Tiger-Cats and the Calgary Stampeders, and it marked the fifth time in a decade that Ticats coach Wally Buono had brought his team to the Grey Cup. Perhaps fifth time lucky?

It started well for them as Buono's Tabbies came roaring out and were first to get on the board after Danny McManus hit Ron Williams for a 35-yard gain that landed them on Calgary's 15-yard line. Three plays later, Williams plunged from the one-yard line. The Osbaldiston convert was successful and it put the Tiger-Cats up 7–0. Another drive into Calgary territory resulted in a 46-yard Osbaldiston field goal at the end of the first quarter.

The kicker missed his next attempt, but was granted a point. However, his second field goal several minutes later — a

41-yarder — was successful, and was followed by a 13-yard touchdown pass from Darren Flutie to Danny McManus. The convert meant that going into the break, Hamilton was leading 21–0. The Stamps remarkably had only 51 yards in total offence in the first half.

That situation improved in the third quarter with a couple of Calgary touchdowns. The first came after Dave Dickenson eyed Travis Moore behind the Hamilton defence and completed a 57-yard pass. On the next play, Dickenson passed to Vince Danielsen, who hauled it in for the touchdown, finally putting the Stamps on the board. On their next possession, the Stampeders ushered the ball down the field once more and Dickenson found Allen Pitts wide open in the end zone, narrowing the gap to 22–14.

Osbaldiston closed the third quarter with a field goal. This must have taken away some of Calgary's momentum, because not a minute into the fourth, a quick drive assembled by McManus ended with Flutie catching a seven-yard pass, extending the Hamilton lead to 32–14. Trying to regain some ground, Dickenson drove deep into Tiger-Cat territory and, on a third down, Duane Forde plunged over the Hamilton goal line. But that would be the end of the scoring; there would be no Stamps comeback. Final score 32–21 in favour of the Ticats. With the win, Hamilton could say they won the Grey Cup in each decade of the century except the first. It was a sweet victory for the team, for fans of the Cats, and for all Hamiltonians.

In an open poll launched on Labour Day by *The CFL on CBC* in which fans could vote online for their favourite all-time CFL players from a list compiled by football writers, broadcasters, and former players, it was Russ Jackson, perhaps Hamilton's greatest football son, who came out on top. Normie Kwong placed second and Tony Gabriel, a Tiger-Cat from the early 1970s, was third.

# 12

## 2000–2011:
## A NEW GOLDEN AGE

It was more than evident by the turn of the century that, while the pulse of Canadian football may have been weak over the last decade and a half, its heart never stopped beating. In fact, now it was stronger than ever. There was even talk of expansion again — but not into the United States.

Early in November, the incoming CFL commissioner, Michael Lysko, was introduced at a news conference. There were the usual questions about the current state of the league as well as its future. Regarding the latter, Lysko replied that he would like to be in 10 Canadian cities within the next three years, though he wouldn't divulge which markets he had his eye on.

The 88th Grey Cup would mark the first time that the B.C. Lions and the Montreal Alouettes would meet at the championship. They would compete on the field at McMahon Stadium in Calgary in front of a 44,382, about 2,300 shy of a sellout. Conditions were ideal: a crisp, blue autumn sky with temperatures hovering at the freezing level.

There was positive energy building around this game, despite the fact that the host city had lost the Western final to the rival Lions a week before. In some ways, it must have resembled a sort of CFL homecoming. Stamps fans still turned out in red and white, and there were, of course, plenty of Lions fans painted orange and black. But there was also a complement of Alouettes colours, and representatives of Saskatchewan and Winnipeg showed up as well.

All eyes seemed to be on Damon Allen of the Lions who, like the CFL, had been written off several years before but was coming into his own as an all-around player and top-notch quarterback. At the opposite end of the field, leading the Alouettes offence, was Mike Pringle, winner of six of the last seven CFL rushing titles and a new record-holder with 19 touchdowns in a season.

The Lions were the first to get on the scoreboard after a failed field goal by Lui Passaglia produced a single. Minutes later, Damon Allen scored a touchdown on a one-yard run making it 8–0 for B.C. The quarter was almost up before Montreal registered with a 19-yard field goal courtesy of Terry Baker.

Another missed field goal by Passaglia resulted in the only point scored in the second quarter. At the half, it was 9–3 for the Lions.

In a third-quarter drive, Montreal slotback Jock Climie caught a one-yard toss from quarterback Anthony Calvillo, narrowing the gap to 12–10 Lions. The Als continued their chase but the Lions wouldn't rest. Barely a minute into the fourth quarter, Robert Drummond broke through the Alouettes defence for a 44-yard touchdown to increase the Lions lead to 19–10.

A field goal from the toe of Terry Baker, his second of the day, inched the Als three points closer. However, Damon Allen followed that with his second touchdown of the day. Although the conversion failed, the Lions were now leading by 12 points: the score was Lions 25, Alouettes 13. But there were still 11 minutes on the clock, and this catch-and-chase game still felt wide open to possibilities.

Mike Pringle ran in a five-yard touchdown to shrink the differential once again, and it was 25–20 with just 3:42 left. But Grey Cup final minutes were like geological time, and there was still room for a whole new football species to evolve.

Lui Passaglia's 29-yard field goal with 1:25 left gave the Lions eight points of breathing room. But Calvillo knew he and the Als still had a chance of at least tying up and taking the game into overtime. The quarterback hit receiver Ben Cahoon across the middle, and Cahoon flew 59 yards to pull the Alouettes to within two points with 44 seconds remaining. The Alouettes went for a two-point conversion to tie it up but Calvillo's pass sailed prettily over the head of a falling Thomas Haskins. After that, Montreal attempted an onside kick, but Lions receiver Alfred Jackson leapt over various and sundry Alouettes and recovered, affording the Lions the opportunity to run out the clock.

Final score: B.C. Lions 28, Montreal Alouettes 26. Fireworks lit up the night sky over McMahon Stadium. Robert Drummond was chosen Most Valuable Player, while Sean Millington was selected Top Canadian.

Containing all of the elements of a classic Grey Cup match, it was another positive shot in the arm for the league. Fans of all stripes spilled out of B.C. Place Stadium and headed to Robson Street for a peaceful gathering that seemed just as much a celebration of Canadian football as it was of the Lions' victory.

• • •

In 2001, during his annual address, Canadian Football League commissioner Michael Lysko paid tribute not only to the Calgary and Winnipeg teams' skills on the field, but their respective clubs' business acumen as well. He praised the marketing job being done by both organizations. He made an example of them and then, alluding to the franchises in the two largest markets, he went on to say: "We need consistent, sustained effort by [Toronto and Vancouver] and a few others to start to level off damage. We have to be a year-round business, not with one or two people in the marketplace selling tickets, but ten."

It was almost another west-of-the-Great Lakes sweep at the CFL awards in 2001, with top rookie honours going to Barrin Simpson of the B.C. Lions and three of the other awards going to Winnipeg players: Khari Jones for Outstanding Player; Dave Mudge for Top Lineman, and Doug Brown for Outstanding Canadian. This trio would meet with their Western Division counterparts from the Calgary Stampeders on the field at Olympic Stadium in Montreal to do battle for the 89th Grey Cup.

Attendance was estimated at 65,255 — the best Grey Cup turnout since 1977 when the Alouettes had defeated the Eskimos here by a score of 41–6, and the second-largest crowd in CFL history. But this was different — not only were there no Alouettes, there were no teams from eastern Canada at all in this championship final. Canadian professional football had died a slow death in this city years before but interest in the game never really disappeared. The CFL's core audience in Montreal was returning and bringing with them a new generation of fans.

The Calgary Stampeders had begun the season with four straight losses, and had racked up a mere three wins by Labour Day. But they eventually got it together and finished their season 8–10 for a second-place finish in the Western Division. The Blue Bombers, on the other hand, finished with the CFL's best regular season record: 14–4.

With his team trailing 4–3 late in the second quarter, Calgary quarterback Marcus Crandell hit Marc Boerigter as he flew down the grid for a 68-yard touchdown. Before the end of the half, the Stamps struck again when Crandell hit Travis Moore for a nine-yard touchdown. At the break, the Calgary squad was comfortably leading their Winnipeg opponents 17–4.

The Blue Bombers came to life in the third quarter, however, and on their first possession, quarterback Khari Jones passed to Arland Bruce for a 23-yard touchdown completion.

FOURTH QUARTER: 1983-2011 | 223

At that point, it looked like the Bombers might have some momentum, but then late in the fourth, Calgary's Aldi Henry blocked a Bob Cameron punt attempt. Willie Fells recovered and carried the ball 11 yards for a Calgary touchdown.

With time left on the clock, the Blue Bombers picked up the pieces. Jones let fly a pass that hit Milt Segal for an impressive 23-yard touchdown reception. But the Stampeders pulled ahead once more. Pinned on their own 11-yard line with precious little time left on the clock, Crandell drilled one to Kevin Anderson, whose running skills bought Calgary 44 yards. A few plays later, and with just 48 seconds left on the clock, Mark McLoughlin kicked a 24-yard field goal. The Bombers fought to the end, but all was lost in this game of missed opportunities. The final score was Calgary Stampeders 27, Winnipeg Blue Bombers 19.

It was Calgary's third championship in 10 years and their fifth Grey Cup win. There was already a rally planned for Olympic Plaza.

• • •

There hadn't been a home team in the final in almost a decade and so there was all that much more reason for Edmontonians to be excited. In 2002, Grey Cup fever was taking noticeable hold on the city.

There was a week of well-attended festivities and the "City of Champions" was festooned in green and gold. Mayor Bill Smith, himself a former Edmonton Eskimo, kicked off the events on Wednesday evening in front of more than 5,000 people. Thousands of visiting football fans descended upon the city, and hotels, restaurants, and retailers were expected to take in about $50 million worth of Grey Cup–related business.

The Edmonton Eskimos and Montreal Alouettes had not met on a Grey Cup field since 1977. The pairing in this 90th

*In 2002, quarterback Anthony Calvillo led the Montreal Alouettes to their first Grey Cup victory in 25 years.*

Grey Cup called to mind previous eras in CFL history, and classic matchups like Etcheverry versus Parker in the 1950s, and Moon versus Wade in the 1970s. Alberta premier Ralph Klein and Quebec premier Bernard Landry made a friendly wager: five pounds of Alberta beef or five pounds of Montreal smoked meat.

Attendance at Commonwealth Stadium was an impressive 62,531. It was a slick, frozen field.

More than just notable, and downright spectacular, was a 99-yard touchdown pass in the first half from Anthony Calvillo to Pat Woodcock — the longest completion in Grey Cup history. The Als dominated the half and led 11–0 at the break.

In the third quarter, after the Eskimos had closed the gap to 11–10, Calvillo hit Jermaine Copeland with a 47-yard pass-and-run touchdown. It was now 18–10 for Montreal.

But in typical Grey Cup fashion, it wasn't over until it was over. Edmonton quarterback Ricky Ray hit Chris Brazzell with a 47-yard pass that put the ball on the Montreal two-yard line with a minute to go. After taking a 15-yard sack on second down, Ray then hit Ed Hervey for a touchdown, making the score 18–16 with 19 seconds left to play. But an attempted two-point conversion failed, and then on the ensuing kickoff, Copeland ran the ball back for a Montreal touchdown. Final score: Montreal Alouettes 25, Edmonton Eskimos 16.

Calvillo was named Most Valuable Player. He finished the game 11 for 31 for 260 yards passing.

Fans in Montreal took to Sainte-Catherine Street for a peaceful celebration of their Alouettes' victory. It was a unifying event, not just for Canada but for Montreal as well. Mayor Gerald Tremblay immediately announced that there would be a victory parade on Wednesday.

• • •

The indoor/outdoor debate resurfaced in 2003. Alouettes coach Don Matthews suggested the Grey Cup only be contested in a domed stadium. Regina was perhaps the wrong place on the CFL map to make such a statement. At any rate, weather was not affecting ticket sales adversely: 50,909 seats had already been sold at Taylor Field. It would be the Edmonton Eskimos' 23rd trip to the Grey Cup, and Regina's second turn at hosting the event. The Alouettes would be fighting to retain the title they had won from the Eskimos the previous year.

Edmonton running back Mike Pringle opened the scoring with a four-yard touchdown run on the Esks' opening drive. Edmonton extended their lead in the second quarter when Ricky Ray connected with Jason Tucker on a 41-yard touchdown pass, capping a four-play, 70-yard drive that made it a 14–0 game for the Eskimos.

Later in the quarter, Montreal's Ben Cahoon made a remarkable one-handed catch in tight coverage that put the Als on the Edmonton four-yard line. In an unusual move, Anthony Calvillo pitched the ball to running back Deonce Whitaker who then tossed a four-yard touchdown to a wide-open Pat Woodcock.

On Edmonton's next possession, Pringle fumbled and Montreal went straight to work; Calvillo hit Sylvain Girard on a 32-yard touchdown pass to tie the game. After a Keith Stokes fumble later in the quarter, Ray hooked up with a streaking Tucker on a 20-yard touchdown passing play that restored the Eskimos' seven-point advantage.

Montreal was quick to reply. Calvillo threw a 27-yard touchdown to Cahoon with 50 seconds left in the half to tie it up, but, determined to go out on top, Edmonton capitalized on a Montreal fumble with a Sean Fleming field goal from the Als' 27-yard line. It was 24–21 at the half.

After the break, the Eskimo defence took over, and Montreal was held to a single point in the third quarter. Edmonton's Ray, on the other hand, scored early in the fourth on a one-yard run to give his team a 31–22 lead. Finally, with only 29 seconds left to play, Sean Fleming booted a 27-yard field goal that sealed the victory for Edmonton. The final score was Edmonton Eskimos 34, Montreal Alouettes 22.

It was Don Matthews's sixth Grey Cup championship victory. The MVP nod went to receiver Jason Tucker, who completed two touchdowns and made seven receptions for 132 yards. Ben Cahoon made six catches for 148 yards and was chosen Most Outstanding Canadian. Outstanding contributions also came from Ricky Ray, who completed 22 of 32 passes for 301 yards, and Anthony Calvillo, who was 22 for 37 for 371 yards.

While he may not have taken home any of the individual awards, Mike Pringle did break the record for career yards rushing in the Grey Cup previously set by Winnipeg's Leo Lewis. In this Grey Cup game, Pringle rushed for a total of 359 yards.

• • •

The year was 2004, and it was Ottawa's sixth turn hosting the Grey Cup. Attendance at Frank Clair Stadium was estimated to be just over 51,000. There was at least one Ottawa citizen that found himself at the wrong place at the wrong time: prime minister Paul Martin happened to be in the middle of an Asian-Pacific leaders summit in Chile at the time, and had to settle for watching the game on a television set at a reception hosted by the ambassador to Chile, being held in a tent outside a hotel in Santiago. At least there was cold Moosehead on hand.

Ottawa's own club, the Renegades, had experienced a disastrous season, with dysfunction playing out in the offices as well as on the field. While the CFL was on a definite resurgence, there were still some vulnerable areas.

With regard to football markets, the one in Toronto was definitely looking up and the fans once more seemed to be showing some pride and wearing their colours, even though their team was the underdog going into the 92nd Grey Cup against the Lions.

Out of the gate, B.C. quarterback Dave Dickenson executed a series of short passes that incrementally brought his team from their own 38-yard line down the field for a touchdown and an early lead. The Argos almost made a field goal later in the quarter, but a flag was thrown on Noel Prefontaine's 39-yard attempt. The subsequent kick from 47 yards missed, leaving B.C. pinned near its own goal line. Dickenson engineered a series of first downs as the quarter wound down, moving the Lions to midfield with help from receivers Geroy Simon and Ryan Thelwell and a nine-yard carry by Antonio Warren.

A long completion from Damon Allen to R. Jay Soward moved the Argos to the B.C. 20-yard line. Now within range, Prefontaine put Toronto on the board with a 27-yard field goal.

On the Argos' next drive, Allen hit Robert Baker for a 35-yarder followed by a 20-yarder, moving them ever deeper into the Lions' lair. A pass interference call against the Lions left the ball on the one-yard line. Allen plunged across for a touchdown, vaulting the Argos into the lead. But the Lions responded immediately, positioning themselves into field goal range. Duncan O'Mahony evened the score with a 42-yarder. But just before the half, Allen again connected with Baker for a 23-yard touchdown.

The field position advantage enjoyed by the Argos in the second quarter continued on the opening drive of the third. Allen was on the move once more and for the second time in the game dove into the end zone for a one-yard touchdown to give the Argos a 14-point lead. Dickenson had only marginal success moving the ball for B.C., and all the Lions were able to put together was a 36-yard goal by O'Mahony.

Minutes into the fourth quarter, from his own 10-yard line, Dave Dickenson began to assemble an impressive drive for the Lions. Lyle Green caught two passes for first downs before running back Antonio Warren took over. Warren ran for 30 and 15 yards, setting up a Lions touchdown on Dickenson's five-yard rush and dive into the end zone. Duncan O'Mahony's convert attempt went wide. Toronto took possession again with a short field. Allen found Tony Miles wide open and brought the Argos down to the B.C. 10-yard line with three minutes left on the clock. A resulting field goal by Prefontaine stretched the Argos' lead to eight points. The Lions tried to get something happening. Dickenson attempted a bomb but the pass to Geroy Simon was incomplete. Once more the ball was Toronto's, and all they needed to do was wind down the remaining seconds on the clock. The final score was Toronto Argonauts 27, B.C. Lions 19.

The win marked a new beginning and remarkable moment for so many reasons. At 41 years of age, performing just as strongly as his younger colleagues and opponents, Damon Allen became the oldest quarterback to win either a Grey Cup or a Super Bowl, and was selected Outstanding Player. His coach, Michael Clemons, became the first black head coach to achieve a Grey Cup victory.

Hard to believe that only recently the Argos franchise was facing bankruptcy. Owners David Cynamon and Howard Sokolowski would get to drink from the Cup prior to the victory parade, which was scheduled for Monday morning.

• • •

On the Friday night before the 2005 Grey Cup game, the CFL awards were handed out at the Vancouver Centre for the

Performing Arts, and Toronto Argonauts quarterback Damon Allen was named Outstanding Player. It was a virtually unanimous decision. Too bad he wouldn't be participating in the Grey Cup.

The championship was back in Vancouver for the first time since 1999. The atmosphere was a bit different this time around because there *actually was some*. There had already been a block party going on along Beatty Street adjacent to the stadium for a few days, and the parade was back this year, with Pamela Anderson in the role of grand marshal.

In terms of the telecast, it was a 21st-century Grey Cup: not only would the game be captured in high-definition, but it would be the first time that a Cablecam was used. Suspended above the field, the camera would run along a cable grid and could drop as low as 3.5 metres above the field.

Attendance at B.C. Place Stadium was back up to the numbers it was achieving in the mid-1980s: just over 59,000. Prime minister Paul Martin performed the ceremonial coin toss.

This was a Grey Cup game that took its time unfolding and seemed to be in no particular hurry to finish. It was a scoreless contest until halfway through the first quarter, when Sean Fleming got the Eskimos on the board with an 18-yard field goal. Later, in the final seconds of the period, the Alouettes' Damon Duval managed to boot a 56-yard single.

Fans had to wait until nearly the end of the half to see a touchdown. Eskie Ricky Ray fired a nine-yard pass to receiver Ed Hervey. Fleming successfully converted and the Eskimos went into the break with a comfortable 10–1 lead.

The Alouettes stormed right back in the third, starting with Eric Lapointe's one-yard dash across the goal line and Duval's convert. After this the see-saw game began. Fleming kicked a 35-yard field goal and then Lapointe and Duval repeated their performances, making it 15–13 Montreal. A Duval field goal was followed by Tony Tompkins's incredible 96-yard kickoff return — the longest in Grey Cup history. Fleming's convert made it 20–18 for Edmonton going into the final quarter.

Montreal's third touchdown of the game arrived more than halfway through the period courtesy of Anthony Calvillo. Staring down third and four with a minute to go, Ray connected with Derrell Mitchell for a first down. That and a series of penalties brought the ball to the Als' one-yard line. Ray plunged it through and then teamed with Jason Tucker for the two-point conversion. It was now 28–25 Edmonton. But it wasn't over. With 0:00 on the clock, Duval tied it up and, for only the second time in Grey Cup history, the game was sent into overtime.

ACCORDING TO THE CFL REGULATIONS REGARDING OVERTIME, EACH TEAM IS GIVEN A CHANCE TO SCRIMMAGE FROM THE OPPONENT'S 35-YARD LINE. IF THE TWO TEAMS REMAIN TIED AFTER EACH HAS COMPLETED AN OFFENSIVE SERIES, THEN THEY PLAY ON UNDER THE SAME FORMAT UNTIL A WINNER EMERGES.

Montreal went first in the shootout, Calvillo passing to Dave Stala in the corner of the end zone, giving the Als a 35–28 lead. Ray answered with a successful 11-yard passing score to Tucker. In the second overtime, Edmonton failed to convert on second and four but Fleming managed a field goal, leaving it at 38–35 before Montreal took its turn.

On first down and facing a crush of Edmonton players, Calvillo looked for an Alouette to connect with. Joe Montford knocked the ball out of his hands, but Calvillo caught it and then drilled it to Kerry Watkins who was wide open in the end zone. Watkins dropped it and Montreal was awarded a

10-yard penalty for the illegal forward pass. Charles Alston sacked Calvillo on first and 20, sending the Als back another 13 yards and pushing Duval out of his range. Things went from bad to worse for Montreal. After an incomplete pass, they were left at third and 33 and, facing another Edmonton attack, Calvillo scrambled and then punted the ball, praying for an Alouette receiver somewhere at the other end. But it was Edmonton's A.J. Gass who caught it, thereby securing the Grey Cup for the Eskimos.

The final score was Edmonton Eskimos 38, Montreal Alouettes 35. It was the Eskimos' second Grey Cup win in three seasons.

• • •

The 2006 Grey Cup festival spanned several days and almost as many venues, turning host city Winnipeg into one giant Grey Cup celebration, rounded out by the parade, the annual dinner, special events, live music, and other activities.

The game itself was to take place at Canad Inns Stadium, formerly Winnipeg Stadium, in front of a near-capacity crowd of almost 45,000. The contest was to be played out between the B.C. Lions and the Montreal Alouettes, and was being billed not as a duel between quarterbacks but rather kickers: the Lions' David McCallum versus Damon Duval of the Alouettes. It was the Lions, however, who were favoured to win the 94th Grey Cup.

Naturally, it was one of the footmen who would get his team on the board first. Failing to capitalize on a first down, B.C. had to settle for a McCallum field goal, his first of the game and the only kind of points that would be seen in the opening quarter. The sole touchdown of the half belonged to Lions' running back Ian Smart who made an 18-yard catch before running it another 25 yards and across the goal line. Montreal finally made its mark with a Duval field goal, which in the last minute of the half was followed by McCallum's third. The score at the break was 19–3 for the Lions.

The third period was not without some controversy. Upon being sacked by R-Kal Truluck, Lions quarterback Dave Dickenson fumbled. The ball was recovered by Chip Cox, who proceeded to run it in for a touchdown. Officials, however, observed that Dickenson was actually down before losing the ball. The instant replay confirmed this and, in a Grey Cup first, the call was overturned. This would mean that all of the points in the third quarter would belong to Montreal — a two-point safety conceded by McCallum, succeeded by a two-yard touchdown run by Robert Edwards that Duval was able to convert, making it 19–12 for B.C.

McCallum continued to be a scoring machine, producing his fifth and sixth goals of the game to tie a Grey Cup record. The Lions were now leading 25–12. Montreal continued to press, but were unable to get beyond the Lions' 15-yard line. The final score was B.C. Lions 25, Montreal Alouettes 14. Despite the Alouettes' loss, people continued to talk about the Montreal Miracle — a team that pulled itself back from oblivion to make two trips in two years to the Grey Cup. For the believers, a Cup victory was just around the corner.

• • •

Attendance for the 2007 Grey Cup — the first meeting between the Saskatchewan Roughriders and the Winnipeg Blue Bombers — in the re-christened Rogers Centre in Toronto was estimated to be better than 52,000, nudging the capacity crowd from 1989 and making up for the disappointing turnout in 1992. Things definitely seemed to be turning around, even in jaded Toronto, where football denizens went to sleep with visions of NFL fantasies dancing in their heads.

Mild-mannered market research of football in Canada was becoming very scientific by that time, with surveys, stats, and pie charts mostly telling everyone what they already knew: the CFL was important to Canadians, and while they might not be glued to their sets during the regular season, the Grey Cup represented a coarse thread in our cultural fabric and set us apart — not in terms of better or worse — from the pro-football marketing behemoth to the south.

The 95th Grey Cup game's first points came from the toe of Blue Bomber Troy Westwood in a 16-yard field goal. Winnipeg's lead was widened after Saskatchewan conceded a couple of safeties. An interception by Roughrider defensive back James Johnson resulted in the first touchdown of the game and a tie score of 7–7. The 'Riders closed the half with a three-point lead following a 45-yard Luca Congi field goal.

The defining moments of the game came early in the third quarter. First, when Saskatchewan took a 13–7 lead following another field goal, and then in the next Winnipeg possession, when Ryan Dinwiddie hit Derek Armstrong with a 50-yard pass for a touchdown. It was on the next Blue Bombers possession that Johnson made his second interception of the game on a Dinwiddie pass. What followed was a Saskatchewan drive to the Winnipeg 11-yard line.

Keeping the 'Riders in check, the Winnipeg defence held them to a 12-yard field goal, which gave them only a 16–14 lead with all the time in the world left to play the third quarter. But there was no more scoring until the final fifteen. That's when Saskatchewan quarterback Kerry Joseph hit Andy Fantuz, who caught the ball and went on to break three tackles before reaching the Bombers' end zone. It was now 23–14 Saskatchewan.

The Bombers managed to narrow the lead with a third safety and a 42-yard Westwood field goal, but it wasn't going to be enough. The final score was Saskatchewan Roughriders 23, Winnipeg Blue Bombers 19. The 'Rider victory sent ripples through the green fields lining the stands of Rogers Centre. It was only Saskatchewan's third Grey Cup victory in its long and storied history.

• • •

The 96th Grey Cup would be the first not broadcast by the CBC since they had started communicating the game to the masses back in 1952 — TSN now held exclusive broadcast rights for English Canada, and its sister network, RDS, handled the French-language duties.

The championship was back in Olympic Stadium, and at 66,308, the attendance nearly matched the Grey Cup record set back in the glory days of 1977. The large crowd was due in no small part to the fact that it was the hometown Alouettes who were going to be taking on the Calgary Stampeders. The last time the two clubs had met for the title was in 1970, when the Alouettes had emerged victorious.

The only scoring in the first quarter came in the form of a field goal from Alouette Damon Duval. The Stampeders' Sandro DeAngelis evened it up in the second quarter with a 44-yarder. The first touchdown came after the Alouettes offence managed to drive the ball deep into the Calgary end and create an opportunity for running back Avon Cobourne to carry it in on a 16-yard run. Following that, special teams took over and Duval made good on a 19-yard attempt, stretching the Montreal lead to 13–3.

But before the half, looking for points and an opportunity to hamper the Als' momentum, the Stamps' Henry Burris threw a 20-yard touchdown pass to wide receiver Brett Ralph.

The Calgary squad continued to dominate in the third quarter. DeAngelis kicked his second field goal of the game to tie it up 13–13. And following a punt single from Montreal, the Stampeders assembled a 75-yard drive that incrementally led to a field goal kick and a 16–14 lead.

On the first play of the last quarter, Montreal's Calvillo was intercepted by Dwight Anderson, leading to another DeAngelis field goal and a more comfortable margin for Calgary. After a Calvillo pass was intercepted by Shannon James, DeAngelis stepped up once again and produced another three points for the Stampeders, sealing the victory. The final score was Calgary Stampeders 22, Montreal Alouettes 14.

It was a heartbreaker for the Montreal team, who had failed for the third time in four years to lay claim to the Grey Cup. While Calvillo was despondent, Calgary quarterback Henry Burris was overjoyed, as the win marked the end of a long journey for the Oklahoma native, a journey full of struggles and disappointments. For Burris it was finally time to celebrate.

• • •

Spectators at McMahon Stadium in Calgary had the honour of seeing a CFL legend and Hall of Famer perform the ceremonial coin toss: Norman "Normie" Kwong, then lieutenant governor of Alberta. Attendance at McMahon to see the Saskatchewan Roughriders take on the Montreal Alouettes was 46,020.

Saskatchewan controlled the game from the get-go. On his second attempt, Luca Congi managed a field goal, which gave the 'Riders a 3–0 lead early in the first quarter. Later, quarterback Darian Durant hit Andy Fantuz for an eight-yard touchdown, stretching Saskatchewan's lead to 10–0. A Damon Duval field goal narrowed the lead to 10–3, but before the end of the half, Congi would kick two more field goals and increase his team's lead to 17–3.

In the third quarter, a nine-play drive by the Alouettes was capped with a touchdown when Calvillo completed an eight-yard pass to wide receiver Jamel Richardson that cut the lead to 17–10. However, less than seven minutes later, Congi kicked his fourth field goal, putting Saskatchewan ahead 20–10.

The 'Rider offensive continued in the fourth quarter. A drive that took all of about three minutes resulted in Durant rushing 16 yards for a touchdown. The single-point convert gave Saskatchewan a 27–11 lead. The Montreal defence was ineffective against the dominant 'Rider offence. But Calvillo bounced back. He threw a spiral from the Montreal 43-yard line that was caught by Brian Bratton on the Saskatchewan three. Avon Cobourne ran the ball in for the touchdown. Calvillo's pass to fullback Kerry Carter was good for a two-point convert, narrowing the gap to 27–19.

With 2:34 left to play, Calvillo took a chance on a third down. He completed a pass to Jamel Richardson who reached the Saskatchewan 11-yard line for a first down. Calvillo then hit an uncovered Ben Cahoon for a touchdown. However, the two-point convert that would have tied the game was missed.

The game was down to its last 10 seconds and the Als had possession. Calvillo once again threw to Kerry Watkins, who caught the ball but was tackled on the Saskatchewan 36-yard line. There were only five seconds to go. The decision was made to try for the field goal; Damon Duval missed on the attempt. But there was a miscommunication among the 'Riders players and they were called for having too many men on the field. A 10-yard penalty was assessed, which moved the Alouettes to the Saskatchewan 26. Duval could now make another attempt, this time at closer range. With no time left on the clock (a game cannot end with a penalty), Duval made good, scoring three points for a 28–27 Alouettes victory. All the Saskatchewan team could do was look on with shock and disbelief.

• • •

Saskatchewan wanted desperately to erase the memory of the previous year's monumental last-second loss with a rematch with the Montreal Alouettes. The 98th Grey Cup would be played at Commonwealth Stadium in Edmonton in front of another sizeable audience: more than 63,000 would be packing the stands. Tickets had sold out one week after they went on sale — a record for the quickest sellout in the history of the Grey Cup. Over six million Canadians tuned in to the game.

Montreal got on the board first with a three-yard touchdown by Avon Cobourne. Damon Duval got the convert and also scored a single some minutes later. In the last seconds of the first quarter, Saskatchewan's Wes Cates scored a touchdown, making it an 8–7 Alouettes lead.

But the second quarter was all Saskatchewan, with a field goal from Warren Kean and a single from Eddie Johnson. The score was 11–8 at the half, Saskatchewan now leading.

One of the most remarkable plays of the game happened early in the third quarter when Montreal's Marc Trestman gambled with a fake punt with the ball on the Montreal 41-yard line. The direct snap went to receiver Eric Deslauriers, who ran 10 yards for the first down, setting up a Damon Duval field goal to tie the game 11–11.

Montreal dominated the final quarter, racking up another 10 point with a field goal from Duval and a touchdown from Marc Parenteau. The 'Riders managed a touchdown in the final minutes of play, but was not able to close the gap. The final score was Montreal Alouettes 21, Saskatchewan Roughriders 18.

For Calvillo, Flory, Stewart, and Cahoon it was now their third Grey Cup together. Avon Cobourne had a strong game for the Alouettes, scoring two touchdowns — including what turned out to be the game-winner. Anthony Calvillo passed for over 300 yards for the second consecutive Grey Cup. The game MVP was Montreal's Jamel Richardson, and Keith Shologan of the 'Riders was named the game's Most Valuable Canadian.

It was the first back-to-back win for a team since the Argonauts pulled it off in 1996 and 1997. For the first time in a long while, people were talking dynasty.

• • •

The 99th Grey Cup would only be the second time that the Winnipeg Blue Bombers and the B.C. Lions had met at the final — the last time being at the 76th Grey Cup in 1988.

The contest would be played out at B.C. Place Stadium in Vancouver in front of 54,313 spectators. The game had been announced a sellout by mid-July, a mere month after tickets went on sale.

PRIOR TO THE START OF THE 99TH GREY CUP GAME, THE SIDELINE CHAINS BECAME ENTANGLED. IN A SCRAMBLE, GAME OFFICIALS RESORTED TO BORROWING A SET FROM A VANCOUVER HIGH SCHOOL. A POLICE ESCORT MADE SURE THAT THE EQUIPMENT ARRIVED WELL BEFORE THE OPENING KICKOFF.

With the hometown crowd behind them, the Lions opened swiftly, driving to an 11–0 lead in the first quarter. Tailback Andrew Harris made a 19-yard touchdown run after the Lions offence cracked open the Winnipeg defensive line. Paul McCallum was good for a field goal and a single.

Winnipeg tightened their game in the second quarter before things got out of control. They held the Lions to a field goal from McCallum, while the Bombers narrowed the gap with two Michael Palardy field goals, the last coming just seconds before the end of the half. By the break, the Lions were leading 14–6.

The first touchdown of the game didn't come until the end of the third quarter. Travis Lulay's 66-yard touchdown strike to Kierrie Johnson pushed B.C. even further ahead and the quarter ended 24–9 for the Lions.

Eight minutes into the fourth quarter, B.C.'s 82-yard drive downfield was capped with a six-yard touchdown strike after Travis Lulay found Arland Bruce, giving B.C. a commanding 31–9 lead. But Winnipeg continued to bring it on, with two late Buck Pierce touchdown passes. He hit Greg Carr on a 45-yard touchdown strike at 11:22, and then found Terrence Edwards on a 13-yard scoring pass with 1:37 remaining to make it 31–23. Palardy succeeded in both of the converts, but it wasn't enough, and in the dying minutes of the game a B.C. field goal courtesy of Paul McCallum made the final score 34–23 for the B.C. Lions.

Travis Lulay was named the game's Most Valuable Player and Andrew Harris was voted Most Outstanding Canadian. It was the Lions' sixth Grey Cup win. They were the first team to win the Grey Cup at home since 1994, and have so far been only the fourth team in CFL history to do so. They were also the first team in history to win the Grey Cup after starting their regular season 0–5. Never say die.

# EPILOGUE

The story of Canadian football competition and its ultimate prize, the Grey Cup, is a story of survival against overwhelming odds, and while some of its adversaries may have been anticipated, others tended to come from unexpected quarters. In the early years the game struggled to find an audience, while at the same time it was working to define itself. Even within football ranks, the championship was sometimes met with indifference. A world war and an admitted lack of organization in the years that followed nearly led to the quick demise of the Dominion Championship and its trophy.

When the West entered the picture, the Grey Cup game evolved and began to take on a more national complexion. Despite the naysayers, the audience actually grew. As East and West battled, skills were exchanged and the playing field levelled. Popularity would wax and wane but it was becoming clear that there was a core audience and room for the sport somewhere between baseball and hockey. Seasons turned and while it looked at times like the game might suffer by its own hands, the clumsy upstart quickly became Canada's Fall Classic. Legends were born, and so was the Canadian Football League. It seemed the visionaries would finally be having their day.

Indeed, there were moments when it seemed the Canadian game was just living in the shadow of its America cousin. From very early on, colleges in the American Midwest were exporting fine football players who contributed greatly. But it was a difficult dance and there was the occasional resentment toward the number of American players on the teams and the prominence they were given, not to mention the ever-present fear that the Canadian game might get watered down or even replaced by the American one. All of this came to a head during the expansion into the U.S., a failed marriage that left the CFL beating a costly retreat north.

What followed was years of uncertainty and near-collapse, but in time the league and the tradition of the Grey Cup seemed to come back even stronger. The Grey Cup game had now transcended sport, having become a cultural event now regularly watched on television by millions of Canadians each year and attended by die-hard fans and entire families who, never wanting to miss a Grey Cup game, would travel across the country to take part in the festivities.

Now when the camera sweeps the stadium audience, occasionally a fan will be seen to be sporting the colours of the U.S. franchise that briefly invaded their hometown and, having shown them something new, something very exciting, left an indelible mark. Also seen are the fans wearing the faded colours of defunct Canadian teams or those teams that didn't make it to the final. Regardless of their allegiances, when the game is through they will wait for the moment that the Grey Cup is brought out onto the field and the victors will hoist it in the air.

Earl Grey's cup itself has become a national icon, symbolic not only of our unique football heritage but of what sets us apart as Canadians. It has suffered abuses and near-destruction over the years and so itself has become a survival story. There is a reverence for it and an understanding that while professional hockey's ultimate trophy is shared between two nations, the Grey Cup is uniquely Canada's own, and has been passed not merely from team to team but from generation to generation, each leaving its mark on it — both literally and figuratively.

In 2012, Canadian football fans will once again descend upon Toronto, the way they did in 1909 for the inaugural Grey Cup game. Visitors will no doubt exchange their personal memories of Grey Cup games past, and will be anxious to introduce the next generation of enthusiasts and aspiring players to what has become a great tradition, one of the oldest in modern times.

Following the 100th Grey Cup game, the existing base of the Cup, a veritable storybook of names and events, will be retired and replaced with a newly designed base. In 2013, Canadians will be able to look upon the Cup with fresh dreams, dreams of filling it with another century's worth of pride and victories.

# APPENDIX 1

## GREY CUP WINNERS
## 1909–PRESENT

| Date | Site | Winning Team | Score | Opponent | Score |
|------|------|--------------|-------|----------|-------|
| 1909 | Toronto | University of Toronto | 26 | Toronto Parkdale | 6 |
| 1910 | Hamilton | University of Toronto | 16 | Hamilton Tigers | 7 |
| 1911 | Toronto | University of Toronto | 14 | Toronto Argonauts | 7 |
| 1912 | Hamilton | Hamilton Alerts | 11 | Toronto Argonauts | 4 |
| 1913 | Hamilton | Hamilton Tigers | 44 | Toronto Parkdale | 2 |
| 1914 | Toronto | Toronto Argonauts | 14 | University of Toronto | 2 |
| 1915 | Toronto | Hamilton Tigers | 13 | Toronto R.A.A. | 7 |
| 1916–1918 | No games played due to wartime | | | | |
| 1919 | No playoff games | | | | |
| 1920 | Toronto | University of Toronto | 16 | Toronto Argonauts | 3 |
| 1921 | Toronto | Toronto Argonauts | 23 | Edmonton | 0 |
| 1922 | Kingston | Queen's University | 13 | Edmonton | 1 |
| 1923 | Toronto | Queen's University | 54 | Regina Roughriders | 0 |
| 1924 | Toronto | Queen's University | 11 | Toronto Balmy Beach | 3 |
| 1925 | Ottawa | Ottawa Senators | 24 | Winnipeg | 1 |
| 1926 | Toronto | Ottawa Senators | 10 | University of Toronto | 7 |
| 1927 | Toronto | Toronto Balmy Beach | 9 | Hamilton Tigers | 6 |
| 1928 | Hamilton | Hamilton Tigers | 30 | Regina Roughriders | 0 |
| 1929 | Hamilton | Hamilton Tigers | 14 | Regina Roughriders | 3 |
| 1930 | Toronto | Toronto Balmy Beach | 11 | Regina Roughriders | 6 |
| 1931 | Montreal | Montreal A.A.A. | 22 | Regina Roughriders | 0 |
| 1932 | Hamilton | Hamilton Tigers | 25 | Regina Roughriders | 6 |
| 1933 | Sarnia | Toronto Argonauts | 4 | Sarnia Imperials | 3 |
| 1934 | Toronto | Sarnia Imperials | 20 | Regina Roughriders | 12 |
| 1935 | Hamilton | Winnipeg 'Pegs | 18 | Hamilton Tigers | 12 |

| Date | Site | Winning Team | Score | Opponent | Score |
|------|------|--------------|-------|----------|-------|
| 1936 | Toronto | Sarnia Imperials | 26 | Ottawa Rough Riders | 20 |
| 1937 | Toronto | Toronto Argonauts | 4 | Winnipeg Blue Bombers | 3 |
| 1938 | Toronto | Toronto Argonauts | 30 | Winnipeg Blue Bombers | 7 |
| 1939 | Ottawa | Winnipeg Blue Bombers | 8 | Ottawa Rough Riders | 7 |
| 1940 (Nov. 30) | Toronto | Ottawa Rough Riders | 8 | Toronto Balmy Beach | 2 |
| 1940 (Dec. 7) | Ottawa | Ottawa Rough Riders | 12 | Toronto Balmy Beach | 5 |
| 1941 | Toronto | Winnipeg Blue Bombers | 18 | Ottawa Rough Riders | 16 |
| 1942 | Toronto | Toronto RCAF Hurricanes | 8 | Winnipeg RCAF | 5 |
| 1943 | Toronto | Hamilton Flying Wildcats | 23 | Winnipeg RCAF | 14 |
| 1944 | Hamilton | Montreal HMCS Donnacona-St. Hyacinthe | 7 | Hamilton Flying Wildcats | 6 |
| 1945 | Toronto | Toronto Argonauts | 35 | Winnipeg Blue Bombers | 0 |
| 1946 | Toronto | Toronto Argonauts | 28 | Winnipeg Blue Bombers | 6 |
| 1947 | Toronto | Toronto Argonauts | 10 | Winnipeg Blue Bombers | 9 |
| 1948 | Toronto | Calgary Stampeders | 12 | Ottawa Rough Riders | 7 |
| 1949 | Toronto | Montreal Alouettes | 28 | Calgary Stampeders | 15 |
| 1950 | Toronto | Toronto Argonauts | 13 | Winnipeg Blue Bombers | 0 |
| 1951 | Toronto | Ottawa Rough Riders | 21 | Saskatchewan Roughriders | 14 |
| 1952 | Toronto | Toronto Argonauts | 21 | Edmonton Eskimos | 11 |
| 1953 | Toronto | Hamilton Tiger-Cats | 12 | Winnipeg Blue Bombers | 6 |
| 1954 | Toronto | Edmonton Eskimos | 26 | Montreal Alouettes | 25 |
| 1955 | Vancouver | Edmonton Eskimos | 34 | Montreal Alouettes | 19 |
| 1956 | Toronto | Edmonton Eskimos | 50 | Montreal Alouettes | 27 |
| 1957 | Toronto | Hamilton Tiger-Cats | 32 | Winnipeg Blue Bombers | 7 |
| 1958 | Vancouver | Winnipeg Blue Bombers | 35 | Hamilton Tiger-Cats | 28 |
| 1959 | Toronto | Winnipeg Blue Bombers | 21 | Hamilton Tiger-Cats | 7 |
| 1960 | Vancouver | Ottawa Rough Riders | 16 | Edmonton Eskimos | 6 |

| Date | Site | Winning Team | Score | Opponent | Score |
|---|---|---|---|---|---|
| 1961 | Toronto* | Winnipeg Blue Bombers | 21 | Hamilton Tiger-Cats | 14 |
| 1962 | Toronto | Winnipeg Blue Bombers | 28 | Hamilton Tiger-Cats | 27 |
| (*Played over two days because of fog) | | | | | |
| 1963 | Vancouver | Hamilton Tiger-Cats | 21 | B.C. Lions | 10 |
| 1964 | Toronto | B.C. Lions | 34 | Hamilton Tiger-Cats | 24 |
| 1965 | Toronto | Hamilton Tiger-Cats | 22 | Winnipeg Blue Bombers | 16 |
| 1966 | Vancouver | Saskatchewan Roughriders | 29 | Ottawa Rough Riders | 14 |
| 1967 | Ottawa | Hamilton Tiger-Cats | 24 | Saskatchewan Roughriders | 1 |
| 1968 | Toronto | Ottawa Rough Riders | 24 | Calgary Stampeders | 21 |
| 1969 | Montreal | Ottawa Rough Riders | 29 | Saskatchewan Roughriders | 11 |
| 1970 | Toronto | Montreal Alouettes | 23 | Calgary Stampeders | 10 |
| 1971 | Vancouver | Calgary Stampeders | 14 | Toronto Argonauts | 11 |
| 1972 | Hamilton | Hamilton Tiger-Cats | 13 | Saskatchewan Roughriders | 10 |
| 1973 | Toronto | Ottawa Rough Riders | 22 | Edmonton Eskimos | 18 |
| 1974 | Vancouver | Montreal Alouettes | 20 | Edmonton Eskimos | 7 |
| 1975 | Calgary | Edmonton Eskimos | 9 | Montreal Alouettes | 8 |
| 1976 | Toronto | Ottawa Rough Riders | 23 | Saskatchewan Roughriders | 20 |
| 1977 | Montreal | Montreal Alouettes | 41 | Edmonton Eskimos | 6 |
| 1978 | Toronto | Edmonton Eskimos | 20 | Montreal Alouettes | 3 |
| 1979 | Montreal | Edmonton Eskimos | 17 | Montreal Alouettes | 9 |
| 1980 | Toronto | Edmonton Eskimos | 48 | Hamilton Tiger-Cats | 10 |
| 1981 | Montreal | Edmonton Eskimos | 26 | Ottawa Rough Riders | 23 |
| 1982 | Toronto | Edmonton Eskimos | 32 | Toronto Argonauts | 16 |
| 1983 | Vancouver | Toronto Argonauts | 18 | B.C. Lions | 17 |
| 1984 | Edmonton | Winnipeg Blue Bombers | 47 | Hamilton Tiger-Cats | 17 |
| 1985 | Montreal | B.C. Lions | 37 | Hamilton Tiger-Cats | 24 |
| 1986 | Vancouver | Hamilton Tiger-Cats | 39 | Edmonton Eskimos | 15 |
| 1987 | Vancouver | Edmonton Eskimos | 38 | Toronto Argonauts | 36 |

| Date | Site | Winning Team | Score | Opponent | Score |
|------|------|--------------|-------|----------|-------|
| 1988 | Ottawa | Winnipeg Blue Bombers | 22 | B.C. Lions | 21 |
| 1989 | Toronto | Saskatchewan Roughriders | 43 | Hamilton Tiger-Cats | 40 |
| 1990 | Vancouver | Winnipeg Blue Bombers | 50 | Edmonton Eskimos | 11 |
| 1991 | Winnipeg | Toronto Argonauts | 36 | Calgary Stampeders | 21 |
| 1992 | Toronto | Calgary Stampeders | 24 | Winnipeg Blue Bombers | 10 |
| 1993 | Calgary | Edmonton Eskimos | 33 | Winnipeg Blue Bombers | 23 |
| 1994 | Vancouver | B.C. Lions | 26 | Baltimore Football Club | 23 |
| 1995 | Regina | Baltimore Stallions | 37 | Calgary Stampeders | 20 |
| 1996 | Hamilton | Toronto Argonauts | 43 | Edmonton Eskimos | 37 |
| 1997 | Edmonton | Toronto Argonauts | 47 | Saskatchewan Roughriders | 23 |
| 1998 | Winnipeg | Calgary Stampeders | 26 | Hamilton Tiger-Cats | 24 |
| 1999 | Vancouver | Hamilton Tiger-Cats | 32 | Calgary Stampeders | 21 |
| 2000 | Calgary | B.C. Lions | 28 | Montreal Alouettes | 26 |
| 2001 | Montreal | Calgary Stampeders | 27 | Winnipeg Blue Bombers | 19 |
| 2002 | Edmonton | Montreal Alouettes | 25 | Edmonton Eskimos | 16 |
| 2003 | Regina | Edmonton Eskimos | 34 | Montreal Alouettes | 22 |
| 2004 | Ottawa | Toronto Argonauts | 27 | B.C. Lions | 19 |
| 2005 | Vancouver | Edmonton Eskimos | 38 | Montreal Alouettes | 35 |
| 2006 | Winnipeg | B.C. Lions | 25 | Montreal Alouettes | 14 |
| 2007 | Toronto | Saskatchewan Roughriders | 23 | Winnipeg Blue Bombers | 19 |
| 2008 | Montreal | Calgary Stampeders | 22 | Montreal Alouettes | 14 |
| 2009 | Calgary | Montreal Alouettes | 28 | Saskatchewan Roughriders | 27 |
| 2010 | Edmonton | Montreal Alouettes | 21 | Saskatchewan Roughriders | 18 |
| 2011 | Vancouver | B.C. Lions | 34 | Winnipeg Blue Bombers | 23 |
| 2012 | Toronto | TBA | | TBA | |
| 2013 | Regina | TBA | | TBA | |

# APPENDIX 2

## GREY CUP MOST VALUABLE PLAYER AWARD WINNERS, 1959–PRESENT

| Year | Player | Club |
|------|--------|------|
| 1959 | Charlie Shepard (RB) | Winnipeg Blue Bombers |
| 1960 | Ron Stewart (RB) | Ottawa Rough Riders |
| 1961 | Ken Ploen (QB) | Winnipeg Blue Bombers |
| 1962 | Leo Lewis (RB) | Winnipeg Blue Bombers |

*Not awarded between 1963 and 1965*

| Year | Player | Club |
|------|--------|------|
| 1966 | George Reed (RB) | Saskatchewan Roughriders |
| 1967 | Joe Zuger (QB) | Hamilton Tiger-Cats |
| 1968 | Vic Washington (RB) | Ottawa Rough Riders |
| 1969 | Russ Jackson (QB) | Ottawa Rough Riders |
| 1970 | Sonny Wade (QB) | Montreal Alouettes |
| 1971 | Wayne Harris (LB) | Calgary Stampeders |
| 1972 | Chuck Ealey (QB) | Hamilton Tiger-Cats |
| 1973 | Charlie Brandon (DE) | Ottawa Rough Riders |

*Between 1974 and 1990, the Offensive Player of the Game and Defensive Player of the Game were awarded separately*

| Year | Player | Club |
|------|--------|------|
| 1974 | Offence: Sonny Wade (QB) | Montreal Alouettes |
|      | Defence: Junior Ah You (DE) | Montreal Alouettes |
| 1975 | Offence: Steve Ferrughelli (RB) | Montreal Alouettes |
|      | Defence: Lewis Cook (DB) | Montreal Alouettes |
| 1976 | Offence: Tom Clements (QB) | Ottawa Rough Riders |
|      | Defence: Cleveland Vann (LB) | Saskatchewan Roughriders |
| 1977 | Offence: Sonny Wade (QB) | Montreal Alouettes |
|      | Defence: Glen Weir (DT) | Montreal Alouettes |
| 1978 | Offence: Tom Wilkinson (QB) | Edmonton Eskimos |
|      | Defence: Dave "Dr. Death" Fennell (DT) | Edmonton Eskimos |
| 1979 | Offence: David Green (RB) | Montreal Alouettes |
|      | Defence: Tom Cousineau (LB) | Montreal Alouettes |

| 1980 | Offence: Warren Moon (QB) | Edmonton Eskimos |
|---|---|---|
| | Defence: Dale Potter (LB) | Edmonton Eskimos |
| 1981 | Offence: J.C. Watts (QB) | Ottawa Rough Riders |
| | Defence: John Glassford (LB) | Ottawa Rough Riders |
| 1982 | Offence: Warren Moon (QB) | Edmonton Eskimos |
| | Defence: Dave "Dr. Death" Fennell (DT) | Edmonton Eskimos |
| 1983 | Offence: Joe Barnes (QB) | Toronto Argonauts |
| | Defence: Carl Brazley (DB) | Toronto Argonauts |
| 1984 | Offence: Tom Clements (QB) | Winnipeg Blue Bombers |
| | Defence: Tyrone Jones (LB) | Winnipeg Blue Bombers |
| 1985 | Offence: Roy Dewalt (QB) | B.C. Lions |
| | Defence: James "Quick" Parker (DE) | B.C. Lions |
| 1986 | Offence: Mike Kerrigan (QB) | Hamilton Tiger-Cats |
| | Defence: Grover Covington (DE) | Hamilton Tiger-Cats |
| 1987 | Offence: Damon Allen (QB) | Edmonton Eskimos |
| | Defence: Stewart Hill (DE) | Edmonton Eskimos |
| 1988 | Offence: James Murphy (WR) | Winnipeg Blue Bombers |
| | Defence: Michael Gray (DT) | Winnipeg Blue Bombers |
| 1989 | Offence: Kent Austin (QB) | Saskatchewan Roughriders |
| | Defence: Chuck Klingbeil (DT) | Saskatchewan Roughriders |
| 1990 | Offence: Tom Burgess (QB) | Winnipeg Blue Bombers |
| | Defence: Greg Battle (LB) | Winnipeg Blue Bombers |
| 1991 | Raghib "Rocket" Ismail (WR) | Toronto Argonauts |
| 1992 | Doug Flutie (QB) | Calgary Stampeders |
| 1993 | Damon Allen (QB) | Edmonton Eskimos |
| 1994 | Karl Anthony (DB) | Baltimore CFLers |
| 1995 | Tracy Ham (QB) | Baltimore Stallions |
| 1996 | Doug Flutie (QB) | Toronto Argonauts |
| 1997 | Doug Flutie (QB) | Toronto Argonauts |
| 1998 | Jeff Garcia (QB) | Calgary Stampeders |
| 1999 | Danny McManus (QB) | Hamilton Tiger-Cats |
| 2000 | Robert Drummond (RB) | B.C. Lions |
| 2001 | Marcus Crandell (QB) | Calgary Stampeders |

| 2002 | Anthony Calvillo (QB) | Montreal Alouettes |
|------|------------------------|------------------------|
| 2003 | Jason Tucker (WR) | Edmonton Eskimos |
| 2004 | Damon Allen (QB) | Toronto Argonauts |
| 2005 | Ricky Ray (QB) | Edmonton Eskimos |
| 2006 | Dave Dickenson (QB) | B.C. Lions |
| 2007 | James Johnson (DB) | Saskatchewan Roughriders |
| 2008 | Henry Burris (QB) | Calgary Stampeders |
| 2009 | Avon Cobourne (RB) | Montreal Alouettes |
| 2010 | Jamel Richardson (SB) | Montreal Alouettes |
| 2011 | Travis Lulay (QB) | B.C. Lions |

# INDEX

*Page numbers of images are in italics*

AAA Grounds (Hamilton Amateur Athletic Association), 22, 23, 27, 28, 30, 59, 60, 91, 109

Ah You, Junior, 161

Allen, Damon, 186, 188, 203, 219, 220, 228, 229, 230

Anderson, Kelvin, 214, 223

Anthony, Karl, 204, 205

Austin, Kent, 193, 194, 195, 204

Baker, Bill, 189, 192

Balmy Beachers (Toronto), 48, 49, 55, 56, *63*, 64, 81–82, 86, 88

Baltimore Football Club (*see also* Baltimore Stallions), 204–08

Baltimore Stallions (*see also* Baltimore Football Club), 204–08

Barnes, Joe, 167, 178, 179

Barrow, John, 131, 138

Batstone, Harry, 43, 45, 47

Bawel, Ray, 122

B.C. Lions, 115, 122, 128, 137–41, 177–78, 183–85, 189–91, 198, 204, 205, 217, 219–22, 228, 229, 232, 233, 239, 240

B.C. Place Stadium, 177, 185, 186, 187, 204, 217, 221, 230, 239

Bell, Jimmy, 18

Bethea, Willie, 138, 143

Blatz, Bill, 36

Boadway, Ray, 61, 62, 66

Boivin, Bill, 122

Boone, David, 165, 170

Box, Albert "Ab," 64

Braley, David, 192, 193

Breen, Joe, 37, 133

Bright, Johnny, 118, 120

Brock, Dieter, 181, 182

Brown, Doug, 222

Brown, Eddie, 209

Buono, Wally, 217

Burnside, Thrift (Burnside Rules), 11

Burris, Henry, 235, 236

Cahoon, Ben, 220, 226, 227, 237, 238

Calgary Stampeders, 92–97, *93*, 99, 116, 134, 148–50, 153–56, 183, 185, 197–202, 206, 207, 213–15, 217, 218, 219, 222, 223, 235, 236

Calvillo, Anthony, 220, 221, *224*, 225, 226, 227, 231, 232, 236, 237, 238–39, 251

Camelleri, Chuck, 90

Cameron, Bob, 191, 223

Campbell, Bill, 47

Campbell, Hugh, 144, 167, 170, *173*, 174

CBC (Canadian Broadcasting Corporation), 106, 112, 113, 123, 169, 181, 186, 187, 215, 218, 235

Canadian Football Hall of Fame, 20, 111, 128, 133, 150, 152, 154, 174, 186, 187, 236

Canadian Football League (CFL), 116, 123, 126, 132–34, 137, 139, 141, 145, 152, 155–57, 163, 174, 177, 179, 180, 184, 185, 187, 188, 190, 192, 195, 196, 199, 200, 202–04, 208, 210, 211, 214, 215, 217–22, 225, 226, 228, 229, 231, 232, 234, 236, 240

Candy, John, 197, 199, 200

Cassels, "Laddie," 38

Champion, Tony, 194

Clair, Frank, 105, 149

Clemens, Mike "Pinball," 213, 215, *216*, 229

Clements, Tom, 163, 164, 181

Cobourne, Avon, 235, 237, 238

Cochrane, "Shrimp," 43, 45

Commonwealth Stadium (Edmonton; formerly Clarke Stadium), 166, 171, 181, 211, 212, 225, 238

Conacher, Lionel, 42, 43, *44*, 45

Congi, Luca, 234, 236, 237

Copeland, Royal, 90

Coulter, DeWitt "Tex," 120, 157

Cox, Chip, 233

Craig, Ross "Husky," 28, 29, 30, 43, 170

Crandell, Marcus, 222, 223

Cronin, Carl, 67

Crowe, Clem, 101

Cunningham, Jimmy, 209

Cutler, Dave, 159, 166, 169–72, 174

Dewalt, Roy, 183, 184

Dickenson, Dave, 218, 228, 229, 233

Diefenbaker, Prime Minister John, 122

Drapeau, Mayor Jean, 113

Drummond, Robert, 209, 211, 220, 221

Dunigan, Matt, 186, 188, 190, 197, 198

Duval, Damon, 230, 231, 232, 235, 236, 237, 238

Ealey, Chuck, 156, 157

Edmonton Elks, 45, 46

Edmonton Eskimos, 39–43, 45, 105, 107, 108, 112–15, 117–21, 128, 129, 150, 159, 160–62, 165–74, 185–88, 195, 196, 202, 203, 208–11, 215, 217, 222, 223, 225–27, 230–32

18th Manitoba Reconnaissance, 83

Empire Stadium (Vancouver), 115, 117, 124, 128, 133, 137, 138, 144, 155, 160

Estay, Ron, 165

Etcheverry, Sam, 118, 120, 150, 201, 225

Exhibition Stadium (Toronto), 97, 120, 126, 130, 139, 134, 140–42, 148, 152, 162, 166, 169, 174

Faloney, Bernie, 112, *124*, 130, 131, 132, 135, 138, 183, 186

Faragalli, Joe, 188, 196

Fargo, North Dakota, 108, 112

Fear, Alfred Henry "Cap," 62

Fennell, Dave, 165, 166, 168

Fleming, Dave, 158

Fleming, Sean, 203, 226, 227, 230

Flory, Scott, 238

Flutie, Doug, 199, 201, 202, 206, 207, 209, 210, 211, *212*, 213, 215

"Fog Bowl," *134*, 136, 141, 179

Ford, Alan, 144, 151, 198

Foulds, William C. "Billy," 17, 20, 40, 75, 76, 109

Frayne, Trent, 124, 187

Fritz, Bob, 71, 77, 83

Gabriel, Tony, 158, 163, 163, 218

Gage, Charlie, 18

Gainor, Martin, 77, 79

Gall, Hugh, 15, 16, 17, 18, 19, 20, *23*, 24, 30, 38

Garcia, Jeff, 214, 215

Gaudaur, Jake, 133, 134, 154, 156, 168, 177

Getty, Don, 119, 120

Goldston, Ralph, 125, 131

Gotta, Jack, 159

Grant, Harry "Bud," 126, 132, 135, 141

Grant, Tommy, 135

Gray, Herb, 126

Green, David, 167, 168

Gregory, John, 193

Gretzky, Wayne, 182, 197, 199–201

Grey, Lord Albert Henry George, 12, 15, 18, 21

Grey Cup parade, 99, 106, 113, 119, 124, 130, 142, 162, 180, 208, 230, 232

Grey Cup Winners, 1909–Present, 245–48

Griffith, Harry, 15, 17, 20, 109

Halter, Sydney, 126, 129, 134, 137, 141

Ham, Tracy, 196, 204, 207

Hamilton Alerts, 27–29, 33, 170

Hamilton Flying Wildcats, 85, 86, 87
Hamilton Tigers, 13, 20, 22, 24, 28–34,
  50, 59–62, 65–67, 69–71, 82, 91, 96
Hamilton Tiger-Cats, 108–11, 119, 121–
  28, 130–35, 137–41, 143, 145, 147,
  156–58, 169, 170, 180, 181, 183–87,
  192–95, 213–18
Hanson, Fritz, 71, 72
Harrison, Herm, 155
Hayman, Lew, 68, 76, 77, 83, 84, 96, 97,
  119
Hewitson, Bob, 48
Hobart, Ken, 183, 184
Holloway, Condredge, 172, 178
Huffman, Dick, 111
Hughes, Billy, 47
Humphrey, Dave ("The Tripper"), 123

"Ice Bowl," 165
Isbister, Bob, 30, 45, 76, 78
Ismail, Raghib "Rocket," 197, 198
Ivor Wynne Stadium (Hamilton; formerly
  Civic Stadium), 87, 124, 156, 157,
  192, 208, 216

Jackson, Mayor Lloyd, 109, 122, 123, 132,
  133
Jackson, Russ, 128, 144, 148, 149, 150,
  151, 152, 169, 183, 202, 218
James, Gerry, 110, 111, 122, 127, 131
Jauch, Raymond, 159

Kauric, Jerry, 188
Kennerd, Trevor, 181, 191
Kerrigan, Mike, 186, 194, 195, 196
Keys, Eagle, 115, 149
"The Kick," 194
Killaly, Percy, 16, 19
King Edward Hotel (Toronto), 14, 99,
  106, 109, 115, 119, 121
Krol, Joe "King," 85, 86, 89, 90, 91, 98, 99
Kwong, Normie, 107, 114, 117, 118, 150,
  218, 236

Lamport, Mayor Allan, 105, 107, 109, 121

Lancaster, Ron, 144, 151, 152, 158, 163,
  193, 215
Lansdowne Park (Ottawa), 51, 79–81,
  145, 147, 189
Larson, Frank, 97
Lawson, Smirle "Big Train," 17, 19, 20,
  74, 109
Leadley, "Pep," 47
Lefebvre, Garry, 154, 159
Lieberman, Moe, 40, 42
Lumsden, Neil, 172

Malton airport (Toronto), 105, 108
Marquardt, Bud, 79
Martin, Prime Minister Paul, 230
Massucci, Art, 69
Matheson, A.S., 52
Matthews, Don, 183, 210, 211, 226, 227
Mazza, Vince, 111
McBrien, Harry, 141, 145, 146
McCallum, Mayor Hiram, 93, 100, 122
McCance, Chester "Ches," 83, 96
McCann, Dave, 51
McGill University, 22, 27, 34, 35, 36, 46,
  64, 139, 152
McKelvey, "Gib," 47
McLoughlin, Mark, 206, 207, 213, 214,
  215, 223
McMahon Stadium (Calgary), 160, 161,
  202, 219, 221, 236
McManus, Danny, 201, 209, 210, 214,
  215, 217, 218
McNall, Bruce, 197, 199, 200
McPherson, Don, 126
Meigham, Tom, 16
Milne, Howie, 47
Milne, Stan, 54
Miss Grey Cup, 106, 122, 132, 139, 152
Mitchell, Doug, 185, 187
Mogul, Lou, 91
Molson Stadium (Montreal), 64, 116
Montreal Alouettes, 96, 97, 112–18, 120,
  139, 150, 152–54, 160–63, 165–69,
  187, 189, 208, 217, 219–27, 230–33,
  235–39, 246–49, 251

Montreal HMCS Donnacona–St. Hyacinthe, 87, 246
Montreal Winged Wheelers, 34, 65
Moon, Warren, 170–72, 174, 225
Morris, Teddy, 68, 90, 92
Mosca, Angelo, 138, 157
Most Valuable Player Award Winners, 1959–Present, 249–51
"Mud Bowl," 128

Nairn, Bill, 89
National Football League (NFL) Super Bowl, 106
Nesbitt, Gerry, 124
Newton, Jack, 16, 20, 109

O'Billovich, Bill, 144, 172, 178, 179
Olympic Stadium (Montreal), 165, 168, 170, 182, 184, 222, 235
Oneschuk, Steve, 123, 127
Organ, Gerry, 159, 163
Osbaldiston, Paul, 186, 187, 193, 213, 214, 217, 218
"Oskee-wee-wee," 86
Ottawa Rough Riders, 12–15, 20, 28, 50, 51, 73, 76, 79–82, 94, 99–101, 122, 128–30, 144, 148–51, 159, 160, 163, 164, 170, 171, 207, 246, 247, 249, 250, 261
Ottawa Senators, 51–54, 245

Parker, Jackie, 114, 118, 119, 128, 170, 202, 225
Passaglia, Lui, 184, 204, 205, 220
Patrick, Steve, 132
Patterson, Hal, 117, 120, 138
Perry, Norm, 69, 110
Phillips, Mayor Nathan, 116, 121, 122
Ploen, Ken, 126, 127, 128, 131, 132, 143
Poley, Bob, 194
Poplowski, Pop, 84
Priestly, Bob, 62
Pringle, Mike, 207, 220, 226, 227
Pullen, Tom, 154

Queen's University, 22, 46, 47, 48, 49, 51, 61, 169, 245
Quinn, Karl, 47

Radio broadcast, 60, 63, 64, 87, 93, 9, 106, 107, 109, 112, 117, 119, 181, 187
"Rain Bowl," 174
Ray, Ricky, 225, 226, 227, 230, 231
Reeve, Ted, 50, 64, 88
Regina Roughriders (see also Saskatchewan Roughriders; Regina Rugby Club), 52, 59–67, 63, 69, 70, 73, 88, 99–101
Regina Rugby Club, 47, 100, 169
Ridgway, Dave, 194, 195
Ritchie, Alvin, 62–64, 66, 106
Ritchie, Bill, 16–19
Rogers Centre (formerly SkyDome), 191, 193, 200, 233, 235
Roseborough, Gary, 122
Rosedale Field (Toronto), 13, 14, 16, 31
RCAF (Royal Canadian Air Force), 86, 100, 112, 113
Royal York Hotel (Toronto), 83, 93, 95, 99, 105, 108, 112–15, 120, 127, 131, 139, 141, 143, 147, 158, 162

Sapunjis, Dave, 201, 207, 214
Sarnia Imperials, 67–70, 72, 73, 75, 77, 79
Saskatchewan Roughriders (see also Regina Roughriders; Regina Rugby Club), 100, 101, 144–47, 149, 151, 156, 158, 163, 164, 192–94, 198, 211–13, 217, 219, 233–39
Sazio, Ralph, 138, 139
Schenley Awards, 150, 156, 157, 168, 172, 190
Sckrien, Dave, 131
Simpson, Bobby, 130
Smith, Adrion, 213
Smith, Harry "Blackjack," 99
"Snow Bowl," 210
Snyder, Warren, 37, 54
Sprague, Dave, 66
Stala, Dave, 231

Stevenson, Art, 75, 76, 78, 80, 150
Stevenson, Bill, 165
Stewart, Anwar, 238
Stirling, Hugh "Bummer," 68, 70, 71
Storey, Red, 78, 79, 170
Strode, Woody, 94, 95
Stukus, Annis, 78, 141
Stukus, Bill, 78, 83
Suitor, Glen, 194
Sutherin, Don, 140, 141, 143, 148, 151
Sweet, Don, 161, 162, 165, 169

Television broadcast, 106, 107, 109, 112, 113, 117, 124, 126, 127, 129, 130, 134, 139, 145, 157, 178, 187, 195, 213, 227
Thompson, Eddie, 83
Thomson, Murray, 17–19
Threlfall, Reg, 78, 80, 82, 85, 89, 108
Timmis, Brian, 60, 66, 86, 133
Tinsley, Robert "Bud," 126–28
Tommy, Andy, 74
Tompkins, Tony, 231
Toronto Argonauts, 11, 12, 22, 24, 26–28, 31, 32, 35, 37, 38, 40–43, 45–47, 50, 67, 68, 74–79, 88–92, 98, 99, 105, 107, 108, 116, 117, 119, 121, 131, 150, 155, 156, 162, 170, 172, 174, 177–79, 182, 185, 187, 188, 191, 197–200, 208–13, 216, 217, 221, 227–30, 239
Toronto Maple Leafs, 121
Toronto Parkdale Canoe Club, 13–17, 19, 20, 29–31, 40–42, 245
Toronto RCAF Hurricanes, 83, 84
Toronto Rowing and Athletic Association (T.R. & A.A.), 27, 32–34
Trafton, George, 111
Trudeau, Prime Minister Pierre Elliott, 148, 152–54, 154
Trestman, Marc, 238
Trimble, Jim, 131, 133, 135, 142
Tucker, Jason, 227, 231
Tucker, Whit, 144
Turville, Frank, 65–67, 71

University of Toronto Rugby Football Club, 19
Union Station (Toronto), 42, 46, 85, 99, 105, 108, 113, 127

Vail, Howard "Red," 79
Vanderjagt, Mike, 209, 210, 211
Varsity (Blue and White; Blues), 11, 12, 14–20, 22–24, 26, 27, 31, 32, 34, 36–38, 40, 41, 46, 53, 54, 59, 66, 69, 109, 245
Varsity Stadium, 13, 25, 31, 32, 36, 37, 42, 43, 47–50, 50, 62, 63, 69, 70, 75, 78, 81–83, 85, 88, 90, 91, 96–99, 101, 105–07, 113, 121–23, 128
Veale, Fred, 70

Wade, Sonny, 153, 161, 165, 225
Walker, Mike, 192
Warrington, Don, 170
Washington, Vic, 148, 149
West, Jack, 91, 92
Westwood, Troy, 201, 203, 234
Whitton, Mayor Charlotte, 100, 101
Wilkinson, Tom, 159, 166, 167, 170, 171, 172
Williams, David, 190
Williams, Henry "Gizmo," 188, 209
Winnipeg Blue Bombers, 75–83, 88–92, 97–99, 108–11, 121–28, 130–35, 141, 143, 162, 170, 172, 180, 181, 183, 189, 190, 191, 195, 196, 197, 200, 201, 202, 203, 217, 219, 221, 222, 223, 233, 234, 235, 239, 240
Winnipeg RCAF Bombers, 83–86
Winnipeg Tammany Tigers, 50–52
Winnipeg Winnipegs ('Pegs), 70–72
Woodcock, Pat, 225, 226
Wright, Chris, 206
Wright, Joe, 121

Young, Scott, 124, 127, 142

Zuger, Joe, 135, 140, 143, 147

**Now You Know Football**
Doug Lennox
9781554884537
$19.99

It's easy to be a Monday-morning quarterback, but the true football fan has the answers all week long. Doug Lennox, the all-pro of Q&A, leads the drive as he tells us why a touchdown is worth six points, who first decided to pick up the ball and throw it, and how a children's toy changed the sport's biggest championship. Along the way we'll meet players great and not-so-great and encounter the various leagues that have come and gone throughout the world.

- Why is the sport called "football"?

- Who first used the term *sack*?

- Why did one American president consider banning football?

- What football team was named after a Burt Reynolds character?

- Why are footballs shaped the way they are?

- How many times have NFL and CFL teams squared off?

- Which came first, the Ottawa Rough Riders or the Saskatchewan Roughriders?

- Whose Super Bowl ring is a size 25?

# OTHER GREAT DUNDURN SPORTS BOOKS

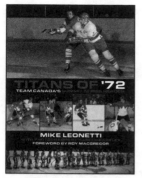

**Titans of '72**
*Team Canada's Summit Series Heroes*
Mike Leonetti
9781459707665
$14.99

Phil Esposito, Ken Dryden, Frank Mahovlich, Yvan Cournoyer, Bobby Clarke — these are some of the Team Canada hockey heroes who struggled to defeat the Soviet Union in the September 1972 Summit Series. Here are profiles of each Canadian who played on that fabled Team Canada, showcased with superb photographs by Harold Barkley.

**Hope and Heartbreak in Toronto**
*Life as a Maple Leafs Fan*
Peter Robinson
9781459706835
$24.99

Being a Toronto Maple Leafs fan requires a leap of faith every year, girding against inevitable disappointment. *Hope and Heartbreak in Toronto* tells what that's like, how it got to be that way, and what the future holds for all who worship the Blue and White.

*Available at your favourite bookseller.*

## VISIT US AT
*Dundurn.com*
*Definingcanada.ca*
*@dundurnpress*
*Facebook.com/dundurnpress*